Stuffing the Ballot Box

Stuffing the Ballot Box is a pioneering study of electoral fraud and reform. It focuses on Costa Rica, a country where parties gradually transformed a fraud-ridden political system into one renowned for its stability and fair elections by the mid-twentieth century. Lehoucq and Molina draw upon a unique database of more than thirteen hundred accusations of ballot-rigging to show that, independently of social structural constraints, parties denounced fraud where electoral laws made the struggle for power more competitive. They also explain how institutional arrangements generated opportunities for several executives to assemble legislative coalitions to enact far-reaching reforms. This book argues that nonpartisan commissions should run elections; it explains why splitting responsibility over election affairs between the executive and the legislature, as classical constitutional theory suggests, is a recipe for partisan rancor and political conflict.

Stuffing the Ballot Box will interest a broad array of political and social scientists, constitutional scholars, historians, election specialists, and policy makers interested in electoral fraud and institutional reform.

Fabrice E. Lehoucq is research professor, Division of Political Studies, Centro de Investigación y Docencia Económicas (CIDE), A.C., México, D.F.

Iván Molina is professor, School of History, and researcher, Centro de Investigaciones en Identidad y Cultura Latinoamericanas (CIICLA), University of Costa Rica.

Cambridge Studies in Comparative Politics

General Editor
Margaret Levi   *University of Washington, Seattle*

Associate Editors
Robert H. Bates   *Harvard University*
Peter Hall   *Harvard University*
Stephen Hanson   *University of Washington, Seattle*
Peter Lange   *Duke University*
Helen Milner   *Columbia University*
Frances Rosenbluth   *Yale University*
Susan Stokes   *University of Chicago*
Sidney Tarrow   *Cornell University*

Other Books in the Series

Continued on page following the index

Stuffing the Ballot Box

FRAUD, ELECTORAL REFORM, AND DEMOCRATIZATION IN COSTA RICA

FABRICE E. LEHOUCQ

Centro de Investigación y Docencia Económicas, A.C.

IVÁN MOLINA

University of Costa Rica

CAMBRIDGE
UNIVERSITY PRESS

CAMBRIDGE UNIVERSITY PRESS
Cambridge, New York, Melbourne, Madrid, Cape Town, Singapore, São Paulo

Cambridge University Press
The Edinburgh Building, Cambridge CB2 2RU, UK

Published in the United States of America by Cambridge University Press, New York

www.cambridge.org
Information on this title: www.cambridge.org/9780521810456

First published 2002
This digitally printed first paperback version 2006

A catalogue record for this publication is available from the British Library

Library of Congress Cataloguing in Publication data
Lehoucq, Fabrice Edouard, 1963–
    Stuffing the ballot box : fraud, electoral reform, and democratization in Costa Rica /
Fabrice E. Lehoucq, Iván Molina.
        p.   cm. – (Cambridge studies in comparative politics)
    Includes bibliographical references and index.
    ISBN 0-521-81045-0
    1. Elections – Costa Rica – History – 20th century.   2. Democratization – Costa
Rica – History.   3. Political ethics – Costa Rica – History.   4. Costa Rica – Politics
and government – 1821–1948.   I. Molina Jiménez, Iván.   II. Title.   III. Series.
JL1458 .L44   2002
324.97286'05–dc21   2001037364

ISBN-13 978-0-521-81045-6 hardback
ISBN-10 0-521-81045-0 hardback

ISBN-13 978-0-521-03456-2 paperback
ISBN-10 0-521-03456-6 paperback

For Mariana

Contents

Tables and Figures

Tables

Tables and Figures

Preface

After a decade in power, Peruvian President Alberto Fujimori (1990–2000) fell amid charges of fraud, voting irregularities, and the abuse of power. In Southern Europe, Slobodan Milosevic (1990–2000) finally lost an election in 1999; his efforts to reverse the results of the ballot box led to a popular revolt that finished his nationalist regime. At the dawn of the new millennium, an extremely close election generates a storm of protest in Florida. Indeed, the entire world looks upon the U.S. 2000 presidential race in disbelief as confused procedures, faulty and antiquated equipment, and racial bias fail to produce an obvious victor.

These are only three examples of how electoral fraud is very much a part of the contemporary world. Few would deny that ballot-rigging has taken place in most systems and that it remains a problem in many democracies. Yet, for a phenomenon that was and remains central to democratic politics, we really know very little about how parties go about fabricating votes. Sure, there are lots of anecdotes; former U.S. President Jimmy Carter's memoirs of personally observing his opponents stuffing the ballot box and depriving him of an electoral victory in rural Georgia is a noteworthy case in point.[1] Aside from colorful (and valuable) accounts like these, we can draw upon only a handful of studies of fraud to make sense of an illegal but ubiquitous electoral activity.

This book aims to fill the gap in our comprehension of electoral fraud and reform. It focuses on a fifty-year period in Costa Rica, when politicians used fraud, violence, and ballots to obtain public office. Over the next five decades, parties gradually (and reluctantly) gave up their right to

[1] Jimmy Carter, *Turning Point: A Candidate, a State, and a Nation Come of Age* (New York: Times Books, 1992).

fabricate fraudulent votes. One of the important puzzles therefore animating *Stuffing the Ballot Box* is why presidents and legislators passed a series of laws that eliminated their ability to rig the ballot box. To understand why they did the unimaginable, this book evaluates office-seeking, sociological, and institutionalist theories of electoral reform. *Stuffing the Ballot Box* also assesses the usefulness of sociological and institutional explanations of the nature, spatial basis, and magnitude of electoral fraud. By explaining why parties change electoral laws and assessing the impact of these changes on political behavior, our study hopes to contribute to debates about the origins and consequences of political corruption, institutional change, and democratization.

Why did we write this book? While doing research in Costa Rica during the late 1980s, Fabrice E. Lehoucq stumbled across a rather peculiar collection of documents known as the petitions to nullify electoral results (*demandas de nulidad*). Commonly published in *La Gaceta* – the official record of laws and government announcements – the petitions were the legal vehicle for aggrieved parties to file complaints about the electoral behavior of their opponents. Though couched in the dry, technical language of litigation, the petitions contain a wealth of material about the nature and amount of fraud and its geographical location. Thanks to the classical theory of electoral governance – an institutional blueprint we evaluate in this book – parties had no choice but to file complaints with Congress, the constitutionally sanctioned body responsible for reviewing all complaints of electoral misconduct. Five years later, we decided to collaborate to analyze the petitions and to explain why parties gradually relinquished their ability to manufacture electoral fraud. *Stuffing the Ballot Box* is the fruit of our efforts.

This was not an easy book to write. Much to our surprise, no more than a handful of studies of fraud were available to guide our project. Neither Costa Ricans nor foreign specialists produced more than a few articles and books about institutional dynamics and political behavior in this country. When we began this study, we had little more than educated guesses about, for example, the size of the electorate, party platforms, the rules and by-laws of electoral governance, and the nature of public opinion. To fill these gaps, we had to read thousands of newspapers, U.S. State Department files, census and registry records, and legal and government documents. So, in studying fraud and reform, we ended up studying myriad topics. We cite the results of these studies throughout this book.

Iván Molina took the lead in the study of fraud and electoral behavior. He examined all 123 petitions and developed the methods for quantitatively and qualitatively analyzing more than 1,300 accusations of ballot-rigging. He produced the estimates of the size of the electorate, assembled voting returns, and identified electoral tendencies. He also analyzed the behavior of the Credentials Committee. Molina also wrote (in Spanish) the initial versions of Chapters 1, 3, and 5, of the section on fraud in the 1948 elections, and of key portions of the discussion of electoral fraud for the introduction and the conclusion.

Lehoucq analyzed Congressional and public debates about electoral reform. He assembled the roll-call data on deputy behavior and led the effort to identify the partisan affiliation of congressmen. Lehoucq took the lead in putting *Stuffing the Ballot Box* together. He wrote the introduction, Chapters 2, 4, and 6, and the conclusion. He translated Molina's initial versions of the remaining chapters of this book. Throughout this arduous process, Lehoucq and Molina met on several occasions in Costa Rica, Mexico, and the United States. They exchanged literally hundreds of e-mail messages about this manuscript.

This book would not have been possible without the generous support of the National Endowment for the Humanities (Collaborative Projects Grant No. RO-22864-95). We are also grateful to the University of Costa Rica, Christopher Newport University, Indiana University, and Wesleyan University for support of this project. We are especially indebted to Patricia Fumero and Paulina Malavassi for research assistance beyond the call of duty. Without their hard work, much of the data we needed to carry out this project would simply not have been available.

Stuffing the Ballot Box benefited from several public presentations of its findings. We thank the participants at the seminar series at the Workshop in Political Theory and Policy Analysis at Indiana University, the Center for Latin American and Caribbean Studies at Indiana University, the Division of Political Studies, Centro de Investigación y Docencia Económicas (CIDE), the Departments of Political Science at Kent State and Texas Tech Universities, the Public Affairs Center at Wesleyan University, the David P. Rockefeller Center for Latin American Studies at Harvard University, the Centro de Investigación en Identidad y Cultura Latinoamericanas (CIICLA) and the Centro de Investigaciones Históricas de América Central (CIHAC) at Universidad de Costa Rica, and the Instituto de Historia de Nicaragua y Centroamérica at Universidad Centroamericana in Managua, Nicaragua. We also thank the American Political Science

Association, the Latin American Studies Association, and the Instituto Panamericano de Geografía e Historia for opportunities to present our findings in their annual meetings and gatherings.

Different people read parts or the entire manuscript. We thank Barry Ames, Robert H. Bates, Kirk Bowman, Jonathan Hartlyn, James Mahoney, John R. Markoff, Elinor Ostrom, Steven Palmer, Eugenia Rodríguez, Andreas Schedler, Charles Tilly, Kurt Weyland, Eduardo Zimmerman, and several anonymous reviewers for helpful comments. Clark Gibson provided incisive feedback on the final drafts of the book. We, of course, are entirely responsible for any limitations that *Stuffing the Ballot Box* contains.

We also thank our respective families for support while we researched and wrote this book. Lehoucq also could not have produced this book without Aída Vaca-Guzmán and Mariana's love, support, and patience.

Introduction

Central Questions

Why do politicians reform the institutions that keep them in power? Why do they relinquish the ability to rig electoral results? The nonfraudulent 2000 Yugoslavian elections triggered the collapse of President Slobodan Milosevic's nationalist regime. The fairness of the 2000 elections in Mexico signaled the end of the PRI's sixty-year stranglehold on the presidency. Yet, for every occasion when dictators respect the results of the ballot box, there are many examples of regimes that rig elections in their favor. Why incumbents would consent to having – and respecting the outcomes of – fair elections, however, is far from clear.

This book explains the development of fair electoral practices in Costa Rica to shed light on the politics of institutional reform. As in Chile, England, Sweden, and Uruguay, politicians in nineteenth century Costa Rica gradually transformed a competitive but fraud-ridden republic into a modern democracy – one that, since 1949, has held regularly scheduled, fair elections and where every adult is entitled to vote.[1] Party politics took

---

[1] For recent discussions of the postwar political system, see John A. Booth, *Costa Rica: Quest for Democracy* (Boulder, CO: Westview Press, 1998); Fabrice Lehoucq, *Lucha electoral y sistema político en Costa Rica, 1948–1998* (San José: Editorial Porvenir, 1997); and Bruce Wilson, *Costa Rica: Politics, Economics and Democracy* (Boulder, CO: Lynne Rienner Pubs, 1998). For studies that place the Latin American cases in broader perspective, see Jonathan Hartlyn and Arturo Valenzuela, "Democracy in Latin America since 1930," in Leslie Bethell, ed., *Latin America: Politics and Society since 1930* (New York: Cambridge University Press, 1998), pp. 3–66, John Markoff, *Waves of Democratization* (Thousand Oaks, CA: Pine Forge Press, 1996), John A. Peeler, *Building Democracy in Latin America* (Boulder, CO: Lynne Rienner Pubs, 1998), J. Samuel and Arturo Valenzuela, "Los orígenes de la democracia: reflexiones teóricas sobre el caso de Chile," *Estudios Públicos* (Santiago de Chile), No. 13 (Spring 1983), pp. 3–37.

off in 1889, when the incumbent liberals, under pressure of a popular uprising, reluctantly ceded power to an opposition liberal-clerical alliance. Since the turn of the century, politics became increasingly competitive even as presidents and their opponents did not stop using fraud and violence to shape election results.[2] Indeed, the widespread use of fraud often threatened to snowball into armed confrontations between government and opposition forces.

Yet, throughout this period, politicians passed several key reforms, including the establishment of direct elections in 1913 and the enactment of the secret franchise in 1925. By 1946, parties wrote a new Electoral Code that cleaned up the registry of voters and made election administration a responsibility of a semi-autonomous court system. Negotiated in an atmosphere of political polarization, this Code remains the foundation of electoral legislation in Costa Rica.

We also analyze a unique database on electoral fraud to assess the impact of reform on political competition. From the 123 petitions to nullify electoral results parties submitted to Congress between 1901 and 1946, we extract more than 1,300 individual accusations of ballot rigging. Charges range from parties accusing their adversaries of procedural violations of electoral law to complaints detailing the brazen intimidation of opposition voters. Our study of the petitions generates a portrait of electoral fraud many social scientists thought impossible to obtain. Furthermore, we look at the geographic distribution of fraud to determine whether regions with different ethnic and social structures had dissimilar experiences with ballot-rigging. By allowing causal factors to vary across space and time, we can assess the impact of social structure and institutional arrangements on the nature and rhythm of electoral fraud.

Our study of electoral reform and fraud therefore contributes to the study of institutions that has taken on increased importance in comparative politics. We expand the institutionalist concern for measuring the impact of legal change on behavior by analyzing activities that were not supposed to have left their footprints on the historical record. We combine this account with a theoretically grounded explanation of why parties relinquish their ability to manipulate election results for partisan advantage. By

---

[2] Fabrice Lehoucq, "The Institutional Foundations of Democratic Cooperation in Costa Rica," *Journal of Latin American Studies*, Vol. 26, No. 1 (May 1996), pp. 329–55 and his *Instituciones democráticas y conflictos políticos en Costa Rica* (Heredia: EUNA, 1998).

pursuing both goals, we explain why parties transform fraud-ridden political systems into full-fledged democratic regimes.

This introduction begins by showing how the structure of Costa Rican presidentialism encouraged executives and their opponents to use violence and fraud during electoral competition. In this section, we also examine several approaches that seek to explain why parties would limit their ability to rig the ballot box. In the second section, we review our findings about the impact of institutional reform on ballot-rigging. The third section discusses how the "new institutionalism" and the study of prereform, republican systems shaped our own approach of electoral fraud and reform. We conclude with an overview of the remaining chapters of the book.

Presidentialism, Collective Dilemmas, and Institutional Reform

Government and opposition factions might have preferred to live in a world where rigging the results of the ballot box was not possible. The threat of violence and civil war would conceivably dissipate, and politics, with fixed institutional arrangements, would become a more predictable affair. Yet, the long-term interest in political stability held by citizens and many politicians did not necessarily coincide with the short-term interests of parties and machines. Unless *all* parties were going to respect new rules governing electoral competition, *each* had an interest to defect from an agreement that it may have judged not to be in its interests.[3] Few liked the idea of surrendering favored practices for a roulette wheel whose results were unknowable, uncontrollable, and, in all likelihood, worse. There was no guarantee that, under new electoral laws, every faction would continue to prosper, much less exist. Predictions of defeat could no longer trigger efforts to stuff the ballot boxes, orchestrated either from the presidency or from civil society.

---

[3] By framing issues in this way, we are using some elementary game theoretic notions to identify the issues that merit empirical analysis. For a defense of this strategy, see Randall L. Calvert, "The Rational Choice Theory of Social Institutions: Cooperation, Coordination, and Communication," in Jeffrey S. Banks and Eric A. Hanushek, eds., *Modern Political Economy: Old Topics, New Directions* (Cambridge, UK: Cambridge University Press, 1996), pp. 216–67. The fundamental text of this literature remains Mancur Olsen, *The Logic of Collective Action: Public Goods and the Theory of Groups* (Cambridge, MA: Harvard University Press, 1965). Also, see Russell Hardin, *Collective Action* (Baltimore, MD: Johns Hopkins University Press, 1982). A recent attempt to grapple with this problem is Mark Lichbach, *The Rebel's Dilemma* (Ann Arbor, MI: University of Michigan Press, 1995) and his *The Cooperator's Dilemma* (Ann Arbor, MI: University of Michigan Press, 1996).

Political Competition and Electoral Reform in Costa Rica: An Overview

By the end of the nineteenth century in Costa Rica, politicians jostled for power in what was becoming a highly competitive political system. A vaguely worded property requirement facilitated the enfranchisement of most males twenty years or older.[4] In 1885, 63 percent of adult males were registered to vote; by 1913, nearly 100 percent of all men twenty years or older were registered to vote.[5] Voter turnout rates also were comparatively high: An average of 71 percent of the electorate voted in presidential elections between 1897 and 1948.

Citizens cast ballots for both chief executives and legislators in Costa Rica. Presidents were elected to four-year terms and could run for reelection, though not consecutively. A candidate needed to attract the support of an absolute majority (more than 50 percent) of electors or, after 1913, of the popular vote to become president. Should no one meet this requirement, the constitution empowered members of the new Congress – half of whom ran for office with the president – to select the president in early May from among the two individuals receiving the largest pluralities of the vote.[6] Legislators, however, could stand for consecutive reelection and represented one of the seven provinces of the republic. Until 1913, provincial Electoral Assemblies selected the other half of Congress, though citizens voted for these electors only every four years. Through-

---

[4] Men only needed to have an "adequate" standard of living, either because of property or employment, to become eligible to vote. Comparing the numbers of registered voters with those from census-based estimates of the economically active male population twenty years or older – which is the population possessing suffrage rights – indicates that, in ten of fifteen elections, demographic estimates are 5.4 percent above or below the number of registered voters. Our figures tend to be slightly lower than the official size of the electorate because census limitations prevent estimating the number of men eighteen years or older who were constitutionally empowered to vote if they were married or "professors of some science." Such a discrepancy also suggests that the electoral rolls were only slightly padded with the names of nonexistent citizens or with citizens who had passed away – a charge frequently made about this period, but about which no reliable figures exist. See Iván Molina, "Estadísticas electorales de Costa Rica (1897–1948): Una contribución documental," *Revista Parlamentaria* (San José, Costa Rica), Vol. 9, No. 2 (August 2001), pp. 354–67; see also http://ns.fcs.ucr.ac.cr/~historia/bases/bases.htm.

[5] Iván Molina, "Elecciones y democracia en Costa Rica (1885–1913)," *European Journal of Latin American and Caribbean Studies*, No. 70 (April 2001), pp. 45–50.

[6] After 1926, a runoff popular election would be convened by Congress should no party obtain an absolute majority of the vote. This threshold was lowered to 40 percent in 1936. Since then, candidates become president if they obtain this minimum share of the popular vote and more votes than their rivals. No runoff election has been necessary since this constitutional reform.

4

out the period under study, a de facto closed-list system of proportional representation selected approximately four-fifths of all deputies running in multimember (three members or more) districts.[7] Parties that obtained pluralities won the remaining deputies, who ran in one- or two-member districts.

The 1871 constitution invested the executive with the administration of elections and Congress with the certification of election results. By splitting the organization from the approval of the vote, legal theorists hoped to encourage executives to be impartial by empowering Congress to review their work. Yet, in a world of competitive political parties, the separation of these functions led presidents to manipulate electoral laws to pack the legislature with their followers. Electoral law, for example, authorized the secretary of the interior (whom the president appointed) to select the local officials responsible for producing the Electoral Registry. They also made this secretariat responsible for organizing polling stations. Finally, the laws made the executive responsible for the initial tally of the vote.[8] As we shall see, the classical approach to electoral governance heightened partisan

---

[7] We say "de facto" because proportional representation did not allocate some seats during this period and because closed lists became necessary only after 1946. If a province was sending three or more deputies to Congress, seats were allocated by proportional representation; if a province sent one or two representatives to San José, deputies were elected either by absolute or relative majorities. Since 1946, all deputies have been elected through the largest remainders version of proportional representation in seven provincial electoral districts. For more discussion of these rules, see Fabrice Lehoucq, "The Origins of Democracy in Costa Rica in Comparative Perspective," unpub. Ph.D. Dissertation (Duke University, 1992), pp. 62–3, 71–3. Few voters chose to vote outside of party lists before closed lists became a legal norm in 1946. See Iván Molina, "Estadísticas Electorales de Costa Rica (1897–1948)," pp. 345–435.

[8] This paragraph draws upon Fabrice Lehoucq, "Can Parties Police Themselves? Electoral Governance and Democratization," *International Political Science Review*, Vol. 23, No. 1 (January 2002), pp. 29–46. The president, with the support of the Permanent Commission (an agent of Congress), could also declare states of siege – a practice that, until 1910, the executive typically used during election campaigns. A more detailed examination of how the executive suspended the constitutional order is Orlando Salazar Mora, "La Comisión Permanente y la suspensión del orden constitucional," *Revista de Ciencias Jurídicas* (San José, Costa Rica), No. 44 (May–August 1981), pp. 19–48. Also, see his book, *El apogeo de la república liberal en Costa Rica, 1870–1914* (San José: EUCR, 1990), esp. pp. 171–241. The Permanent Commission was dismantled in 1910; a related constitutional reform also forced the president to seek the approval of Congress for any suspension of the constitutional order. For comparative notes on this topic, see Brian Loveman, *The Constitution of Tyranny: Regimes of Exception in Spanish America* (Pittsburgh, PA: University of Pittsburgh Press, 1994) as well as, more recently, José Antonio Aguilar, *En pos de la quimera: reflexiones sobre el experimento constitucional atlántico* (Mexico City: Fondo de Cultura Económica, 2000).

animosities and, in hotly contested elections, failed to produce the impartial verdicts necessary to generate compliance with democratic institutions.

In a society without severe class or ethnic conflicts, the concentration of authority in the executive transformed the race for control of this office into the central cleavage of politics. As Dana Munro noted long ago, control of the executive and other state offices led to employment, pork, and the kind of distributive politics public authority typically conferred.[9] Loss of the presidency, in contrast, deprived parties of access to such goods and the use of administrative levers to consolidate their hold on state power. Incumbents, as a result, faced few incentives to hold fair electoral contests.

Excluded from power, opposition parties fought back by attempting to overthrow the president. Between 1882 and 1948, opposition movements launched twenty-six rebellions against central state authorities – three of which succeeded in installing new incumbents to the presidency.[10] Chronic political instability, however, encouraged presidents to begin to trade access to Congress for consent to their rule. During this period, presidents were much less likely to become targets of coups as the number of opposition politicians in Congress increased.

Seeking to deter additional rebellions against his rule, President Cleto González (1906–10) of the National Union Party (PUN) did not prevent the Republican Party (PR) from increasing its share of Congressional seats in the 1908 midterm elections and from winning the 1909 general elections. Once in power, PR President Ricardo Jiménez (1910–4) endorsed fundamental changes, including the creation of the secret ballot. Despite the PR's control of both branches of government, reformers were forced to settle for a constitutional amendment establishing direct elections for all public officials and in promulgating a new, slightly revised electoral law.

Upon returning to the presidency a decade later, Jiménez (1924–8) managed to obtain legislative approval of two new electoral laws. Safeguards against the use of fraud increased in 1925 with the creation of a tribunal to adjudicate electoral conflicts, with the development of a national registry of

---

[9] Dana Gardner Munro, *The Five Republics of Central America*, 2nd ed. (New York: Russell, 1967), pp. 185–203. To judge from bibliographies, few studies of twentieth century Central American politics have relied upon this classic – which is a pity. It remains a foundation of ideas, observations, and hypotheses about the political trajectories of Central America countries.

[10] Lehoucq, "The Institutional Basis of Democratic Cooperation in Costa Rica."

voters and, most important, with the enactment of the secret ballot.[11] The 1927 Law of Elections eliminated the ability of local electoral juntas to include names in or strike names from the Civic Registry. This law also centralized the production of paper ballots within the secretariat of the interior. This innocent enough sounding provision stripped parties of their ability to distribute ballots and thus to monitor the behavior of voters.

Despite the promulgation of these reforms, existing laws did not deter parties and machines from trying to subvert the results of the ballot box. Despite the requirement that citizens needed to exhibit photographic identification on election day, governments continued to postpone this reform. Unless public officials waived this requirement, politicians argued that it would unfairly deprive voters not possessing identification cards of their suffrage rights.

These facts make the promulgation of the 1946 Electoral Code a remarkable achievement. Under the threat of an opposition-led insurrection, President Teodoro Picado (1944–8) and his secretary of the interior, Fernando Soto, sponsored a reform bill that promised to overhaul the electoral registry and require voters to provide photographic identification. The bill also strengthened the newly named National Electoral Tribunal (TNE) by making it entirely responsible for the organization of the electoral process. The 1946 Electoral Code remains the cornerstone of electoral legislation, even though most accounts of the 1948 civil war and the 1949 constitution neglect to discuss it.[12] Table 1 summarizes these reforms.

Theories, Approaches, and Hypotheses

Political scientists possess two main types of theories to explain the behavior of parties and politicians. Office-seeking theories suggest that the desire to hold office shapes the behavior of parties. In the words of Anthony Downs, the first exponent of this approach, parties develop policies to win elections, not the other way around.[13] By assuming that parties

---

[11] Some useful notes on the origin of a national registration system are contained in Rafael Villegas Antillón, "El Registro Civil y el proceso electoral en Costa Rica," *Estudios CIAPA*, No. 2–3 (1980): 48–62.

[12] A legal analysis of the current law, though slightly out of date, makes this point. See Rubén Hernández Valle, *Derecho electoral costarricense* (San José: Editorial Juricentro, 1990).

[13] This remark is from Anthony Downs, *An Economic Theory of Democracy* (New York: Harper & Row, 1957). This paragraph draws from Michael Laver and Norman Schofield, *Multiparty Democracy: The Politics of Coalition in Europe* (New York: Oxford University Press,

Table 1. *Principal Electoral Reforms, 1913–49*

Year	Electoral Reforms
1913	Direct elections held
1925	Secret franchise enacted Electoral registry established Grand Electoral Council established
1927	A single paper ballot printed
1946	Electoral registry revamped Electoral tribunal strengthened and renamed
1949	Supreme Tribunal of Elections made completely autonomous of the executive branch and legislature

will do whatever is necessary to obtain and hold public office, office-seeking accounts suggest that parties hold no ideological allegiances. They search for support wherever they can get it. They are pragmatic or, in the words of their critics, opportunistic.

Though office-seeking theories were not initially formulated as explanations of institutional change, they imply that parties will only endorse reforms that favor their ability to obtain or retain control of public offices. They will maintain prevailing arrangements or, at most, create "efficient" institutions, that is, changes that benefit all parties. If this approach is valid, parties will support "efficient" reforms because they expect their political standing to improve with tendered reforms. However, parties are unlikely to agree to back "redistributive" reforms because these changes promise to benefit other parties at their expense.[14] Parties will also oppose bills whose consequences are uncertain because they want to avoid the possibility of suffering a reduction in their share of state power.

That, over a fifty-year period, almost three-quarters of all presidents and their legislative counterparts never proposed electoral reforms

1994), which distinguish between office-seeking and policy-making theories. Policy-making theories hypothesize that parties seek office to transform their preferences into public policy. Though similar in formulation, these theories lead to different sorts of expectations. Policy-making theories imply that parties are accountable to constituencies. Unless they deliver on their promises, they will lose electoral support.

[14] We borrow this way of characterizing institutions from George Tsebelis, *Nested Games: Rational Choice and Comparative Politics* (Berkeley, CA: University of California Press, 1990), chap. 4.

upholds the validity of office-seeing perspectives. Furthermore, only a handful of presidents obtained legislative approval of reform bills. By emphasizing their interest in maximizing access to state power, office-seeking models of party behavior therefore do explain why most politicians did not seek to change the status quo. Nevertheless, they cannot explain why *some* presidents did break ranks with their counterparts and members of their party. Nor is it clear if they can explain the behavior of legislators during key periods of reform, when enough of them decided to back far-reaching institutional changes.

Sociological approaches start from the premise that office-seeking approaches cannot explain why parties adopt reforms with long-term benefits *and* short-term costs. That parties make such choices, according to proponents of this line of reasoning, is evidence against office-seeking theories of institutional change. A social class might spearhead institutional change as part of a larger strategy to obtain political power. An oligarchy can veto reforms that threaten to reduce its control of the political system. The adoption of certain reforms in some countries can make them more acceptable in many other countries. Or reform could simply be the result of the actions that visionary leaders take. A variety of background and cognitive factors can therefore generate preferences for reform not reducible to the logic of electoral competition.[15]

If these approaches are useful, parties that consistently support electoral reform should also be those that support social reform. Similarly, certain reforms – like, for example, expanding suffrage rights – should become more attractive as politicians in advanced countries enact them. These factors can also congeal to explain the counterintuitive behavior of strategically placed individuals.

As we will see, efforts to combine electoral with social reform dissipated by the early 1910s, when the Republican Party largely abandoned calls to help peasants and workers. Furthermore, during this and subsequent periods, the party's respective positions on social reform and property rights could not distinguish the friends from the foes of electoral reform. The international diffusion of ideas about the practice of republican

---

[15] The work of Seymour Martin Lipset is perhaps the most representative of this approach. See, for example, his "The Centrality of Political Culture," *Journal of Democracy*, Vol. 1, No. 4 (Fall 1990), pp. 80–3, as well as his *Political Man: The Social Bases of Politics*, 2nd ed. (Baltimore, MD: Johns Hopkins University Press, 1981). His latest thoughts on democratization are to be found in *Three Lectures on Democracy* (Norman, OK: University of Oklahoma Press, forthcoming).

politics also did shape public debates about electoral reform. While proponents of democratic reform referred to such changes in other countries, their arguments did not blunt the opposition of those who openly rejected these arguments. Furthermore, while key reformers such as Jiménez may have been extraordinarily gifted individuals, they had to struggle in a world with politicians concerned with reelection and the distribution of pork. Both powerful ideas and remarkable individuals helped the cause of reform. Nevertheless, they did not determine when, why, and how presidents and legislatures agreed to transform the rules governing access to state power.

To explain counterintuitive choices, institutionalist models factor in the impact of the rules governing the acquisition and retention of electoral offices. A key assumption of such studies is that reforms, like any other type of legislation, require politicians to make choices. Depending on the rules governing access to state offices, politicians – even those from the same party – will face different incentives. Institutional constraints, therefore, may very well encourage politicians to make choices that seem irrational for other public officials.[16]

A powerful way to explain political outcomes is by using formal models – abstract representations of the key features of a political system that identify behaviorial patterns and trends. In an analysis of civil service reform in presidential systems, Barbara Geddes argues that legislators enact far-reaching reforms when two or more evenly balanced coalitions dominate Congress. Her game-theoretic model suggests that a stalemate produces an equilibrium where key factions have equal access to political patronage.[17] As a result, each party may consider supporting major reforms because each believes that proposed changes will not benefit its rivals at its expense.

As we will see, electoral reform in Costa Rica offers support for these propositions. With one exception, evenly balanced coalitions existed in the

---

[16] This is the central message of the new institutionalism. See Tsebelis, *Nested Games*, chap. 4, which also emphasizes the importance of institutional arrangements for theories of reform. Also, see Kenneth Shepsle, "Institutional Equilibrium and Equilibrium Institutions," in Herbert Weisberg, ed., *Political Science: The Science of Politics* (New York: Agathon Press, 1986), pp. 51–81, and his "Studying Institutions: Some Lessons from the Rational Choice Approach," in James Farr, John S. Dryzek, and Stephen T. Leonard, eds., *Political Science in History: Research Programs and Political Traditions* (Cambridge, UK: Cambridge University Press, 1995), pp. 276–95. Also, see Randall L. Calvert, "The Rational Choice Theory of Social Institutions."

[17] Geddes, *Politician's Dilemma: Building State Capacity in Latin America* (Berkeley, CA: University of California Press, 1994).

Congressional sessions where legislators approved redistributive reforms. Congress never got around to establishing the secret franchise and creating other safeguards for voters until the mid-1920s because majorities had killed it when it came up for debate. Indeed, legislators only succeeded in amending the constitution to create direct elections for all public offices in 1913 because enough PR deputies opposed all other reforms. As a prototypical efficient reform – one that promised to improve the situation for all or most players – eliminating indirect elections promised to prevent "agents" (second-stage electors) from voting against their "principals" (parties).

We build upon these findings by showing why presidents assembled coalitions in support of reforms that most politicians opposed. First, we show that a handful of presidents favored institutional change because they saw the political advantages of advancing institutional reform. Unlike running for legislative or municipal office, obtaining the support of a majority to be elected president requires appealing to national – that is, common – interests. Democratic reform is precisely such an issue; while perhaps not of interest to legislators concerned with reelection and pork, forging such appeals is indispensable for winning high office. The growth in the size of the electorate, in fact, served to enlarge the constituency for reform and encouraged presidents to promote causes unpopular with locally oriented legislators. That presidents could run for reelection – but not consecutively – also empowered some incumbents to focus on the long-term benefits of democratic reform.

Second, we identify another set of reasons why a legislative stalemate advances the cause of reform. If no party has a majority in Congress, the president can use his or her veto to amplify his or her influence by acting as a "pivot" between rival legislative factions.[18] Even if legislators are uninterested in far-reaching reforms, the president can assemble coalitions of independent and opposition deputies to reform electoral laws because each wants to expand its share of state power. Under threat of a presidential veto, pro- and antigovernment deputies will back reforms they may not otherwise support because they prefer enactment of some to none of their policies.

---

[18] We thank Robert H. Bates for bringing this point to our attention. For more on pivoting, see Robert H. Bates, et al., *Analytic Narratives* (Princeton, NJ: Princeton University Press, 1999), especially pp. 231–8. For a path-breaking study of presidential vetoes, see Charles M. Cameron, *Veto Bargaining: Presidents and the Politics of Negative Power* (New York: Cambridge University Press, 2000).

Finally, we argue that only the additional incentive of a threat of civil war empowered a president to complete the reformist project. Despite the opposition of his party, Picado (1944–8) assembled makeshift coalitions of pro- and antigovernment legislators to back the 1946 Electoral Code. Fearing the consequences of civil war more than the possible loss of state power, a handful of majority party legislators decided to endorse reform. When combined with the support of opposition deputies, who were concerned with facilitating their party's access to elected office, his presidential administration mustered a bare majority to approve the Code that remains the cornerstone of existing electoral legislation in the Republic.

Electoral Fraud: Patterns and Issues

Asking whether changes negotiated in the capital affected political behavior throughout the predominately rural districts of the Republic is important. For a time and place that did not generate polling data, the use of other information sources is indispensable to determine whether institutional change had any impact on the struggle for power. An obvious source of information consists of reports of electoral fraud. Thankfully, we can draw upon the petitions to nullify electoral results (*demandas de nulidad*) that parties submitted to Congress in the weeks after election day. Containing a wealth of material about the frequency, nature, and geographical basis of ballot-rigging, the petitions were one of the weapons the opposition most frequently used to combat arbitrary presidents.

Existing Research

With only a few exceptions, however, researchers have largely ignored the petitions or other legal documents to understand electoral fraud. Indeed, some social scientists believe that assessing the effects of ballot-rigging is impossible because partisanship taints legal materials and newspaper accounts on electoral fraud.[19] While only a few analysts draw this conclu-

---

[19] Peter H. Argersinger quotes four scholars of U.S. politics, including Walter Dean Burnham, who claim that fraud is an intractable problem to study. See his "New Perspectives on Election Fraud in the Gilded Age," in his *Structure, Process and Party: Essays in American Political History* (New York: M. E. Sharpe, 1992), pp. 107–8. For a similar statement from a historian of Argentina, see Paula Alonso, "Politics and Elections in Buenos Aires, 1890–1898: The Performance of the Radical Party," *Journal of Latin American Studies*, Vol. 25, No. (1993), p. 473.

sion, the consensus among students of prereform political systems is that the topic is too difficult to study. The best books on such systems refer elliptically to fraud, even if it emerges as a crucial part in the complex mixture of campaigning, competition, and threat-making that characterized "elections before (full) democracy."[20]

Despite these difficulties, some analysts have succeeded in making sense of electoral fraud. In the most systematic study to date, Gary Cox and J. Morgan Kousser analyze more than three hundred newspaper reports of ballot-rigging in rural New York during the late nineteenth century. They show that parties went from buying votes to paying voters to stay home with the establishment of the secret franchise in 1890 in New York.[21] In perhaps the most detailed examination of any prereform electoral system, Frank O'Gorman briefly considers the impact of fraud on English elections in the eighteenth and nineteenth centuries. He shows that the number of complaints about election results sent to the House of Commons declined during this period, in large part because of the high costs of documenting accusations and getting them to Parliament before the Commons convened.[22] Loomis Mayfield argues that fraud could not have affected the accuracy of the Pittsburgh electoral registry. After the establishment of a personal registration system in 1906, voter turnout rates actually increased. If the voter registry had been padded, Mayfield concludes, absolute turnout rates would have declined in the aftermath of progressive-era reforms.[23]

These studies, however, are the exceptions. In a wide-ranging overview of the subject of fraud, Peter Argersinger suggests that students of U.S. elections – in the South, North, and West – have barely begun to tap into the wealth of personal testimonies and the judicial, congressional, and executive records that exist on electoral fraud.[24] With a history of elections as long and as rich, Latin Americanists have typically neglected the study of political institutions in prereform systems. Eduardo Posado-Carbó's

---

[20] We borrow this phrase from Eduardo Posada-Carbó, ed., *Elections before Democracy: The History of Elections in Europe and Latin America* (New York: St. Martin's Press, 1996).

[21] Gary W. Cox and J. Morgan Kousser, "Turnout and Rural Corruption: New York as a Test Case," *American Journal of Political Science*, Vol. 25, No. 4 (November 1981), pp. 646–63.

[22] Frank O'Gorman, *Voters, Patrons and Parties: The Unreformed Electoral System of Hanoverian England, 1734–1832* (Oxford, UK: Clarendon Press, 1989), pp. 166–8.

[23] Loomis Mayfield, "Voting Fraud in Early Twentieth-Century Pittsburgh," *Journal of Interdisciplinary History*, Vol. 24, No. 1 (Summer 1993), pp. 59–84. For a comprehensive review, see Fabrice Lehoucq, "Electoral Fraud: Causes, Types, and Consequences," *Annual Review of Political Science*, Vol. 6 (2003), forthcoming.

[24] Peter H. Argersinger, "New Perspectives on Election Fraud in the Gilded Age."

exhaustive review of electoral corruption in Latin America uncovered only a handful studies in a region with two centuries of democratic experience and institutional innovation.[25] With a few exceptions, even Europeanists have ignored a key source of information vital for linking institutional reform with political behavior, "high" with "low" politics, and the legal with the illegal in the formation of democratic forms of government.[26]

Sources and Methods

We use the 123 petitions parties submitted to Congress between 1901 and 1946 to explain the impact of institutional change on ballot-rigging strate-

[25] Eduardo Posada-Carbó, "Electoral Juggling: A Comparative History of the Corruption of Suffrage in Latin America, 1830–1930," *Journal of Latin American Studies*, Vol. 32, No. 3 (November), pp. 611–44. We found the following books and articles especially useful in thinking about prereform electoral politics and fraud: Paula Alonso, *Between Revolution and the Ballot Box: The Origins of the Argentine Radical Party in the 1890s* (Cambridge, UK: Cambridge University Press, 2000); Antonio Annino, ed., *Historia de las elecciones en Iberoamérica, siglo XIX* (Buenos Aires: Fondo de Cultura Económica, 1995); Jorge Basadre, *Elecciones y centralismo en el Perú: Apuntes para un esquema histórico* (Lima: Universidad del Pacifico, 1980); Natalio R. Botana, *El orden conservador: la política argentina entre 1880–1916* (Buenos Aires: Editorial Sudamericana, 1979); Todd Eisenstadt, "Courting Democracy in Mexico: Party Strategies, Electoral Institution-Building, and Political Opening," unpub. Ph.D. Dissertation in Political Science, University of California, San Diego, 1998; Richard Graham, *Patronage and Politics in Nineteenth-Century Brazil* (Stanford, CA: Stanford University Press, 1990); Carlos Malamud, ed., *Partidos políticos y elecciones en América Latina y la Península Ibérica, 1830–1930* (Madrid: Instituto Universitario Ortega y Gasset, 1995); Hilda Sabato, *La Política en las Calles: entre el voto y la movilización, Buenos Aires, 1862–1880* (Buenos Aires: Editorial Sudamericana, 1998); Hilda Sabato, ed., *Ciudadanía política y formación de las naciones: perspectivas históricas de América Latina* (Mexico, D.F.: Fondo de Cultura Económica, 1999); Hilda Sabato y Elías Palti, "¿Quién votaba en Buenos Aires? práctica y teoría del sufragio, 1850–1880," *Desarrollo Económico*, Vol. 30, No. 119 (October–December 1990), pp. 395–424; Germán O. E. Tjarks, "Las elecciones salteñas de 1876 (un estudio del fraude electoral)," *Anuario de Historia*, Vol. 1 (1963), pp. 417–75; and, J. Samuel Valenzuela, *Democratización vía reforma: la expansión del sufragio en Chile* (Buenos Aires: IDES, 1985).

[26] Some of the best recent studies are Margaret Lavinia Anderson, "Voter, Junker, Landrat, Priest: The Old Authorities and the New Franchise in Imperial Germany," *American Historical Review*, Vol. 98, No. 5 (December 1993), pp. 1448–78, as well as her *Practicing Democracy: Elections and Political Culture in Imperial Germany* (Princeton, NJ: Princeton University Press, 2000); Malcolm Crook, *Elections in the French Revolution* (New York: Cambridge University Press, 1996); Theodore K. Hoppen, *Elections, Politics and Society in Ireland, 1870–1980* (Oxford, UK: Clarendon Press, 1984); Marcus Kreuzer, *Institutions and Political Innovation: Mass Politics, Political Organization, and Electoral Institutions in France and Germany, 1870–1939* (Ann Arbor, MI: University of Michigan Press, 2000); O'Gorman, *Voters, Patrons and Parties*; Jonathan Sperber, *The Kaiser's Votes: Electors and Elections in Imperial Germany* (New York: Cambridge University Press, 1997).

gies. To obtain the most accurate portrait of electoral fraud possible, we classify each request to annul votes at each polling station as an individual accusation because petitions were generally platforms to present a multiplicity of charges against one or several polling stations. A remarkable 1,131 accusations exist for the period under study. To this total, we add another 235 accusations formulated during the tally of the vote that Provincial Electoral Councils conducted. Both generate a database containing a total of 1,366 allegations of electoral fraud.

Some critics might question the ability of these materials to shed light on what was really happening throughout the Republic. Are the petitions simply rhetorical devices that politicians used to discredit each other, a source that does nothing more than shed light on their prejudices? We argue that there are two reasons to suggest that the petitions are a valid way to understand how institutional change shaped electoral behavior.

First, electoral laws demanded that litigants prove that their rivals had violated specified sections of the law. To quote from article 101 of the 1893 Law of Elections,

Citizens have the right to present accusations to nullify electoral results; but, they must describe the events that occurred and present evidence. Without such requisites, the denunciation will not be accepted.[27]

That petitioners need to prove their accusations is, in fact, why we analyze the petitions and largely eschew analysis of newspaper reports of electoral fraud. Free of any such requirements, newspaper writers were more likely to engage in the sort of hyperbole useful for discrediting opponents and rationalizing defeats to supporters.

The 1908 and 1909 amendments to the 1893 Law modified these procedures by allowing petitioners to appeal the rulings of Provincial Electoral Councils. Starting in 1905, if plaintiffs disagreed with the Council's tally of the popular vote, they could file a complaint with the Supreme Court's Chamber of Repeal (*Casación*). The 1913 Law of Elections dropped this measure so that only Congress, as the 1871 constitution stipulated, could rule on the validity of presidential and legislative results. Again, despite its length, it is worth citing article 72 of the 1913 Law:

[27] República de Costa Rica, *Decretos relativos a elecciones, instrucciones para praticar las de segundo grado, conforme al sistema de voto proporcional numérico y división territorial electoral* (San José: Tipografía Nacional, 1893), p. 29. Lehoucq is responsible for all translations from Spanish into English in this and subsequent quotations. For a preliminary version of those results, see Iván Molina and Fabrice Lehoucq, "Political Competition and Electoral Fraud: A Latin American Case Study," *Journal of Interdisciplinary History*, Vol. 30, No. 2 (Autumn 1999), pp. 199–234.

Every citizen has the right to denounce or identify cases for nullification. . . . The petition should be written and addressed to the body that must consider it, but it will not be judged unless it is presented within ten working days after election day or the act constituting grounds for nullification. Furthermore, to admit the petition or accusation, the events, circumstances, or conditions should be identified that impugned the legality of the act, vote, resolution, vote total, or election. Admission also requires the infringed laws to be cited and the grounds for nullification be identified upon which the accusation is based. It also requires that each charge be accompanied by documentary evidence that is adduced to justify the charge or to present the reasons that make it comprehensible to excuse the omission of such evidence.[28]

The 1913 Law also required that Congress publish petitions in the daily government gazette so that citizens could present arguments against them or in their favor. The electoral laws of 1925 and 1927, which regulated the elections between 1926 and 1946, essentially maintained the provisions of the 1913 Law.

The second reason the petitions shed light on the clandestine activities of parties is that the very struggle for power encouraged parties to document infractions committed by their adversaries. Especially in an era without public opinion polls, the uncertainty so characteristic of electoral competition forced parties to seek any advantage to discredit their rivals and, of course, to stay ahead in the race for public offices. As legislators amended electoral legislation to make fraud more difficult to perpetrate, the probability that an act of fraud would go undetected was, at the very least, declining.

Parties therefore faced incentives to solve the collective action problem of organizing and coordinating their actions to denounce the illegal behavior of their rivals. In the months or weeks before election day, party representatives supervised the revision of the lists of voters put up for public scrutiny in every district to ensure that local registrars included supporters who had come of age or had recently settled in the district. They worked to ensure that local registrars removed the names of deceased or nonexistent voters from the electoral rolls. They also inspected polling stations to ensure they were appropriate places for holding elections. On election day, parties sent poll watchers (*fiscales*) throughout the country to monitor the behavior of their rivals. Should infractions occur, poll watchers drew up the list of charges that became the basis of the petitions

---

[28] República de Costa Rica, "Ley de elecciones (7 August 1913)," *Colección de Leyes y Decretos, 1913* (San José: Tipografía Nacional, 1914), pp. 310–1.

parties submitted to Congressional authorities. The Credentials and Resignations Committee then evaluated these complaints before Congress as a whole voted on them.

Definitions and Scales

In this book, fraud consists of activities that can alter the results of the ballot box and that violate electoral laws. This legal definition permits identifying, both qualitatively and quantitatively, acts that public officials, judges, and parties considered fraudulent at the time they occurred. Since standards change over time, this ostensibly narrow view possesses the advantage of revealing how legal definitions of fraud change according to the compromises parties negotiate about what is and is not an acceptable electoral activity. Unlike broader conceptions, it does not assume that any constraint or act that encourages or compels voters to behave against their interests (as the analyst conceives them to be) is fraudulent.

We are also mindful of the fact that not every act of fraud was a product of a plot to overturn election results. As we will see, parties often denounced polling stations for failing to complete poll books accurately, for not appropriately signing their deliberations, or even for starting or closing out of schedule. These activities are best seen as irregularities that, nevertheless, could favor a party during the tally of the vote when election officials held the authority to annul votes. Similarly, parties criticized their rivals for, among other things, distributing liquor on election day. These activities, however, may have represented the culmination of public celebrations – especially before the enactment of the secret franchise in 1925 – rather than attempts to intoxicate and therefore bribe citizens.

To distinguish between acts of fraud, we create a fourfold classification of electoral fraud. The first dimension determines whether impugned acts are fraudulent or irregular – that is, whether parties are denouncing acts that are clearly intended to defile the results of the ballot box. The second dimension assesses the intensity of the act parties decry. This procedure permits assessing the severity of 1,321 accusations of fraud between 1901 and 1948; this total does not include the forty-five charges where the nature of the fraudulent act remains unclear or which did not involve an accusation of fraud.

We place all procedural violations in the first category. Illustrative examples include the absence of signatures and the late swearing in of members of polling stations. Accusations like this, of course, are not conclusive proof of the perpetuation of electoral fraud. Such violations may have been the product of the carelessness or inexperience of polling station officials that may or may not have favored one party at the expense of another. No better example of a procedural violation exists than that lodged during the 1921 campaign in the Province of Limón, "where the [polling station] remained unassembled for long periods and where, for half an hour, all of its members lunched in different places. [During their absence], they left the polling station in solitude."[29]

Another common procedural violation was the questionable use of quotation marks (*comillas*). Before the establishment of the secret franchise, polling station officials used quotation marks to record any vote that was identical to the one cast before it. Petitioners often claimed that this policy was illegal because it surreptitiously inflates the number of votes that their rivals amassed. As in the lunch example, this practice could have stemmed from carelessness or inexperience. It may not have necessarily favored one party over another. Defeated parties, nevertheless, often exploited these shortcomings to impugn election results. Thirty-nine percent of the accusations against polling stations between 1901 and 1946 were of this variety.

In the second category, we include charges that could favor a party without necessarily inferring that fraud occurred. Examples of such accusations include placing a polling station closer to the headquarters of one party, distributing liquor on election day, and questioning the impartiality of polling station officials. Another frequently heard charge involved starting or ending a polling station's hours of operation at variance with the law. A colorful example of this type of fraud involved the commander of the Saint Lucas Prison in Puntarenas. During the 1921 midterm elections, a petitioner claimed that the commander used the prison boat "for the exclusive benefit of Interim President Francisco Aguilar. As a result, everyone could see Commander Guevara travel up and down the coast, openly drawing attention to his cause by transporting people interested in his candidate."[30]

The third category consists of accusations that undeniably involved fraudulent practices. They include charges like voting by individuals not

---

[29] Miguel Angel Veláquez, "Demanda de nulidad (12 December 1921)," *La Gaceta*, No. 18 (22 January 1922), p. 68. He claimed that this occurred in Estrada, District of Matina, Central Canton of Limón.

[30] Francisco Conejo Calvo, "Demanda de nulidad (10 December 1921)," Ibid., No. 19 (24 January 1922), p. 72. Congress had named Aguilar temporary president in 1919 in the aftermath of the Frederico Tinoco dictatorship's collapse.

meeting suffrage requirements and the surreptitious substitution of votes. We also place the destruction of poll books or otherwise altering the preferences of voters in the third category. A particularly noteworthy example is the accusation a Reformist Party petitioner made in Guanacaste after the 1930 midterm elections: "The rain [chorreo] of votes was scandalous; even the dead voted."[31]

The final category contains charges that the authorities or individuals coerced voters into not voting or casting ballots for their candidates. These charges were especially common during hotly contested races. A typical example occurred during the 1915 midterm elections in the first district of the Canton of Moravia of San José, where members of the polling station claimed that

from 6 A.M., when the voting began to elect deputies for San José, we noted the strong pressure exercised by the police against citizens. The police forced them to vote for the governing ticket and were responsible for distributing ballots to citizens. When, by 2:05 P.M., the opposition had more votes than the government, a citizen presented himself to vote for the opposition. His vote, however, was rejected because the police had orders to prevent voting against the government.[32]

Over the long term, parties switched from committing largely procedural violations of electoral laws to blatantly stuffing the ballot box. The share of category three and four types of fraud increased from 31 percent of all accusations between 1901 and 1912 to 70 percent by the 1940s. Curiously enough, even as electoral reform was closing the possibilities for fabricating votes, it was abetting the flagrant manipulation of the electoral process. This trend, as we now will see, stemmed more from institutional arrangements than from the social structural conditions associated with the worst types of fraud.

Explaining Electoral Fraud

We assess the usefulness of two approaches to explain why parties try to stuff the ballot box. The first argues that parties are more likely to violate electoral laws in societies where social and economic power is unequally

---

[31] "Demanda de nulidad (February 1930)," Ibid., No. 96 (30 April 1930), p. 618. "Chorreo" was slang for a rain of fabricated votes at a single location. It could, for example, include surreptitiously stuffing a ballot box or amassing voters with illegal identification cards to cast ballots.
[32] "Demanda de nulidad (5 December 1915)," Ibid., No. 2 (5 January 1916), p. 9.

distributed. In such places, this approach contends, a wealthy class dominates society and, as a result, will coerce or otherwise persuade citizens to vote in certain ways. In these settings, more powerful individuals will be more tempted to steal or otherwise fabricate votes to maintain their position in society. If these hypotheses are valid, we should see petitioners accuse their rivals of more numerous and more flagrant acts of fraud in areas with more social and ethnic stratification. The second approach argues that fraud varies in response to political competitiveness and institutional arrangements. The struggle for power, as defined by the rules governing the acquisition of state offices, will determine where and how parties try to rig election results. As competition becomes more intense, parties will resort to more and increasingly blatant acts of electoral fraud.

Our analysis reveals that social structure played a fundamental role in shaping the nature and magnitude of electoral fraud. Until the 1940s, the periphery generated half of all accusations of electoral fraud, though only about a fifth of the electorate resided in the outlying Provinces of Guanacaste, Limón, and Puntarenas. During this period, the core Provinces of Alajuela, Cartago, Heredia, and San José accounted for the other half of the accusations, but contained close to three quarters of the electorate.

These findings reveal the existence of two different societies in Costa Rica. Besides housing the most important urban centers and the largest share of newspapers, the center held important numbers of small and medium-sized coffee growers. The center was also more ethnically homogeneous: It consisted of a mestizo population that considered itself white. In contrast, social differentiation was much more pronounced in the predominately rural periphery, where laborers were typically illiterate, landless, and worked on large cattle or banana estates. The periphery also contained large numbers of mulattos, indigenous peoples, and English-speaking Afro-Caribbeans – all of whom suffered discrimination at the hands of "white" Costa Ricans. Possessing few economic resources and inhabiting a world where acts of coercion were more commonplace, citizens in the periphery more often became targets of officially sponsored and partisan acts of fraud.

Yet, it would be misleading to argue that social structure single-handedly determined the rhythm of electoral fraud. First, electoral laws created a more competitive environment in the periphery and therefore encouraged parties to commit and, most important, to denounce acts of fraud. In contrast to the center, majority rule allocated close to three-fourths of the periphery's legislative seats because most of its races involved only one or two representatives. Proportional representation apportioned more than 90 percent of the legislative seats in the core because parties competed for three or more deputies per election. Under the pre-1946 system of proportional representation, only parties that obtained a quotient – a number produced by dividing the total number of votes by available seats – could use their leftover votes to compete for seats for which no party had a quotient. Not surprisingly, once we control for the respective sizes of the periphery's electorates, parties in the periphery competed for about three times fewer eligible voters than in the center. In the periphery, it was, simply put, easier to win legislative seats by outpolling rivals than by winning quotients.

Second, institutional reforms did change the magnitude and nature of ballot-rigging. Though the denunciation of electoral fraud continued to increase between 1901 and 1948, rates of accusation actually declined because the size of the electorate was expanding. It fell by 50 percent after the establishment of the secret franchise: The number of eligible voters per accusation of fraud climbed from an average of 1,083 between 1901 and 1925 to an average of 1,990 between 1928 and 1946. Judged by the nature of the offense, however, the electoral laws of the mid-1920s seem to have encouraged parties to expand their repertoire of illegal actions. Paradoxically enough, just as legislation was making it more difficult to fabricate votes, parties increasingly began to coerce voters, to steal ballots, and to get away with holding elections publicly. Parties committed more blatantly coercive acts of fraud precisely because electoral reform eliminated the ability of parties to get away with the easiest types of fraud.

Third, the dynamics of electoral competition at the national level decisively shaped the nature, magnitude, and spatial basis of electoral fraud. By the 1940s, parties reversed their historic patterns. The center went from being the target of less than half of all accusations to more than two-thirds of all accusations of electoral fraud between 1940 and 1946. Containing 74 percent of the registered electorate by 1946, the center was a region that was, for the first time, experiencing its proportional share of electoral fraud.

A crisis of political succession fueled the unusually rapid increase in the frequency and intensity of fraudulent activity in the center during the 1940s. The 1927 electoral law's concentration of disciplinary authority over electoral matters, along with the responsibility for safeguarding the electoral registry, in the hands of the presidency produced a set of incentives too tempting for President Rafael Angel Calderón (1940–4) of the National Republican Party (PRN) to ignore. Once the regime's popularity began to wane, the PRN employed the powers of the executive branch for partisan advantage. Even if electoral misconduct was not responsible for Picado's 1944 victory, the apparent scale of electoral fraud scandalized society and fomented the development of hardline sectors dedicated to overthrowing the government.

Indeed, the geographic shift in the concentration of fraud helps to explain why ballot-rigging became a rallying cry for the opposition during the 1940s – and sheds light on the riddle of why political competition became so polarized during this crucial decade of Costa Rican politics.[33] Simply put, once acts of political arbitrariness spread to the center – where most literate, sophisticated, and supposedly "white" voters lived – such acts became a highly contentious issue, one potent enough to create what became the central cleavage of Costa Rican politics. The redistribution of fraud from the periphery to the center, therefore, is another argument against any sort of sociological determinism about the rhythm and nature of electoral fraud. The very struggle for power, as shaped by institutional arrangements, can foment behavior associated more with political polarization than with political moderation.

The Magnitude of Electoral Fraud

Despite widespread accusations of fraud, we find that ballot-rigging was only infrequently the cause of electoral defeat. Between 1901 and 1948, fraud did put two candidates in the presidency whom otherwise fair elections would have not. In both cases, ballot-rigging helped one party gain control of the presidency because election races were unusually close and because institutional arrangements created opportunities for fraud to be important. Despite obtaining a plurality of votes in the 1905 popular elections, the PUN jailed hundreds of opposition electors to fabricate a majority in second-stage elections to install its candidate on the presidency in 1906. In 1924, questionable tallying procedures deprived the Agricultural Party (PA) of two legislative seats, and thus created a bare majority for the PR to send its candidate to the presidency.[34]

---

[33] See Lehoucq, "The Origins of Democracy in Costa Rica in Comparative Perspective," unpub. Ph.D. Dissertation, Duke University, 1992, especially pp. 162–336, and his "Class Conflict, Political Crisis and Democratic Practices: Reassessing the Origins of the 1948 Civil War," *Journal of Latin American Studies*, Vol. 21, No. 1 (February 1991), pp. 37–60.

[34] We do not mention the highly controversial 1948 elections here because no one alleges that the incumbent National Republican Party (PRN) stole the election. Indeed, it lost

This conclusion hinges upon the reliability and validity of the petitions to nullify electoral results. Critics, however, can argue that the petitions vary systematically with regime competitiveness. Indeed, a central finding of our study is that charges of fraud increase with the intensity of the struggle for power. In authoritarian regimes, fraud is not a problem because dictators do not hold competitive elections. Furthermore, complaints about incumbent behavior may fail to record the fact that fewer opposition voters turned out to vote if they believed the opposition stood no chance of winning elections. A smaller turnout, in fact, would help governments win elections and would, interestingly enough, provide fewer reasons to denounce its behavior on election day. Concluding that the absence of accusations is evidence that incumbents behaved impartially in electoral competition might therefore be fallacious.

One way to avoid committing this fallacy is to develop a formal model of electoral fraud.[35] A model permits identification of how institutional arrangements affect turnout rates and thus the efficacy of ballot-rigging. By varying institutional features, the model will show how changes in voters expectations and party strategies change turnout and ballot-box stuffing efforts. A model can therefore pinpoint when parties will channel their resources into, on the one hand, mobilizing or demobilizing voters and, on the other hand, stuffing the ballot box. We decided not to develop a formal model of fraud because, for the period we study, preelection and exit polls are simply not available.

Another way to avoid this inference is to compare the conclusions from other sources of evidence with our findings of the petitions to nullify electoral results. First, we can use a naturally occurring experiment to gauge the effects of fraud on political outcomes. At the height of presidential omnipotence (before 1913, when elections were indirect), we know when incumbents stole elections because second-stage election outcomes wildly diverged from popular election results. Despite having more ways of distorting elections, presidents at the beginning of the twentieth century were unable to fabricate enough votes to win popular elections. As we will see, incumbents often jailed electors so that the incumbents could remain or

the presidential election to the opposition, a verdict that the PRN-dominated Congress refused to certify. As we show in Chapter 6, there are powerful reasons to believe that Congress acted correctly; available evidence suggests that the opposition may have stolen the election from the PRN. Also, see Iván Molina, "El resultado de las elecciones de 1948 en Costa Rica. Una revisión a la luz de nuevos datos," *Revista de Historia de América* (México, D. F.), No. 130 (January–June 2001).

[35] We thank Bruce Buena de Mesquitia for this suggestion.

impose their successors on the presidency *precisely because* they could not manufacture favorable popular majorities. As the electorate increased in size, we argue, it became virtually impossible to steal an election. Only the flagrant violation of civil rights and election procedures could succeed in throwing a popular election – precisely the features that a dictatorship suspends through the liberal use of violence.

Second, we draw on primary and secondary sources to understand the nature of politics during each election we examine. We compare our petition-based conclusions about the significance of fraud with newspaper and diplomatic appraisals of political competition. Petitions never contradicted other reports about the fairness of elections. Third, we use overly "liberal" interpretations of the extent of fraud: In all of our calculations, we assume that every ballot at an impugned polling station was fraudulent, even if petitioners only claimed that their rivals had fabricated only some votes. Even with such an assumption, ballot-rigging does not often surpass the margin of victory separating winners from losers.

We, however, do find that fraud is greater than the victor's margin of victory on *some* occasions. That ballot-rigging could throw an election is what is ultimately so corrosive of democratic stability. Even if fraud typically failed to be decisive, the threat that it could influence and possibly even decide election outcomes is what unhinges political competition. Uncertainty about the effects of ballot-rigging encourages losers to claim that fraud was responsible for their rivals' victory. Precisely because measuring the extent of an illegal set of activities is not easy, the real or perceived use of fraud prevents the consolidation of democratic systems. Until parties reform electoral laws, the possibility that fraud could be decisive discourages parties from abandoning nondemocratic ways of obtaining power.

Theoretical Guideposts

Despite some obvious possibilities for mutual exchange and growth, two research traditions isolated from each other have nourished our thinking about the transformation of fraud-ridden republican systems into democracies. The first is concerned with the role played by political institutions in society, which has witnessed a revival within recent years under the rubric of the "new institutionalism." The other, even more recent intellectual project, is the study of the electoral processes in predemocratic, republican political systems. By wrapping both with an interest in democratization, this book hopes to draw these and related literatures closer together to answer substantive questions about the consolidation of democratic regimes.

This book builds upon this insight by borrowing from – and, hopefully, contributing to – the "new institutionalism." At the core of this approach is the search for "microfoundations" and so a rigorous theory of institutional development. The use of game theory permits us to show why politicians, in their struggles for power, find themselves making similar choices when faced with roughly similar situations. It is institutions that are responsible for establishing the regularity of circumstances that encourage politicians to make the same decisions over an extended period. By punishing violators and rewarding the compliant, they generate expectations about the behavior of rivals. Institutions, in other words, fix time horizons so that agents can plan and invest for the future.

Our book also builds upon the other variant of institutionalism that many political scientists espouse. Historical institutionalists tend to play closer attention to how "critical junctures" can restructure the circumstances in which parties and other players struggle for domination.[36] In such moments, parties can set their societies on new "paths" – or what rational choice analysts refer to as stable equilibria. We hope that our effort to explain institutional reform during multiple "critical junctures" and its consequences on party behavior can bring new and historical institutionalists closer together.

A key puzzle for such approaches is why institutions change. If institutional arrangements help to generate what microeconomists call equilibria   that is, a set of mutually beneficial agreements from which no one has an incentive to defect unilaterally – a change in conditions must be responsible for their transformation.[37] Economic development or demographic change, for example, can alter the distribution of resources between groups and thus their interest in change. Politicians can also

---

[36] See Sven Steinmo, Kathleen Thelan, and Frank Longstreth, eds., *Structuring Politics: Historical Institutionalism in Comparative Politics* (New York: Cambridge University Press, 1992). Two very good reviews that examine historical institutionalism are Paul Pierson and Theda Skocpol, "Historical Institutionalism in Contemporary Political Science," in Ira Katznelson and Helen Milner, eds., *Political Science: The State of the Discipline* (Washington, D.C.: APSA, forthcoming), and Kathleen Thelan, "Historical Institutionalism and Comparative Politics," *Annual Review of Political Science*, Vol. 2 (1999), pp. 369–404.

[37] For a discussion of how institutions sustain equilibria, see Kenneth A. Sheplse, "Institutional Equilibrium and Equilibrium Institutions."

become aware of possibilities within prevailing institutional arrangements to advance their own careers. We explore such changes, endogenous to the political system itself, in this book.

Little work exists on how theories of institutional change can answer perennial questions about the development of nonfraudulent institutions. A handful of works explore the ebb and flow of suffrage reform and electoral fraud in the United States.[38] In his magisterial study of suffrage restriction in the eleven former states of the confederacy, J. Morgan Kousser reveals how the Democratic Party used the powers of incumbency to exclude Populists and Republicans from the political arena between the late nineteenth and mid-twentieth centuries. By depriving African Americans and poor whites of their voting rights, the Democratic Party eliminated its rivals' constituency – a process that included massive amounts of fraud that remain largely unanalyzed.[39]

The most studied electoral reform is, of course, the First Reform Bill of 1832 in England. The analysis of electoral practices in England is perhaps the most developed of any country. Frank O'Gorman's comprehensive treatise on the English electoral system before the first great reform conveys the impression that a well-developed historiography exists on institutional politics.[40] Yet, aside from numerous studies of electoral politics in different corners of the United Kingdom, no comprehensive study of fraud and reform exists.

What is true for the electoral politics of First World countries is even more true for Latin America. Though Latin American countries have had republican systems since their independence from Spain and Portugal in the 1820s, historians and social scientists have paid comparatively little attention to the "nuts and bolts" of political action in this region.[41] Critics would no doubt respond by pointing out that dictatorship, civil war, and coups d'etat in Latin American history make a study of electoral competition irrelevant to making sense of basic patterns of development. Yes,

---

[38] For a recent overview, see Peter H. Argersinger, *Structure, Process and Party: Essays in American Political History*.

[39] J. Morgan Kousser, *The Shaping of Southern Politics: Suffrage Restriction and the Establishment of the One-Party South, 1880–1910* (New Haven, CT: Yale University Press, 1974).

[40] Frank O'Gorman, *Voters, Patrons and Parties*.

[41] This point is also made, most recently, by Francois-Xavier Guerra, "The Spanish-American Tradition of Representation and its European Roots," *Journal of Latin American Studies*, Vol. 26, No. 1 (February 1994): 1–35. For a discussion of consequences of ignoring the role played by formal institutions in politics, see Jonathan Hartlyn and Arturo Valenzuela, "Democracy in Latin America since 1930."

they might concur, electoral politics, like all other aspects of the human experience, merits examination. But, they would probably add, electoral politics serve only as a complement to more enduring economic and social issues.

Happily, not everyone agrees. Many recent studies demonstrate that electoral laws and the structure of presidentialism shape not only the nature of the party system, but also the very survival of democracy itself.[42] Indeed, in their studies of Brazilian democracy, Barry Ames and Scott Mainwaring show that chief executives cannot enact policies to solve recurring fiscal deficits, eliminate corruption, and redistribute income because institutions fragment political power. Even in control of the presidency, Brazilian reformers cannot overcome the centrifugal dynamics unleashed by federalism, personalistic party systems, and candidate-centered electoral laws.[43]

There has even been a revival of the study of institutions and elections among historians. Even in as violent a place as nineteenth-century Colombia, Eduardo Posada-Carbó discovers that electoral fortunes of candidates and parties shaped their decision to start, to pursue, and to end civil wars.[44] Twenty years ago, Natalio Botana wrote a now classic study of what he called the Argentine "conservative order." His book explains why and how incumbents manipulated institutional mechanisms – in which all adult male citizens were entitled to vote – to retain control of the state, and how Argentina's reform opened the Pandora's box that led to the opposition

---

[42] Among other studies, see Mark P. Jones, *Electoral Laws and the Survival of Presidential Democracies* (Notre Dame, IN: University of Notre Dame Press, 1995); Juan J. Linz and Arturo Valenzuela, eds., *The Failure of Presidential Democracy* (Baltimore, MD: Johns Hopkins University Press, 1994); Scott Mainwaring and Matthew Shugart, eds., *Presidentialism and Democracy in Latin America* (Cambridge, UK: Cambridge University Press, 1997); and, Mathew Shugart and John M. Carey, *Presidents and Assemblies: Constitutional Design and Electoral Dynamics* (Cambridge, UK: Cambridge University Press, 1992). Useful reviews of institutionalist research include Joe Foweraker, "Review Article: Institutional Design, Party Systems and Governability – Differentiating the Presidential Systems of Latin America," *British Journal of Political Science*, Vol. 28, No. 2 (July 1998), pp. 651–76; and Jonathan Hartlyn and Arturo Valenzuela, "Democracy in Latin America since 1930."

[43] Barry Ames, *The Deadlock of Democracy in Brazil* (Ann Arbor, MI: University of Michigan Press, 2000), and Scott Mainwaring, *Rethinking Party Systems in the Third Wave of Democracy: The Case of Brazil* (Stanford, CA: Stanford University Press, 1999). Also, see Kurt Weyland, *Democracy Without Equity: Failures of Reform in Brazil* (Pittsburgh, PA: University of Pittsburgh Press, 1992).

[44] Eduardo Posada-Carbó, "Elections and Civil Wars in Nineteenth-Century Colombia: The 1875 Presidential Campaign," *Journal of Latin American Studies*, Vol. 26, No. 3 (October 1994).

Radical victory in the 1916 elections.[45] More recently, Hilda Sabato shows how parties, social organizations, and citizens created a vibrant public sphere in late nineteenth-century Buenos Aires.[46]

No better example of the importance of electoral politics, however, exists than that of nineteenth-century Brazil. In his masterful study of politics of prereform Brazil, Richard Graham shows that local, state, and national-level elections were typically competitive and involved the use of fraud and violence. Even in a society that had an emperor until 1889 and that based large sectors of its agricultural economy upon slave labor, Graham estimates that the electorate consisted of ". . . 50.6 percent of all free males, 20 years of age or older, regardless of race or literacy."[47] The fight for seats in parliament, in fact, determined which factions and parties controlled the cabinet and thus shaped national-level policies. What is important about these and related studies is that electoral politics included many participants and decisively shaped state behavior.

These remarks, of course, do not claim that elections were the only routes to power. Nor do they mean that balloting procedures and the tally of the vote complied with standards demanded by electoral observers of the late twentieth century. These studies of Colombia and Brazil, along with ours on Costa Rica, emphasize how the decision to rebel or to form coalitions with military officers hinged upon performance in the electoral arena itself. As the number of votes and public offices obtained in elections increased, the willingness of party leaders to entertain other ways of influencing public policy decreased. That insurrection might fail encouraged parties and factions to fabricate as many votes as possible to avoid having to plan for such contingencies.

Methodological Reflections

This book is comparative and historical in scope. It is comparative because its research design examines four efforts to reform electoral laws and more than 1,300 individual accusations of fraud. Comparisons between four periods of reform allow us to assess the validity of alternative approaches

---

[45] Natalio R. Botana, *El orden conservador*. On the openness of the franchise, see Sabato y Palti, "¿Quién votaba en Buenos Aires?"

[46] Hilda Sabato, *La política de las calles.*

[47] Richard Graham, *Politics and Patronage in Nineteenth Century Brazil*. Graham notes that it is not clear how many of these men actually voted. Large numbers of men, however, were voting, despite the existence of income, occupation, and residence requirements.

to institutional change. During each of these periods, we will examine multiple roll-call votes to shed light on the factors that prompt legislators to support or oppose electoral reform.

By looking at fraud over a fifty-year period, we also can identify shifts in behavior and determine whether proposed reforms achieved intended effects. And, by looking at differences between central and peripheral provinces of the republic, we determine whether and how social structure shaped the rhythm and scope of electoral fraud. So, while this book does look at developments in one country, it does not have an "N" of one. It is an effort to maximize variation, on both independent and dependent variables, to answer important questions about electoral reform and its impact on political behavior.

This book is historical in scope because we chart these changes, and their impact, through time. Our notion of history, however, is not of a compilation of events and individual actions described in minute detail. Nor can it be conceived of as a collection of individuals incapable of moving because of the burdens of time and place. Rather, to continue with our metaphor, we can imagine history as a collection of travelers loaded with luggage whose movements are restricted and rechanneled by obstacles and opportunities. The centrality of time, and of its analysis, will be revealed in this book.

We present our findings in the form of an analytic narrative.[48] Like any other story, our narrative contains actors and changes in scenery. Our study starts at the beginning of the twentieth century and ends fifty years later. Parties using fraud and violence to come to power appear in act one. Several acts later, these actors have relinquished the stage to parties willing to accept the results of competitive elections. Unlike a conventional historical narrative, however, the chronological course of events does not drive our story. Rather, we arrange the actors and the set to evaluate alternative interpretations of their behavior.

An Overview of the Book

In **Chapter 1**, we argue that obtaining – and retaining – control of the state was vital for securing jobs and beneficial public policies. Since politics revolved around control of the executive branch of government, we

---

[48] Robert H. Bates, et al., *Analytic Narratives*.

29

identify its dynamics and its principal outcome: the fraud and violence so characteristic of electoral competition in Costa Rica at the beginning of the twentieth century. We then chart the behavior of the electorate since the late nineteenth century.

This chapter then shows that most infractions of electoral law were procedural in nature even as some petitions denounced more egregious acts of fraud between 1901 and 1912. It also explains how electoral laws and social structure made the periphery, where only a fifth of the electorate resided, the place where parties lodged a disproportionate number of their complaints of electoral fraud. Chapter 1 ends by discussing how splitting responsibility over elections between the executive and legislature worked only when different parties controlled both of these branches of government. When unified government existed, the executive called upon his partisan allies in Congress to ratify his electoral machinations. Congress, a highly political body, abdicated its responsibility for ensuring that elections were held according to constitutional precepts.

In **Chapter 2**, we explain why legislators largely failed to reform electoral laws between 1910 and 1914. Although most deputies belonged to the PR, a party with a commitment to institutional reform, its factions could not agree to establish the secret franchise, to create direct elections for all public offices, and to democratize local and provincial government. The PR failed to enact most of these reforms because one of its factions did not want to augment the uncertainty of the forthcoming presidential elections. PR factions only established direct elections only because, as an efficient reform, this measure promised to help all parties to eliminate the possibility that electors could vote against the wishes of the party leadership.

In **Chapter 3**, we show that the establishment of direct elections did curtail the ability of incumbents to impose their successors on the presidency. The continuation of public elections also deterred parties from committing no more than a few flagrant acts of fraud because, quite literally, too many people were watching. That citizens voted in front of poll watchers and their peers encouraged parties to stick to committing procedural violations of electoral law. Again, social structure and electoral laws made the periphery the site for about half of all infractions of electoral law.

Though fraud was rarely extensive enough to determine the results of most elections, it did become the source of a major political crisis in the aftermath of the 1923 presidential election. By annulling a small number of votes, two PR-dominated Provincial Electoral Councils succeeded in obtaining two additional Congressional seats for the PR and its allies. Since no candidate had obtained an absolute majority of the popular vote, the PR ruse succeeded in assembling a Congressional coalition just large enough to send Jiménez, amid allegations of fraud, to the presidency for the second time in his life.

In **Chapter 4**, we show how the new president transformed a political crisis into an opportunity to advance electoral reform and therefore to rebuild his political reputation. Instead of rejecting an opposition reform bill, the president expanded its reach by including a set of proposals to establish the secret ballot and to enfranchise women. Though reelection-minded legislators successfully opposed the second provision, the president manipulated the partisan standoff in Congress to his advantage. By vetoing bills he did not to like, he convinced enough pro- and antigovernment legislators to support a bill none of them really wanted. Yet badgering Congress got him only so far: After a certain point, enough deputies from the evenly balanced coalitions could unite to strike items from his bill that threatened their reelection interests.

It was during the last year of Jiménez's presidency – the third period of reform – that legislators passed a bill that made the secret franchise effective. Until 1927, parties continued to supply voters with paper ballots, an innocent enough sounding provision that allowed parties to monitor the behavior of voters. After 1927, the secretariat of the interior (*de Gobernación*) became responsible for the production and distribution of paper ballots. Though the number of progovernment deputies in 1927 was even smaller than in 1925, the president skillfully compensated for his weakened position in Congress by "going public." By using the media to put reelection-minded legislators on the defensive, he exploited a new set of alignments in Congress to gain legislative approval of his reform bill.

In **Chapter 5**, we study how incumbents, parties, and machines developed new ways of manufacturing fraud in the aftermath of the 1920 reforms. We show that accusations of fraud did become less commonplace because electoral laws became more restrictive. Fraud, nevertheless, became qualitatively worse: The intimidation of voters, the false use of identification cards, and other such acts increased from about one-fifth of all charges between 1901 and 1912 to over three-quarters of all accusations in the 1940s. Paradoxically enough, electoral reform encouraged parties to use increasingly coercive and blatant tactics to win elections.

Again, we show how Congress largely abdicated its oversight functions between 1925 and 1948. We also chart the growth of a new party, the National Republican Party (PRN), that succeeded in monopolizing executive and legislative offices. Once the popularity of PRN President Rafael Angel Calderón (1940–4) began to wane, however, the party began to stuff the ballot box flagrantly. We show how the geographic redistribution of fraud from the periphery to the center contributed to the polarization of political competition and put electoral reform back on the national agenda.

In **Chapter 6**, we explain why President Picado (1944–8) succeeded in gaining legislative approval of a far-reaching Electoral Code. His support of a bill that promised to weaken his party's control of both the executive and legislative branches of government remains paradoxical because the PRN was widely suspected of having placed him on the presidency fraudulently. Despite the opposition of the dominant faction of his party, Picado assembled makeshift coalitions of pro- and antigovernment legislators to support enactment of the 1946 Electoral Code. Fearing the consequences of civil war more than the possible loss of state power, a handful of majority party legislators decided to endorse reform. When the support of these legislators was combined with the support of opposition deputies, who were concerned with easing their party's access to elected office, the president was able to muster a bare majority to approve the Code that remains the cornerstone of existing electoral legislation. Yet, we argue, it was only the additional incentive of a threat of civil war that empowered a president to complete the reformist project.

We also discuss how, paradoxically enough, the promulgation of the Electoral Code did not thwart the polarization of political competition. Instead, it paved the way for an opposition victory in the hotly contested 1948 elections and the outbreak of civil war. By analyzing previously neglected sources of information, we discover that there are powerful reasons to doubt that the opposition won these elections. Far from presenting a paradigmatic case of a government preventing its opponents from gain control of the presidency, we suggest that electoral reform succeeded in allowing the opposition to contrive a victory that it might not otherwise have attained. We also outline how, in the aftermath of the opposition's victory in the war, popularly elected delegates attended a Constituent Assembly in 1949 that, among other things, extended voting rights to women. It also strengthened the 1946 Electoral Code by creating the Supreme Tribunal of Elections – the sole body currently responsible for the organization of elections, the interpretation of electoral law, and the tally of the vote.

In the **Conclusions**, we present the principal findings of our research. We summarize the impact of social structure and institutional arrangements on the nature and magnitude of electoral fraud. We demonstrate the inability of the classical theory of electoral governance to generate widely acceptable election results. By comparing major periods of electoral reform, our discussion centers upon how useful office-seeking, sociological, and institutionalist approaches are in explaining the ebb and flow of institutional innovation. Finally, our conclusions identify the ways in which our research can be expanded to grasp the role of electoral fraud and reform in comparative politics.

1

Electoral Fraud during Indirect and Public Elections, 1901–12

Introduction

How did parties compete for power at the height of presidential omnipotence? How did they rig election results? Did sociological and institutional factors shape ballot-rigging strategies? These are the questions we explore in this chapter.

According to conventional wisdom, politics in prereform Costa Rica was no different than in the other so-called oligarchies of Latin America. To stay in power, incumbents will pack the electoral registry with the names of dead or nonexistent individuals to allow their followers to vote repeatedly. They could put polling stations in places inaccessible to their rivals; worse still, they could even stop hostile voters from casting their ballots. In conjunction with their opponents, they could restrict access to the franchise to keep subordinate groups from threatening their control of a largely corrupt political system. Indeed, one analyst has gone so far as to argue that politics in prereform Costa Rica was no different than in Guatemala. However they did so, several analysts claim, it was a relatively straightforward matter for incumbents to manufacture favorable electoral majorities. This is what made politics in prereform Costa Rica the predictable, elite-dominated affairs typical of oligarchic regimes.[1]

---

[1] Despite the fact that their books concentrate upon electoral activity, this is the view taken of elections by Orlando Salazar Mora, *El apogeo de la república liberal en Costa Rica, 1870–1914* (San José: EUCR, 1990) and by Jorge Mario Salazar Mora, *Crisis liberal y estado reformista: análisis político-electoral, 1914–1949* (San José: EUCR, 1995). Also, see Deborah J. Yashar, *Demanding Democracy: Reform and Reaction in Costa Rica and Guatemala, 1870s–1950s* (Stanford, CA: Stanford University Press, 1997), for the surprising argument that the political systems of both countries were remarkably similar oligarchies before the mid-twentieth century. For a different view of the Costa Rican oligarchic republic, see: Iván Molina, "Elecciones y democracia en Costa Rica (1885–1913)," *European Journal of Latin American and Caribbean Studies*, No. 70 (April 2001), pp. 41–57.

The Political Economy of Presidentialism

This chapter sheds light on the validity of conventional portraits by examining the impact of ballot-rigging on political competition when presidents were at their most powerful. It argues that election outcomes during the first decades of the twentieth century were not predetermined affairs. Despite a property restriction on the franchise, virtually all adult males (20 years old and older) had registered to vote. Over 50 percent of the electorate turned out to vote in presidential elections. When opposition parties found reason to complain about the behavior of government officials, they did not typically denounce blatant attempts to throw elections. Instead, they filed petitions charging officials with opening and closing polling stations out of schedule, incorrectly transcribing voters's choices, and other largely procedural violations of electoral law. What we will discover is that the difficulty – if not impossibility – of controlling the male electorate turned incumbents' attention to manipulating second-stage election results. Between popular and second-stage elections, presidents could much more easily shape the general will to their liking.

The main objective of this chapter, however, is to explain why parties commit and denounce acts of fraud. It evaluates two rival, though not mutually exclusive, accounts of electoral fraud. The first claims that parties and landlords violate electoral laws where voters are poorer, more illiterate, and in economically disadvantageous conditions. In such circumstances, voters are less able to defend their civil rights. The second hypothesis suggests that fraud varies with political competitiveness. Parties will use fraud to inflate their vote totals and to decrease those of their rivals to win hotly contested elections. By looking at provincial-level indices of fraud, this chapter argues that differences in electoral laws powerfully shaped the ballot-rigging strategies.

This chapter begins by looking at the role of the state in an agro-exporting economy to understand why the presidency was an object of deep, partisan concern. It then examines how the political structure of the state made retaining or holding the executive the principal objective of national political life. It then identifies central tendencies in electoral behavior. After analyzing allegations of electoral fraud, this chapter examines how the political system failed to deliver legitimate verdicts for hotly contested elections.

The Political Economy of Presidentialism

In a society without severe class and ethnic conflicts, the struggle over the state became the central issue separating allies from opponents. As it does in many other presidential systems, political life in Costa Rica revolved around retaining or gaining control of the presidency. In control of the executive branch of government, a party could reward its followers with jobs and beneficial policies. It could also perpetuate itself in power by manipulating electoral laws for partisan advantage.

Public Finances and Electoral Competition

The Costa Rican state was not revenue rich. It collected less than 5 percent of annual Gross Domestic Product (GDP) between 1901 and 1948. Extracting resources from a largely rural society whose economy was based upon the export of coffee and bananas made the state dependent on indirect forms of taxation for most of its income. An average of 70 percent of state revenues stemmed from taxes on international commerce and the state liquor monopoly between 1890 and 1947.[2]

Despite these limitations, politicians succeeded in using state resources to cultivate support with the electorate. Table 1.1 indicates that expenditures on education, health, and public works increased from 24 percent between 1890 and 1914 to 55 percent between 1940 and 1947. During this same period, military, and police expenditures slowly declined. Table 1.1 indicates that these expenditures went from 26 percent of all public spending between 1890 and 1914 to 16 percent between 1940 and 1947. With only two exceptions, public expenditures never declined during general election years. This trend became evident after 1932, when National Republican Party (PRN) governments increased expenditures during their last year in office. Despite falls in revenue induced by foreign commercial downturns, fiscal deficits did not prevent incumbents from spending to

---

[2] Taxing imports was easy because points of entry were few and required little administrative capacity. The rich and large numbers of small and medium-sized rural and urban property owners – comprising perhaps as much as a third of all adult males – might have been able to pay such an income or property tax, but the electoral costs of creating one deterred most politicians from developing bureaucracies to monitor the behavior of their constituents. According to the 1950 population census, at least a third of all males twenty years or older said they held property. See Republic of Costa Rica, *Censo de población de Costa Rica (22 de mayo de 1950)*, 2nd edition (San José: Dirección General de Estadística y Censos, 1975), pp. 292, 296, and 300. So, public authorities settled for taxing trade and other economic transactions easy to monitor and control. This and following paragraphs draw from Iván Molina, "Ciclo electoral y políticas públicas en Costa Rica (1890–1948)," *Revista Mexicana de Sociologia*, Vol. 63, No. 3 (July–September 2001), pp. 67–98.

Table 1.1. *Composition of State Revenue, 1902–47 (in Percentages)*

Time Period	Taxes on Foreign Trade	Taxes on Goods and Services[a]	Income from FANAL[b]	Income from Railroad[c]	Others
1890–1901	47	12	31	1	9
1902–16	62	1	25	6	8
1917–9	38	1	30	11	21
1920–9	60	5	19	9	9
1930–9	57	8	14	11	11
1940–7	42	14	19	11	14

Notes:
[a] The decrease in the percentage share of taxes on goods and services during 1902–16 stems from the dismantling of the tobacco monopoly in 1908.
[b] National Liquor Factory.
[c] After 1902, this income came only from the Pacific Railroad.
Source: Ana Cecilia Román, *Las finanzas públicas de Costa Rica: metodología y fuentes (1870–1948)* (San José: Centro de Investigaciones Históricas de América Central, 1995), pp. 27–38, 57–64.

help their parties win elections. This trend becomes clear after 1920, when electoral competition became more regular and intense.[3]

Not only did parties manipulate the public purse for partisan advantage, but they also found state employment for their followers. To quote from a bill that Deputy Tomás Soley (later minister of public finance) submitted to Congress in 1920,

... political contests have been converted into struggles for public posts, which are considered the victory booty and, as a result, as patronage to reward the interested adhesion of party followers, friends, and relatives of the triumphant candidate.[4]

Even in a vibrant agro-exporting economy such as Costa Rica's, state employment was significant. It allowed politicians and their parties to offer

---

[3] The relationship between electoral competition and social expenditures only became negative during the Frederico Tinoco dictatorship (1917–19).
[4] Cited in "Dictamen de la Comisión de Legislación (2 June 1924)," *La Gaceta*, No. 123 (6 June 1924), p. 630. Committee members referred to Soley's bill to demonstrate their sympathy for a bill proposing the creation of a civil service. Despite their purported support for the bill, Committee members did not endorse the bill because, they claimed, article 102 of the constitution empowered the president to name and replace all officials contracted by the executive. They did not, however, pursue or recommend a constitutional reform to deal with this vexing issue. Only in 1949 did a Constituent Assembly create a civil service.

Table 1.2. *Sectoral Composition of Public Employees, 1927[a]*

Occupation	Males	Percentage of the Male EAP	Females	Percentage of the Female EAP
Military, police, and soldiers	1,611	1.2		
Executive employees	3,139	2.3	1,284	7.6
Teachers and professors	511	0.4	1,452	8.6
Judicial employees	69	0.1		
Municipal employees	237	0.2	5	0.03
Post office employees	131	0.1	2	0.01
Telegraph employees	271	0.2	19	0.1
TOTAL	5,969	4.4	2,757	16.5

Note:
[a] The number of state employees is slightly underestimated because the 1927 Census does not identify those who worked on the Pacific Railroad, for the Government Printing Office, for the National Liquor Factory (FANAL), nor for autonomous agencies such as the National Bank of Costa Rica or the National Insurance Bank.
Source: Republic of Costa Rica, *Censo de población de Costa Rica 11 de mayo de 1927* (San José: Dirección General de Estadística y Censos, 1960), pp. 54–7.

employment to their followers. It created a ready-made constituency for both government and opposition to recruit as activists and, of course, as voters. As a share of the economically active population in urban areas, the state employed a maximum of 14 percent of the male labor force and a maximum of 26 percent of the female labor force by the mid-1920s. The strategic importance of state jobs increased for the publicists, professionals, and intellectuals who congregated in the capital and whose economic livelihood hinged upon employment as legal advisors, accountants, professors, and librarians, to name a few occupations to which they could aspire.[5] Annual growth in state employment, climbed from slightly more than 2 percent between 1890 and 1901 to over 4 percent between 1902 and 1916 – rates that exceeded the 1.9 annual population growth between 1901 and 1948.[6] Table 1.2 lists selected bureaucratic occupations from the 1927 population census.

[5] Iván Molina, *El que quiera divertirse: Libros y sociedad en Costa Rica, 1750–1914* (Heredia and San José: EUNA-EUCR, 1995), pp. 170–87.
[6] The 1902–16 growth rate is similar to the one in effect between 1950–70. Analysts typically define the postwar period as the heyday of import substitution industrialization and the politicization of state employment. See Molina, "Ciclo electoral y políticas públicas en Costa Rica."

State employment also allowed parties to finance their political campaigns. After the 1909 general elections, Republican Party (PR) President Ricardo Jiménez got Congress – where his party held a majority of seats – to approve a law that deducted a small percentage of each public servant's salary to pay for the PR's campaign expenses. Subsequent governments adopted this measure; it became the way that victorious parties paid debts contracted to pay for increasingly competitive electoral campaigns. Indeed, by the 1930s, parties not only solicited large contributions from wealthy donors, but they also contracted loans from private banks. Especially if a campaign's chances of winning were high, banks apparently willingly lent a campaign money because this quasipublic finance system guaranteed them repayment of the loan, and with interest.[7]

The consequences of politicizing state employment and public expenditures were profound. It shaped both the preferences of voters and politicians. Again, quoting from Deputy Soley's bill,

We do not vote for the man who presents a better program of government nor for him whose qualities we deem superior. We vote for this or that candidate because he is our friend; because he will give us the job we seek; because he will place this or that relative; in a word: for our *mercenary personal interests* and not, as it should be, for the best interests of the fatherland (emphasis in the original).[8]

"Mercenary personal interests" therefore led to the unideological politics so characteristic of Costa Rican society. In a country without significant class and ethnic conflicts, control of the state led to the cleavages that separated political friends from foes. The struggle between incumbents and opposition was not simply the expression of the principal cleavages of society; the conflict between "ins" and "outs" *was* the basis of political identity.

Presidentialism and the Classical Theory of Electoral Governance

Nineteenth-century constitutions typically split election administration between the executive and legislative branches of government.[9] The 1871

---

[7] Alex Solís, "El financiamiento de los partidos políticos," *Revista Parlamentaria*, Vol. 2, No. 2 (December 1994), p. 71.

[8] "Dictamen de la Comisión de Legislación (2 June 1924)," p. 630.

[9] See Fabrice Lehoucq, "The Institutional Foundations of Democratic Cooperation in Costa Rica," *Journal of Latin American Studies*, Vol. 26, No. 1 (May 1996), pp. 329–55.

Costa Rican constitution was no different. It makes the executive responsible for organizing, holding, and tallying the vote. To keep executive officials honest, the constitution empowers the legislature to certify the vote count. The classical approach to election governance therefore relies upon checks and balances to encourage presidents and legislators to produce election results that major political forces find acceptable. It assumes that executives and legislators would jealously guard their respective institutional prerogatives.

As we shall see, entrusting representative bodies with the responsibility for allocating state offices infuses election governance with an enormous amount partisan conflict. We hypothesize that the classical approach generates reasonably acceptable election results under divided government. When different parties control the executive and legislature, the party-less world envisaged by eighteenth-century theorists is roughly approximated.

In a world of competitive parties, however, politicians would not be principally loyal to their branch of government. Instead, politicians would maximize the interests of their parties by forging networks binding leaders and followers in search of employment, benefits, and security. So, if executive and legislators belong to the same party, partisan interests will override their institutional interests. Under unified government, the classical theory of election governance, we hypothesize, will fail to deliver impartial, accurate, and legitimate election verdicts.

Even under divided government, partisanship encourages presidents to manipulate electoral laws for partisan advantage. In control of the executive, parties could appoint progovernment officials to key administrative posts. They could ensure that the tally of the vote produced victories for government parties. They could pack the electoral registry with dead or nonexistent individuals who would "vote" for them on election day. If they also succeeded in gaining control of Congress, they could certify results they found acceptable and ignore the handful of their legislative opponents. Having no guarantees that their rivals would behave any differently, ruling parties therefore preferred monopolizing to sharing power.[10]

---

[10] This section draws upon Fabrice Lehoucq, "Can Parties Police Themselves? Electoral Governance and Democratization," *International Political Science Review*, Vol. 23, No. 1 (January 2002), pp. 29–46.

The Political Landscape of the Early Twentieth Century

Parties spent a great deal of time and energy to gain the support of voters throughout the country. They helped register citizens to vote and got them to the polls. Parties struggled for the support of electors, who met biennially in provincial assemblies to select one-half of Congress and to select presidents quadrennially. Far from being an activity of concern to a limited group of people, electoral politics commanded the attention of society at large.

The Size and Nature of the Electorate

Census and electoral records reveal, as commentators at the time liked to emphasize, that suffrage rights were universal for all adult males. Even though the 1871 constitution had a property (as well as a gender) restriction, its vagueness meant that, by the early twentieth century, all men at least twenty years old were registered to vote. Indeed, the percentage of adult males registered to vote climbed from 50 percent in 1897 to 100 percent 1913. Table 1.3 reveals that demographic estimates, are in ten of fifteen elections, 5.4 percent above or below the numbers of registered voters.[11]

The first reason why the franchise was universal for males stems from the interest that parties had in holding public office. Since it was local political authorities, with the consent of the local citizenry, who produced the electoral registries, parties could sway undecided certifiers by appealing to their kinship ties or political sentiments. In the second place, most adult males probably met the constitutional requirement that citizens have an adequate standard of living, either because they held enough property or had employment that generated an income sufficient to satisfy constitutional requirements. Commonly cited figures indicate that most men did own property during the first decades of the twentieth century. For example, the number of wage laborers (*jornaleros*) only went from 29 to 44 percent of the economically active male population between 1864 and 1927.[12] Even by 1950, when 59 percent of the agricultural workforce

---

[11] See note 4, p. 5.

[12] Republic of Costa Rica, *Censo general de la República de Costa Rica (27 de noviembre de 1864)*, 2nd edition (San José: Dirección General de Estadística y Censos, 1964), pp. 86–99, and Republic of Costa Rica, *Censo de población de Costa Rica (11 de mayo de 1927)* (San José: Dirección General de Estadística y Censos, 1960), pp. 54–7. Also, see Mario Samper, "Los productores directos en el siglo de café," *Revista de Historia* (Heredia, Costa Rica), No. 7 (July–Nov. 1978), pp. 153–94.

Table 1.3. *Size of the Electorate: Official and Estimated,*
1901–48

Year	Official[a]	Estimates	Difference in %
1901	N/A	66,032	—
1905	N/A	70,548	—
1909	N/A	75,291	—
1913	81,971	80,158	2.3
1915	N/A	82,637	—
1917	91,079	85,139	7.0
1919	84,987	87,745	−3.2
1921	N/A	90,149	—
1923	98,640	92,664	6.4
1925	92,760	92,162	0.6
1928	116,993	100,195	16.8
1932	116,855	111,192	5.1
1934	115,180	117,003	−1.6
1936	129,700	123,035	5.4
1938	124,289	129,299	−4.0
1940	139,219	135,803	2.5
1942	142,047	142,561	−0.4
1944	163,100	149,583	9.0
1946	160,336	156,880	2.2
1948	176,979	164,465	7.6

Note:
[a] N/A = Not available. We include at least the estimated size of
the electorate for every election year.
Source: Official figures are from *La Gaceta* (1913–48). Estimates are
from Iván Molina, "Estadísticas electorales de Costa Rica (1897–
1948): Una contribución documental," *Revista Parlamentoria* (San
José, Costa Rica), Vol. 9, No. 2 (August 2001), pp. 354–67.

consisted of "employees," many workers still retained parcels of land upon
which they grew coffee and subsistence crops.

According to Table 1.4, voters largely resided in rural areas during the
first half of the twentieth century. Even by 1950, men twenty years or older
still basically lived in the countryside; only 34 percent of them lived in
cities and villages. And what was true for the electorate was true for the
population as a whole: Its share of urban and semi-urban environments
increased only slightly from 27 to 34 percent between 1892 and 1950.

Table 1.4. *Social and Spatial Characteristics of the Electorate, 1892 and 1950*

Region	Population in Cities and Villages[a]		Males in the Agricultural Sector		Salaried Males in the Agricultural Sector		Population 10+ That Knows How to Read and Write	
	1892	1950	1892	1950	1892	1950	1892	1950
Center[b]	27	38	76	58	52	62	45	83
Periphery[b]	27	22	72	73	58	55	38	73
TOTAL	27	34	75	63	53	59	44	80

Notes:
[a] Population data for cities and villages are slightly underestimated for 1950.
[b] Central provinces include Alajuela, Cartago, Heredia, and San José. Peripheral provinces include Guanacaste, Limón, and Puntarenas.
Source: Republic of Costa Rica, *Censo general de la República de Costa Rica. 18 de febrero de 1892* (San José: Tipografía Nacional, 1893), pp. xix–xlix, liv–lvi, lxxxvi–cix; ídem, *Censo de población de Costa Rica. 22 de mayo de 1950*, 2ⁿᵈ edition (San José: Dirección General de Estadística y Censos, 1975), pp. 108–15, 247–54 and 292–5.

Most men also held typically rural occupations; the percentage of men employed in the agricultural sector declined only from 75 percent in 1892 to 63 percent of the workforce by the mid-twentieth century.

Electors and Second-Stage Elections

Suffrage restrictions were much more explicit for electors than for voters. Instead of applying the vague language used for popular elections, constitutional framers made participation in Provincial Electoral Assemblies contingent upon citizens being at least twenty-year-old males, knowing how to read and write and owning property "not below 500 pesos or having an annual rent of 200 pesos."[13] Popular sovereignty was also limited in another way: While voters chose electors to select presidents and one-half of deputies at four-year intervals, these same electors chose the other half of Congress during midterm elections. In addition to fraying the links between voters and representatives, this rule created the possibility that electors could become independent of the party leadership, especially since electors did cast their ballots in secret.

[13] Article 59, p. 469.

Table 1.5. *Second-Stage Electors: Participation and Occupation, 1898–1910*

Number of Times Elected	Number of Persons	Percentage	Occupation	Number of Persons	Percentage
1	2,335	76.1	Farmer with 3 or more laborers	383	12.5
2	604	19.7	Shopkeeper	179	5.8
3	112	3.6	Writer or journalist	56	1.8
4	19	0.6	Teacher or professor	44	1.4
			Physician	31	1.0
			Lawyer	29	0.9
			Billiard hall owner	27	0.9
			Priest	26	0.9
			Liquor salesman	24	0.8
			Store owner	24	0.8
			Coffee processor	22	0.7
			Merchant	13	0.4
			Artisan	10	0.3
			Cattle rancher	8	0.3
			Others	26	0.9
			Unknown	2,168	70.6
TOTAL	3,070	100.0	TOTAL	3,070	100.0

Source: Iván Molina y Fabrice Lehoucq, *Urnas de lo inesperado. Fraude electoral y lucha política en Costa Rica* (San José: EUCR, 1999), p. 35.

Like voters, approximately 80 percent of electors represented rural districts because population determined their number and distribution. Furthermore, the largest number of electors for which census data exists consisted of rural property owners employing three or more laborers. Other rural occupations represented among electors include coffee processors and cattlemen. As Table 1.5 reveals, Electoral Assemblies also represented significant numbers of lawyers, physicians, and other professionals. And, while many of the priests, billiard hall owners, and merchants who also figured prominently among the occupations in Table 1.5 lived in urban areas, many were from rural areas or in close contact with rural interests. So, while some electors were members of urban political networks, most belonged to local families and machines with interests in agricultural production and in politics, either as district administrators (*jefes políticos*), municipal councilmen, or, of course, electors. From this position of strength, electors were a crucial link in a party system that tied voters to deputies and to presidents, and one that reminded national-level party leaders of the need to build schools, roads, and other infrastructural policies of interest to a largely rural electorate.

Fraud during Indirect Elections

That citizens voted for electors only every four years intensified political competition for state offices indispensable for political survival and financial success. Political uncertainty drove incumbents to manipulate popular and second-stage elections even as opposition parties did not remain above violating the law for partisan advantage.

The Nature and Spatial Basis of Electoral Fraud

Between 1901 and 1912, parties filed twenty-two petitions, complaints (*reclamos*), reports (*memorias*), or protests containing 110 accusations of electoral fraud. Parties generated another seventy-five accusations of fraud when Provincial Electoral Councils met to tally the popular vote. On average, parties cast sixty-two complaints for each of the general elections held between 1901 and 1912.

Perhaps the most striking fact about the denunciations of electoral fraud is that a disproportionate share took place in the peripheral provinces of the republic. Though the provinces of Guanacaste, Limón, and Puntarenas contained a fifth of the electorate, parties made 48 percent (88 of 185) of their charges against electoral activity in the periphery.

Then, as now, the periphery was sparsely settled. With the exception of the ports of Limón and Puntarenas, outlying provinces did not contain any urban centers of national importance (see Figure 1.1). An impoverished peasantry lived in the province of Guanacaste; large-scale cattle ranchers and foreign mineral corporations dominated its economy and society.[14] In the Caribbean coast province of Limón, the United Fruit

---

[14] Marc Edelman, *The Logic of the Latifundio: The Large Estates of Northwestern Costa Rica since the Late Nineteenth Century* (Stanford, CA: Stanford University Press, 1992). This and the following paragraphs draw from Iván Molina, "Un país, dos electorados. El caso de Costa Rica (1890–1950)," *Desacatos. Revista de antropología social* (Oaxaca, México), No. 6 (Spring–Summer, 2001), pp. 165–174, and from Iván Molina and Fabrice Lehoucq, "Political Competition and Electoral Fraud: A Latin American Case Study," *Journal of Interdisciplinary History*, Vol. 30, No. 2 (Autumn 1999), pp. 199–234.

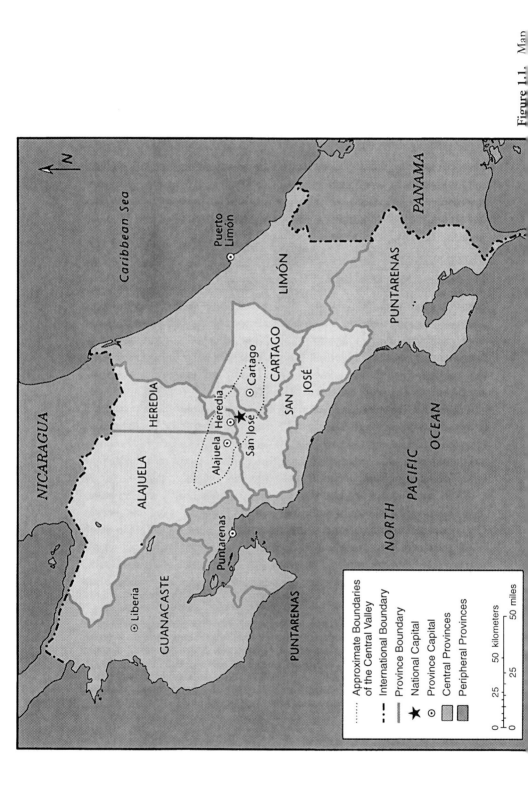

Figure 1.1. Map

Company employed the largest number of agricultural workers. While Guanacaste consisted of mulatto and indigenous populations, Limón held large numbers of English-speaking immigrants from the West Indies and a not insignificant number of Nicaraguans. Finally, after United Fruit left Limón in the 1930s, it settled in the Pacific Coast Province of Puntarenas. A mestizo population of poor peasants and agricultural workers lived in this province.[15]

In outlying provinces, education and public health services were also less abundant. In Guanacaste and Puntarenas, the 1927 population census indicates that literacy rates among individuals ten years or older were 57 and 50 percent, respectively. In Limón, the literacy rate reached a high of 77 percent, largely because many West Indians could read and write in English. Between 1892 and 1950, the population ten years or older that was literate increased from 45 to 83 percent in the center and from 38 to 73 percent in the periphery, respectively. Only 20 percent of the electorate resided in the periphery in 1901; by 1946, only 26 percent of the eligible voters lived in the outlying parts of the republic.

In contrast, the four central provinces contain a region known as the Central Valley. It is approximately 3,200 square kilometers and possesses 16 percent of the land in these four provinces and 6 percent of the national territory. The Central Valley remains the epicenter of the production of coffee, which has an important sector of small and medium-sized coffee producers.[16] The Central Valley houses a largely mestizo population that considers itself to be white and racially superior to its darker compatriots in the periphery. It had been the principal beneficiary of liberal public health and educational reforms launched in the late nineteenth century. By 1927, 68 percent of the population nine years old or above was

---

[15] For more on Limón, see Philippe Bourgois, *Ethnicity at Work: Divided Work on a Central American Banana Plantation* (Baltimore, MD: Johns Hopkins University Press, 1989); Aviva Chomsky, *A Perfect Slavery: West Indian Workers and the United Fruit Company in Costa Rica, 1870–1950* (Baton Rouge, LA: Louisiana State University Press, 1996); and, Ronny Viales, *Después del enclave: un estudio de la región Atlántica costarricense* (San José: EUCR, 1998).

[16] See, in particular, Carolyn Hall, *El café y el desarrollo histórico-geográfico de Costa Rica* (San José: ECR, 1976); Lowell Gudmundson, "Peasant, Farmer, Proletarian: Class Formation in a Smallholder Economy, 1850–1950," *Hispanic American Historical Review*, Vol. 69, No. 2 (May 1989), pp. 221–57. Iván Molina, *Costa Rica (1800–1850): el legado colonial y la génesis del capitalismo* (San José: EUCR, 1991); and Mario Samper, *Generations of Settlers: Rural Households and Markets on the Costa Rican Frontier, 1850–1935* (Boulder, CO: Westview Press, 1990).

literate. And, in 1901, these provinces housed 80 percent of the electorate; by 1946, they contained 74 percent of eligible voters.[17]

That the periphery was responsible for basically half of all accusations of fraud suggests that its citizens were less able to defend themselves against violations of electoral law. Parties committed more acts of fraud where the electorate was more illiterate, dispersed over a larger territory, and where large-scale banana plantations and cattle ranches predominated. Unlike the periphery, the more densely settled and well-connected villages of the Central Valley were also able to detect infractions of electoral law more easily. An electorate that was more literate was also more able to communicate transgressions of electoral law to the newspapers located in the principal cities of the republic. As a result, parties and civil society as a whole deterred rivals from stuffing the ballot box.

Institutional differences, however, also encouraged parties to commit – and to denounce – acts of fraud in greater numbers in outlying provinces than in central provinces. Between 1901 and 1912, it was much easier for parties to elect their candidates to Congress in the periphery because they only had to win more votes than each of their rivals. In contrast, parties could compete for seats in the center only if they attracted the support of at least one electoral quotient – a sum obtained by dividing the total number of votes by contested seats – because core provinces typically sent three or more members to Congress per election. Levels of fraud were three times higher in the periphery than in the center between 1901 and 1912. On average, there were 591 eligible voters per accusation of fraud in the periphery to 1,946 eligible voters per accusation lodged in the center.

Only differences in electoral laws, however, can explain why there were, proportionally, three times as many accusations in the periphery than in the center. Once we control for the size of the electorate, there were 5,320 eligible voters per party in outlying provinces and 21,164 eligible voters per party in the center. And in the periphery it was much easier for parties to win legislative seats because they only had to attract move votes than any of their rivals. Precisely where voters were most vulnerable, politicians and parties had more incentives to commit and to denounce acts of fraud.

According to Tables 1.6 and 1.7, parties filed 85 percent of their accusations against popular elections between 1901 and 1912. More than a

---

[17] Molina, "Un país, dos electorados."

Fraud during Indirect Elections

Table 1.6. *Accusations of Electoral Fraud, 1901–12*

Province	Number of Accusations	Category of Fraud	Accusation	Number
Center			*Popular election*	
San José	8		Officials did not take an electoral census	1
Alajuela	14	2	Against polling stations[a]	80
Cartago	42	4	Officials show favoritism	64
Heredia	33	4	Coercion against polling stations	6
			Coercion against voters	3
			Not specified[a]	3
Periphery				
Guanacaste	38		*Second stage*	
Puntarenas	29	1	Elector not qualified to vote by technical defects	10
Limón	21	1	Technical or legal defects	8
		2	Elections held off schedule	1
		3	Elector excluded	4
		3	Alternate elector illegally voted	1
		4	Coercion against electors	1
			Person elected not qualified for post[b]	3
TOTAL	185		TOTAL	185

Notes:
[a] See Table 1.7.
[b] Theses cases did not apply in our classification.
Source: *La Gaceta* (1901–12).

third of them (65 of 157) contain charges against polling station and other public officials. Parties, for example, accused local government authorities of not having produced a comprehensive electoral registry. They also charged that public officials displayed favoritism toward the progovernment party. Petitioners also leveled charges of a procedural sort against polling station officials. Forty-five percent of the charges (36 of 80) against polling stations officials complained that they had not, for example, affixed

Table 1.7. *Accusations against Polling Stations, 1901–12*

Category of Fraud	Accusations against Polling Stations	Number
1	Technical or legal defects	36
2	Elections held off schedule	2
2	Voting booth in inappropriate place	2
3	Voters did not meet requirements	26
3	Voters excluded inappropriately	8
3	Party representative expelled or threatened	2
3	Voters cast multiple ballots	4
TOTAL		80

Source: *La Gaceta* (1901–12).

the required signatures on tally sheets or had not sworn in their members correctly.

The most serious sorts of violations were significantly less commonplace. Twenty-five percent (40 of 157) of the accusations lodged against popular elections denounced efforts to inflate or deflate the vote totals of rivals. Such charges included expelling party observers from polling stations and preventing citizens from voting. Parties also accused polling station officials of allowing some citizens to vote more than once and of permitting individuals not meeting suffrage requirements to vote. Only 5 percent (9 of 157) of the accusations involved the use of coercion by authorities against voters or polling stations.

Of the 15 percent of the charges against second-stage elections, almost a third (8 of 28) were procedural in nature. The most commonplace charges were that electors had not received the majorities the law required, that the president of the Electoral Assembly had not been legally selected and that the Assembly did not have a legal quorum when it made its decisions. These findings suggest that the denunciation of electoral fraud did not involve the blatant fabrication of large numbers of votes, but procedural infractions and changes in the status of electors.

Most denunciations of second-stage elections concentrated on the alleged shortcomings of electors themselves. Thirty-nine percent (11 of 28) of these charges argued that electors did not satisfy the income or wealth requirements. Other charges were procedural in nature – that electors no longer lived in the district they represented, that they were under legal prosecution or that they held a job, such as police officer, that was incompatible with being an elector. These accusations suggest that parties went to great lengths to monitor electors from rival parties to determine if their economic and residential status changed over the course of their four-year terms.

Rarely did petitions seek to impugn the qualifications of elected officials. Radical PR Deputy Victor Fernández, for example, failed to disqualify the election of Ascención Esquivel to the presidency in 1902. Neither did working-class leader Gerardo Matamoros succeed in overturning the election of Deputy Gregorio Martin in May 1904 by arguing that he was a foreigner and therefore constitutionally barred from holding public office.[18] Only a group of electors from the city of Puntarenas achieved such an objective and its target was the PR deputy, Pablo M. Rodríguez. The group prevented him from taking a seat in Congress by arguing that being a deputy was constitutionally incompatible with being a judge on a civil court. Furthermore, his detractors claimed that he did not obtain the support of the absolute majority the law required – he received the support of only 49 percent (18 of 37) of electors in their provincial Electoral Assembly.[19]

Between 1901 and 1912, only one charge concerned the use of force against electors. PR Deputy Martin criticized the government for taking advantage of a state of siege in 1906 to jail or otherwise prevent 371 opposition electors from voting against their presidential candidate. This petition also denounced the widely reported claim that seventy-six opposition electors were compelled to vote for the progovernment candidate. During this period, the denunciations refer to a total of only four occasions when electors were arbitrarily excluded from Electoral Assemblies; three of these took place in the periphery and one in the center.

Only one of the twenty-two petitions was directed against a president. Radical liberal Deputy Fernández presented the sole petition to overturn the election Esquivel's 1902 compromise candidacy. Curiously enough, the radical liberal congressman did not refer to violations of electoral law committed during the election, but to the charge that Esquivel was not a Costa Rican citizen because he had been born in Nicaragua of "Nicaraguan parents."[20] Sure enough, article 96 did require presidents to

---

[18] O.s. no. 103, *La Gaceta*, No. (6 May 1904), p. 419.

[19] "Dictamen de la Comisión de Credenciales (7 May 1904)," *La Gaceta*, No. 106 (10 May 1904), p. 432, and "Memorial (14 March 1904)," *La Gaceta*, No. 101 (4 May 1904), pp. 408–9.

[20] "Dictamen de la Comisión de Credenciales (n.d.)," *La Gaceta*, No. 101 (5 May 1902), p. 410.

have acquired their citizenship by being born on national territory. But, what the new president's critics did not mention was that article 5 (paragraph four) also naturalized residents of Guanacaste in 1858. Though Esquivel was born in Rivas, Nicaragua, in 1844, his parents moved to Guanacaste before 1858, thus making them and their children citizens of Costa Rica. Over the protests of his detractors, Congress nevertheless voted to declare Esquivel president.[21]

The Intensity and Magnitude of Electoral Fraud

We classify accusations into one of four categories to discern the impact of fraud on political competition. One dimension upon which we categorize acts of fraud is by whether the act is manifestly fraudulent. The other dimension taps the intensity of abuse exercised against voters. Sixty-nine percent of the accusations between 1901 and 1912 fell into the initial two categories. This was a pattern that was true of the center as well as of the periphery: 35 percent of accusations made in the core provinces are fraud types three and four. Twenty-six percent of them in the outlying provinces belong in these categories. Most of the charges, in other words, were procedural in nature.

This finding raises the vexing issue of whether the petitions record all instances of ballot-rigging. While there is no definite way of knowing whether parties neglected to report blatant acts of fraud to the authorities, we doubt that parties refrained from denouncing the worst sorts of fraud because, simply put, they did. The very same reasons that encouraged parties to distort election results – their interest in holding state power – also drove them to monitor and to denounce the behavior of their rivals. Furthermore, the public ballot allowed parties to keep tabs on voters. If citizens, their families, friends, and the party leadership and rank and file were literally watching, their rivals were deterred from committing the worst acts of fraud.

The overall magnitude of fraud remained quite small in most elections. Parties disqualified votes only in a total of 2 percent (9 of 531) of all polling stations in 1901. They impugned votes in 13 percent (75 of 568) and

---

[21] Ibid. On Esquivel's citizenship, see Clotilde Obregón, *El río San Juan en la lucha de las potencias, 1821–60* (San José: EUNED, 1993), p. 244. We thank Daniel Masís for bringing these facts to our attention.

3 percent (21 of 607) of polling stations in 1905 and 1909, respectively. And, because successful presidential candidates in 1901 and 1909 won by margins of 54 and 44 percent, respectively, it is clear that, even if all accusations were true, they would not have changed electoral results.[22] This conclusion also appears to hold for the 1905 elections. Only by assuming that every vote cast at each of these polling stations was fraudulent can we conclude that the National Union Party (PUN) stole this election.[23] Despite the suspension of the constitutional order and official pressure, the PUN candidate obtained the support of only 41 percent of the electorate. What made the 1905–6 election season so scandalous was the way the government treated opposition electors. Indeed, the PUN government repressed electors precisely because it was unable to fabricate a large enough majority to ensure the triumph of its candidate in popular elections.

Official parties were unable to fabricate enough votes during popular elections to impose official candidates on the presidency. This is why presidents who were determined to stay in office or impose their successors resorted to jailing, harassing, or otherwise manipulating the much smaller number of electors. Between 1897 and 1909, there was an average of 798 electors; in contrast, the electorate consisted of an average of 68,397 citizens, 56 percent of which turned out to vote. And, of course, executives had only to cajole or to repress an even smaller group – that is, those electors who identified themselves with the opposition.

Congress, Reform, and Dispute Resolution

The fundamental objective of parties fielding observers, scribes, and legal specialists was to convince Congress to invalidate fraudulent elections. How did they do this? Did they meet with any success?

---

[22] This is a retrospective estimate based on the number and distribution of polling stations in 1913. During the elections of this year, there was an average of 123 and 130 estimated voters per station in the center and the periphery, respectively. Since we could not find the number of polling stations in use in the 1901, 1905, and 1909 elections, we divided the number of estimated voters in the center and periphery for these elections by the number of polling stations in existence in 1913. This figure probably is an underestimate. Figures in the last sentence of the text are based upon percentage of electors in 1901 and the popular vote in 1909.

[23] Salazar Mora, *El apogeo de la república liberal en Costa Rica, 1870–1914*, p. 213.

Institutional Controls

Though the constitution empowered Congress to certify election results, laws and administrative practices transformed Provincial Electoral Councils into de facto oversight committees of election-related activities. The 1893 Law of Elections made Councils responsible for the tally of the vote, a duty that inevitably led them to review election results. Provincial Electoral Councils acted upon 17 percent (or 27 of 157) of the accusations against popular elections made during this period. On average, the Councils of the center and the periphery annulled votes in 42 and 33 percent of the provincial elections held between 1901 and 1912, respectively. And, parties sent Provincial Electoral Councils three of the twenty-two petitions they wrote between 1901 and 1912. The Councils ruled in favor of two of these petitions and rejected the others. Curiously, a Council accepted one of the petitions filed in 1904, despite the fact that it was not legally empowered to do so.[24]

Councils often acted arbitrarily. In 1901, for example, the Electoral Council of San José ruled against the request to annul some votes because citizens too young to vote cast them. It rejected the claim because a priest had issued the supporting birth certificates, a common enough occurrence in a rural, Catholic country where the Civil Registry was only thirteen years old.[25] Conflicts between secular and religious authority, though absent from party politics, still exerted their pull on both legal and political matters.

Yet, the Councils could behave more evenhandedly. In 1901, for example, the Electoral Council of Cartago annulled the vote in two districts because local authorities had incorrectly altered electoral registries. To resolve the problem, it called for new elections at a later date.[26] The Council of Heredia agreed to annul the votes of several citizens when it found that they did not meet suffrage requirements. It also decided not to

---

[24] These figures would have been even higher in 1905, when Congress approved a reform specifying that only the Chamber of Repeal of the Supreme Court was entitled to annul votes. As we shall see, this reform did not stop Provincial Electoral Councils from annulling votes. For more on these issues, see Iván Molina, "La Comisión de Credenciales y Renuncias del Congreso: Un capítulo olvidado de la política costarricense (1902–1948)," in Ronny Viales, ed., *Memoria del IV Simposio Panamericano de Historia* (Mexico: Instituto Panamericano de Geografía e Historia, 2001), pp. 113–31.

[25] "Elecciones de primer grado (24 December 1901)," *La Gaceta*, No. 5 (8 January 1902), p. 22. The Civil Registry was established in 1888.

[26] "Acta electoral (25 December 1901)," *La Gaceta*, No. 12 (16 January 1902), p. 50.

54

tally the votes of two citizens whose preferences were recorded twice. The petition does not mention whether double-voting was intentional or accidental.[27]

Congress ruled on all but two of the remaining fifteen petitions.[28] The PR filed ten, and the Civil Party (PC) presented four of these petitions; the partisan identity of the last petitioner is unknown. The Credentials Committee endorsed only two of them unanimously and rejected eleven of them. The Committee issued both majority and minority reports on the remaining two petitions. And, the record of Congress as a whole was even worse – or better, depending upon the partisanship of the observer. It ruled in favor of only two petitions. In the first, a group of citizens in Puntarenas called for revoking the 1904 election of PR Pablo Rodríguez. In the second, a PR candidate requested that he be named first alternate in the Province of Alajuela. Both the Committee and Congress as a whole voted unanimously in favor of these petitions.

Though the PUN-dominated Credentials Committee and Congress rejected the six PR petitions and one PC petition filed between 1901 and 1906, the behavior of the PR-dominated Committee and Congress between 1908 and 1912 suggests that it could be more evenhanded. Between 1906 and 1912, when the PR controlled the Credentials Committee and, after 1908, Congress as a whole, the Credentials Committee and Congress rejected all eight petitions, even though the PR and PC filed four and three of these petitions, respectively (again, the partisan affiliation of the last one is unknown). Partisan interests did not always prevail because, as the Credentials Committee pointed out and our analysis of the magnitude of fraud corroborates, ruling in favor of these petitions would not have changed election results anyway.

Political Conflict and Electoral Reform

With the executive in control of Congress, coalitions of moderate and hardline opposition sectors plotted to overthrow presidents. Between 1889

---

[27] "Acta electoral (23 December 1901)," *La Gaceta*, No. 14 (18 January 1902), p. 57.

[28] The last one was sent to the secretary of the interior. It asked the secretary to permit PR electors from the Canton of Limón in the Province of Limón to vote in the 1912 midterm elections. The secretary rejected the appeal because the Chamber of Repeal was reviewing the legality of the elections that had made the individuals in question electors.

and 1906, presidents possessed the loyalty of three-quarters of Congress; during these years, they became the targets of seven insurrections.[29]

After surviving an opposition-led rebellion at the end of his first year in office, National Union Party (PUN) President Cleto González sent Congress a modest bill of electoral reforms in May 1907. His action unleashed several years of negotiations between an "imposed" president and an opposition swollen with victims of political repression. His proposed reforms stipulated that residency requirements be tightened to prevent citizens from voting in more than one district, that requests to nullify electoral results be simplified and judged by the judiciary, and that the length of campaigns be restricted.[30]

Over the next three years, the PUN president and his PR opponents passed three sets of amendments to the 1893 Law of Elections. These reforms restricted the executive's ability to interfere in the electoral process. Provincial governors, whom the president named, were no longer to be the presiding officers at Provincial Electoral Assemblies. Instead, the Supreme Court of Justice would hold a raffle among six candidates it nominated; the randomly chosen person would then become the president of an Electoral Assembly. These amendments also incorporated the 1905 law that empowered this Court's Chamber of Repeal (*Casación*) to judge petitions lodged against popular elections; Congress remained responsible for assessing the validity of second-stage elections. These reforms also allowed parties to appoint poll watchers to observe the deliberations of Provincial Electoral Councils and polling stations. Most importantly, they gave electors immunity to prevent the sort of abuse that had led to González's imposition on the presidency in 1906.[31]

---

[29] Lehoucq, "The Institutional Foundations of Democratic Cooperation in Costa Rica," pp. 334, 341.

[30] *Exposición y proyecto de ley para la reforma de la Ley de Elecciones*, presentado al Congreso Constitucional de la República de Costa Rica por P. J. Valverde, Secretario en el Despacho de la Secretaría de Gobernación (San José: Tipografía Nacional, 1907). On the 1906 revolt against the president, see Octavio Quesada, *Sumaria por sedición: noviembre, diciembre de 1906* (San José: Imprenta Nacional, 1906).

[31] They were "Ley No. 28 (1 December 1908)," "Ley No. 30 (22 May 1909)," "Ley No. 73 (26 June 1909)." All reforms of the 1893 Law of Elections in effect for the 1910 general elections are included in *Compilación sobre Leyes de Elecciones* (June 1909) (San José: Tipografía Nacional, 1909).

Politicizing the Judiciary

The legal reform that empowered the Chamber of Repeal to review petitions against first-stage elections was the first attempt to involve judicial institutions in electoral affairs. It, however, was a partial solution to repairing the flaw of splitting election administration between the two political branches of government. That Congress retained the authority to certify both second-stage elections and election results as a whole created another institutional rift that compounded difficulties of adjudicating electoral conflicts.

At first, Electoral Councils and the Credentials Committee respected the Chamber's interventions in electoral affairs. In 1905, the Chamber of Repeal overturned fifteen of the Electoral Council of Heredia's nullifications. This amounted to slightly more than half of all nullifications that Electoral Councils made between 1901 and 1912. Though the president of the Electoral Council of Heredia complained that the Chamber "is removing the faculty of tallying the vote in the true meaning of the word," he and other Council officials accepted judicial interference in their affairs.[32] The PR-dominated Credentials Committee also refused to endorse the petition to overturn the 1912 Congressional election of Francisco de Paula Amador, a member of the *jimenista* wing of the PR. The Committee ruled in favor of a member of the PR because it did not want to contradict the Chamber. In earlier decisions, the Chamber concluded that the popular election responsible for the PR *jimenista* deputy was devoid of irregularities.[33] The PR-dominated Congress voted in favor of the Committee's recommendation.

On other occasions, however, splitting the authority for reviewing two-stage elections between the Credentials Committee, Congress, and the judiciary could lead to conflicting decisions. In 1912, for example, the Credentials Committee again refused to overturn the Chamber's verdict. On this occasion, two PR stalwarts, Antonio Álvarez and Pablo M. Rodríguez, argued that the Electoral Assembly of Guanacaste deliberated without satisfying legal quorum. Though the minimum number of

---

[32] National Archive of Costa Rica, Gobernación, Exp. 1629 (1905), ff. 68–68 v.

[33] "Dictamen de la Comisión de Credenciales (2 May 1912)," *La Gaceta*, No. 103 (10 May 1912), p. 566. We could not find a partisan affiliation for the petitioner, Antonio Peña Rebolledo.

electors were present (fifty-two), they argued that one of them, Rafael Hurtado (who appears to have belonged to the PC), was a nonnaturalized foreigner.[34]

The Credential Committee's recommendation provoked an outcry in Congress. PC Deputy Francisco Faerrón pointed out that the ruling ignored the fact that the Guanacastan Electoral Assembly president had not allowed additional electors to take part in deliberations once the legal quorum was met. According to the PC deputy, the Assembly president wanted to invalidate electoral results. Though the PR dominated Congress, it accepted his arguments because, we suspect, doing otherwise would have cost the civilistas and the PR each a legislative seat.[35] If Congress would have accepted the request for nullification, it would have had to convene new elections in Guanacaste. Furthermore, by rejecting the Credential Committee's opinion, Congress implicitly rebuffed the Chamber of Repeal.

In all fairness to Congress, existing legislation was not clear on whether the president of this Assembly had acted illegally. According to the Committee, article 55 of the 1893 electoral law allowed the president of an Electoral Assembly to restrict the inflow of electors to the legal quorum.[36] Yet, this very same article stated that "on election day, the Assembly could be convened with just electors [and not with their alternates], if all are present, or with the electors present plus alternates", so that electors and their alternates could increase the total number of electors choosing public officials in provincial Assemblies.

Involving the judiciary in one stage of election administration did little to dampen partisan conflict. If the law itself was ambiguous, confusion would contribute to institutional rivalry. Both would be filed to produce impartial and acceptable verdicts. Furthermore, "if the legislature is the first not to respect the rulings of the courts," PR Deputy Alfredo González pointed out, "we will promptly reach a terrible chaos."[37] The use of the judiciary in electoral affairs therefore threatened the impartiality of this branch of government.

---

[34] "Dictamen de la Comisión de Credenciales (2 May 1912)." It was not unusual that foreigners were chosen as electors. A notable case is that of U.S. Geologist William Gabb, who represented a district in Talamanca in 1901. See "Demanda de nulidad (20 December 1901)," *La Gaceta*, No. 15 (19 January 1902), p. 62.

[35] "Dictamen de la Comisión de Credenciales (2 May 1912)," p. 566.

[36] Ibid.

[37] O.s. no. 1 (2 May 1912), art. 2, *La Gaceta*, No. 100 (7 May 1912), p. 544.

Parties and Electors: Principal-Agent Problems

Between popular elections and the meeting of Electoral Assemblies, electors could change their preferences. That so many of them, especially of the opposition, preferred to go to jail or otherwise refrain from voting against the wishes of the electorate suggests that party networks and kinship ties brought pressure to bear on them to hue a partisan line. But, political alliances were always changing: Between general elections, electors were entrusted with selecting one-half of all deputies. Electors and the deputies they chose could tip the Congressional balance of power against presidents. Midterm elections could therefore hasten or halt the decline of a presidency.

Parties began to raise concerns about the loyalty of electors at the beginning of the twentieth century. The letters of accreditation the PUN to its electors in 1901 nicely exhibit these concerns:

> this victory of the National Party, that expressed will of the people . . . this patriotic mandate of the district [which the elector represents] is now dependent upon your loyalty as a powerful covenant, invulnerable to clever tricks and unbreakable in the face of violence. The Esquivelist National Party, which before the popular election placed its trust in you in the hopes of triumphing . . . now is confident, after its victory, that you will remain loyal . . .[38]

For parties, then, the dependability of electors was a central issue. Not even an authoritarian politician like Rafael Iglesias, who had governed the republic for eight years, was able to ensure that all of his followers endorsed Esquivel's compromise candidacy. During the electoral campaign, many PC voters favored sending eighty-one of his electors to the Provincial Electoral Assemblies of Cartago and Guanacaste – against Iglesias's expressed wishes. According to the terms of the self-styled "transaction," they should have voted for the PUN.[39]

The rebellious or "suicidal" PC electors, as they were called, illustrate the challenge parties faced trying to maintain the loyalty of both citizens and electors alike, especially in the aftermath of the 1907 and 1908 reforms that ended up making electors even more independent of the party leadership. The behavior of these representatives also explains why politicians began to clamor for the elimination of indirect elections. Perhaps few were

---

[38] Colección de muestras de la Tipografía de Sibaja, 1901, Cultural Historical Museum, Alajuela, Costa Rica.

[39] Salazar Mora, *El apogeo de la república liberal en Costa Rica, 1870–1914*, pp. 207–8.

as eloquent as Ricardo Jiménez, the PR deputy (1906–10), who had proven himself to be a pragmatic and outspoken member of the opposition and later became president. He proclaimed that

the Electoral Assemblies are antiquated institutions . . . electors can dispose of their votes as they see fit; and that possibility can provoke, between first and second stage elections, the formation of intrigues that serve to deceive the popular will or, at the very least, to maintain a harmful political instability fed by uncertainty. . . . All outcomes depend upon the will of electors; and, since their terms last four years, it can also become the case that the elections made after the first year are completely divorced from the public will because of the emergence of new issues that could not have been taken into account during the selection of electors.[40]

What is striking about this speech is that Jiménez raised a plethora of issues, the most important of which concerned the threats to stability posed by constitutionally empowering a small group of citizens to choose executives and legislators at four-year intervals. His declarations also pointed to another issue, one of significantly less concern to parties, but of vital interest to democratic theory: namely, whether the existing system of indirect elections was an efficient way of ensuring that elected officials remained responsive to public opinion. For reasons both normative and practical, parties began to demand the reform of an institution they found increasingly unacceptable.

Conclusions

The financial resources of the Costa Rican state made holding the presidency the primary goal of political competition. The concentration of so much discretionary authority over electoral matters discouraged incumbents from relinquishing control of the presidency. Quite predictably, the monopolization of state power encouraged opposition moderates to form coalitions with opposition sectors to overthrow the president. This chronic cycle of instability began to break down only by the early twentieth century, when executives started to trade access to power for consent to their rule.

---

[40] "Mensaje inaugural presentado al Congreso por el Licenciado don Ricardo Jiménez (8 de mayo de 1910)," in Carlos Meléndez Chaverri, comp., *Mensajes presidenciales*, 1906–16, t. IV (San José: Biblioteca de la Academia de Geografía e Historia de Costa Rica, 1983), pp. 130–1.

Conclusions

In line with social structural arguments, parties spent more time criticizing the electoral behavior of their rivals in outlying provinces than in central provinces. Though only 20 percent of eligible voters resided in the periphery, close to half of all accusations of electoral fraud were concentrated in the provinces with the greatest ethnic heterogeneity as well as the lowest rates of literacy and urbanization. Unlike the ethnically more homogeneous center, the periphery was dominated by large-scale plantation agriculture and cattle estates. Though large landlords existed in the center, there was also a large sector of small and medium-sized coffee growers in the central provinces of the republic. Moreover, most educated voters lived in the center, and rates of literacy were higher here than in the periphery. For these reasons, the population of the periphery was less able to defend itself from official abuse of electoral laws.

The structure of electoral laws, however, shaped the spatial distribution of fraud between 1901 and 1912. Precisely where voters were the poorest, least literate, and most geographically isolated, politicians had more incentives to commit acts of fraud and to denounce their opponents' infractions of electoral law. That parties in the periphery only needed to attract more support second-stage electors than their rivals oddly enough encouraged them to accuse their rivals of electoral misconduct more often in outlying than in core provinces. Since the difference in votes between winners and losers was typically less in plurality than in proportional representation provinces, it was rational for parties to denounce fraud more often in the periphery than in the center. Differences in electoral laws also explains why, once we control for the size of the electorate, there were four times as many eligible voters per party in the periphery than in the center. Simply put, greater levels of political competitiveness encouraged politicians and parties to commit and denounce acts of fraud precisely where sociological perspectives claimed civil society was too weak to defend its political rights.

Between 1901 and 1912, most violations of electoral law were procedural in nature and occurred during popular elections. Parties denounced public officials for displaying favoritism toward the official party. They accused polling station officials of starting the vote off schedule and/or swearing in their members incorrectly. But, parties also denounced blatant acts of electoral fraud. That most petitions focused on rather petty charges of fraud reflects the fact that voting in public – in front of rivals and supporters – discouraged parties from coercing opposition voters. Simply put, public elections allowed everyone to observe and therefore to deter the worst acts of fraud. Though most allegations of fraud were procedural, parties did lambast the executive for committing more blatant acts of fraud. The PR did file a petition against President Esquivel in 1906. It accused the PUN of jailing large numbers of opposition electors to impose its candidate on the presidency. That the opposition used legal channels to denounce the president's behavior also suggests that filing petitions was rapidly becoming an accepted way of protesting the executive's arbitrary use of power.

We also discover that the magnitude of fraud was less than the margin of votes separating winners from losers. With the exception of the 1906 imposition, subtracting a very liberal estimate of impugned numbers of votes from the total number of votes that presidential candidates obtained would not have changed overall results. Even in 1906, the incumbent party lost the presidential election if we assume that all ballots were fraudulent at polling stations where petitioners claimed that their rivals had stuffed the ballot box.

The classical theory of electoral governance failed to arbitrate disputes about election results. In line with office-seeking approaches to political behavior, the discretionary authority presidents held proved too tempting to ignore. As the 1906 imposition demonstrates, executives used their powers to pack Congress with their supporters and then to certify election results to seal their grip on the state. Only the threat of continued opposition-led rebellions forced the new president to relinquish some of his authority over electoral administration. Even if these reforms strengthened safeguards for electors and opposition parties, they failed to remove partisanship from electoral governance. Indeed, allowing only judicial institutions to review popular elections led to repeated clashes between the three branches of government.

2

Institutional Change, Electoral Cycles, and Partisanship, 1910–4

Introduction

Parties debated a large number of institutional reforms in the 1910s. They analyzed the consequences of creating the secret franchise. They explored the benefits of eliminating two-stage elections for public offices. Politicians identified the merits of the popular election of governors and district administrators. They also considered replacing the proportional representation with the plurality election of legislators. Parties, however, approved only a small number and uncontroversial set of reforms.

This outcome is surprising because two conditions seemed to be ripe to enact far-reaching reforms. First, one party was in control of both branches of government. After more than two decades combating arbitrary presidents, the Republican Party (PR) triumphed in the 1909 general elections. In a field featuring only one other candidate, the PR's Ricardo Jiménez attracted the support of 71 percent of the popular vote. When Provincial Electoral Assemblies met, 91 percent of the electors voted in favor of the PR presidential and legislative candidates. Second, after two decades of political persecution, the PR could credibly claim that it would overhaul the institutional architecture of the republic.

The puzzle we resolve in this chapter is why, despite these advantages, Congress approved so little of the PR's reformist project. Sociologists would suggest that PR deputies representing plantation owners and cattle ranchers sabotaged these efforts. These deputies would oppose these reforms because they had the most to lose from genuinely competitive elections. This approach is not implausible: The PR was split into two factions. Máximo Fernández, the leader of one of its more radical and "popular" factions, led one faction. Most ominously for the dominant class,

63

Fernández had a following among the artisans and workers of the capital and agricultural laborers of the countryside.[1] Centrist politicians led the other faction of the party.

Office-seeking theories, for example, argue that parties will oppose reforms that threaten to augment political uncertainty. In Costa Rica of the 1910s, this approach suggests that the *fernandistas* – as Fernández's supporters were called – would resist democratic reforms that promised to make campaigning for the presidency more difficult. Like other PR deputies, fernandistas would therefore vote against establishing the secret franchise. PR deputies, however, would approve dismantling two-stage elections. Like other efficient reforms, direct elections would help all parties; they would not benefit some parties at the expense of others. This approach helps to explain why many deputies voted to limit reform. Yet, this account does not contribute to understanding why more than 50 percent of all deputies did back some major reforms, including the secret franchise.

Most far-reaching reforms died because, as constitutional reforms, they required the backing of two-thirds of all legislative deputies. Having different requirements for legal and constitutional reforms suggests that institutional arrangements modified short-term electoral interests. That the constitution did not permit incumbents to run for consecutive re-election, curiously enough, created the opportunity for reform even as it reduced its scope. On the one hand, the nonconsecutive election of presidents liberated them from reelection considerations. Being able to run for office only after spending a term outside of the presidency empowered presidents to consider the long-term political benefits of endorsing democratic reforms that most politicians opposed. On the other hand, this constitutional constraint created an electoral cycle that gradually distanced deputies from the president's faction. Unable to run for office, the president was in no position to help members of Congress – who could run for reelection – win party nominations or other remunerative state employment. If institutional perspectives are valid, presidents should advocate far-reaching reforms. Similarly, if they are useful, the size of the legislative coalition in favor of change should decline with the advance of a four-year presidential term.

This chapter evaluates the ability of three models of institutional reform to explain political behavior in the early 1910s. It begins by analyzing why

---

[1] Orlando Salazar Mora, *El apogeo de la república liberal en Costa Rica, 1870–1914* (San José: EUCR, 1990), p. 212.

the PR won the 1909 general elections. This section also explains why the PR, at least at the level of broad programmatic goals, had been endorsing sweeping institutional reforms since the late nineteenth century. The principal sections of this chapter examine the legislative struggles to enact the secret franchise, direct elections for all public offices, and related reforms. The chapter begins to draw to a close by analyzing one last attempt to reform electoral laws. It concludes by summarizing our principal findings and relating them to the rival approaches to institutional reform that we presented in the introduction to this book.

Watershed Elections and Political Mandates

For many citizens, the 1909 elections represented a clash of political arbitrariness with republican principle. In its late edition on election day, *La Prensa Libre* claimed that the elections "were not simply the triumph of one party," but of much greater importance. They signified the "arrival of the Republic, not privileges for some; to the rule of law, not the triumph of partiality . . ."[2]

It is not difficult to understand the clamor around these elections. By not backing a candidate, PUN President Cleto González left the powerful machinery at the executive's disposal with little else but to administer electoral laws impartially. Local polling station officials did not strike the names of opposition voters from the electoral registry. Nor did they seek to prevent them from voting. District administrators, governors, or other public officials also did not jail or otherwise harass the electors chosen in popular elections.

Once he had begun to negotiate with the opposition, the president had, so to say, let the genie out of the bottle. That opposition hardliners organized against his regime during his first year in office encouraged the PUN president to amend the 1893 electoral law. With these safeguards, the opposition won over half of the Congressional seats subject to competition in the 1908 midterm elections. Along with the defection of PUN deputies to the Republican cause, the opposition controlled Congress by 1909.

One of the reasons why the PR performed so well was that it did not have to compete in a race with a regime-sponsored candidate. A second cause of Republican success was the absence of a credible rival: The PR candidate's only opponent was the ex-dictator, Rafael Iglesias of the Civil

---

[2] "Tenemos República," *La Prensa Libre*, No. 6511 (30 August 1909), p. 2.

Party (PC). Finally, the PR selected Jiménez, a moderate liberal, as its presidential candidate, not long-time party member and its perennial favorite, Fernández. Before becoming president, Jiménez had a been a distinguished jurist and an insightful newspaper columnist, and only once held an elected post. Indeed, many within the PR approached him to be their presidential candidate precisely because he did not have a reputation for being a reelection-minded politician.

For weeks and perhaps even months, many newspapers let their pages become vehicles for anti-*civilista* attacks. Columnists reminded readers that Iglesias had forced his reelection to the presidency in 1897, despite constitutional prohibitions to the contrary. Editorialists reinformed the public that Iglesias had, among other things, stolen the 1894 election from the Catholic Union Party and subsequently declared it illegal. He had also imprisoned and exiled scores of opposition leaders, including the PR politician Fernández. In the words of *La Prensa Libre*, "Don Rafael Iglesias, notwithstanding his personal merits, has to become part of the past because he represents, among us, the principle of absolute power, with its tyrannical methods of repression."[3]

The Struggle to Reform the Constitution

Like all executives, President Jiménez faced a set of choices upon assuming power. He could concentrate his energy on endeavors that did not require institutional reform. Many other items were competing for a place on the president's agenda, including dealing with the fallout of the devastating earthquake in Cartago in May 1910, solving the foreign debt crisis, and preparing and sending a new budget to Congress. All required the expenditure of political capital. Though Jiménez had been elected with a great deal of popular support, the honeymoon period of his term was not going to last forever.

It was doubtful that the president would reject the path of reform. His political career in part had been built upon promoting the reduction in the powers of the presidency. He also was unlikely to accept the status quo because of a large number of campaign pledges made to reform electoral laws. In the January 1909 party convention, the first such gathering held in Costa Rica, Republican delegates chose him to become their standard-bearer. Along with every party member, he pledged to work for the enact-

---

[3] "Resultado de las elecciones," Ibid.

ment of suffrage reform, a prohibition on executive ministers running for office in the six months prior to election day, and the direct election of provincial governors and district administrators.[4] And the notion of establishing a commitment with the electorate, a cornerstone of democratic republican thought, was rapidly disseminating in Costa Rica.

Even when an incumbent favored change, tendered reforms often needed the support of supermajoritarian legislative coalitions. Altering or creating electoral laws initially required committee endorsement. Subsequently, a majority of deputies present during each of the three separate debates required of all bills needed to approve evolving versions of a reform bill. In addition to following the rules governing the creation or alteration of ordinary laws, attempts to amend the constitution succeeded only after they had received the backing of two-thirds of all deputies in two different years of the legislative calendar. And, finally, after approval in a third debate, a bill or constitutional amendment was submitted to what was literally called a detailed discussion. During this final phase of discussion, a majority of the deputies present in the chamber had to approve each article of the tendered reforms.

Factionalism and the Reforms

In the aftermath of the 1909 elections, the Republicans controlled virtually all legislative seats. Along with the seventeen seats they picked up in these elections, they held most of the seats not subject to renewal. All together, 79 percent (thirty-three of forty-two) representatives professed allegiance to the PR. The PR was divided into two factions. One identified itself with the president; the other remained loyal to the long-time Republican leader Fernández (the latter faction is hereafter referred to as the PRf). Though the *jimenistas*, as the supporters of Ricardo Jiménez were known (and hereafter referred to as PRj), obtained nine of the nineteen newly elected deputies, they could at most count upon the votes of twenty deputies, two short of an absolute majority. The PRf were thirteen in number. Only four representatives belonged to the PC. Another four declared themselves to be neutral.[5]

---

[4] "El Programa del Partido Republicano se cumple. A propósito de elección popular de Gobernadores y Jefes Políticos y sufragio directo y secreto," *El Republicano*, No. 85 (26 April 1912), p. 2.

[5] "CONGRESO, 1910–1912," *La República*, No. 7856 (5 April 1910), p. 2.

Policy differences among these factions were not great, especially among PR factions concerned with institutional reform. Many criticized the PC not only for the heavy-handed use of public authority, but also the party's willingness to contract foreign debts to build infrastructural projects, especially railroads. Republicans, especially Jiménez, disliked borrowing abroad and giving preferential treatment to the United Fruit Company because of its threats to national sovereignty.

Strategic differences created tensions among Congressional parties and factions. Both Fernández and Iglesias, known for exercising a great deal of influence over their deputies, were eligible to run in the 1914 presidential race. In line with office-seeking approaches, electoral imperatives forced PC and PRf leaders to worry about the impact of legislation, particularly of a reformist kind, on their chances for success and the ability to win elections. Fernández's response, in particular, was to watch his deputies closely to ensure that, from his minority position, he could shape Congressional decisions. In contrast, the nonconsecutive reelection of presidents permitted the president to consider the long-term implications of legislation on his political career.

In this environment, reformers submitted two constitutional reform bills within a month of each other. The first, dated 4 June 1910, called for the direct election of provincial governors and municipal executives. A bipartisan coalition of deputies – nine PRf, seven PRj, and one PC deputy – sponsored this bill.[6] It was a novel proposal, and not only because it shifted appointment of key administrative personnel of the national territory from the executive to the electorate. The proposed amendments of constitutional articles 57, 102, and 131 also circumvented the existing system of indirect elections. A month later, another group of representatives – including five PRj, three PRf, and two *civilistas* deputies[7] – presented a second reform bill to Congress. It called for the direct election of presidents, members of Congress, governors, and district administrators. It also endorsed the secret franchise. While the numbers are too small to permit the use of statistical tests of significance, party affiliations suggest that the PRj was more inclined to support far-reaching reforms than the PRf and PC.

Though the president's imprimatur was nowhere to be seen in these bills, they had his tacit approval. In his inaugural speech before Congress

[6] "Proyecto de Reforma Constitutional (4 June 1910)," *La Gaceta*, No. 130 (10 June 1910), p. 544.
[7] "Proyecto (June 1910)," Ibid, No. 7 (8 July 1910), p. 28.

in May 1910, the new president called for the election of governors and district administrators as well as "the suppression of two-stage elections." He reminded deputies that "it was a political, even if not a legal fact" that "electors can dispose of their vote in the way they wish" during their four-year terms, in part because electors cast ballots in secret. Furthermore, indirect elections, Jiménez pointed out, "created the possibility that – especially when no party obtained a decided advantage – intrigues could be hatched to pervert the popular verdict between the first and second elections or that, for several months, a harmful political climate would be maintained." President Jiménez also recommended the adoption of the secret franchise so that "the elections best represent the popular will."[8]

As proof of his commitment to reform, Jiménez promulgated the constitutional amendments that PR deputies and the outgoing president had negotiated. Procedure required executives to endorse constitutional amendments if reforms had obtained the support of two-thirds of all deputies. These reforms dismantled the Permanent Commission and regulated the executive's ability to declare states of siege. The constitution now required the executive to inform Congress within forty-eight hours of suspending individual rights and guarantees, which the deputies could then rescind.[9]

Committee Reports

It took a while for the Congressional Special Committee to issue its report. Not until the end of July did Congress select its members. Deputies selected one *civilista*, two PRf, and two PRj, including the president's older and politically independent brother, Manuel de Jesús Jiménez.[10] The balance of forces on the committee thus gave the PRf a slight advantage:

[8] "Mensaje inaugural presentado al Congreso por el Licenciado don Ricardo Jiménez (8 May 1910)," in Carlos Meléndez Chaverri, ed., *Mensaje presidenciales, 1906–1916*, vol. IV (San José, Academia de Geografía e Historia de Costa Rica, 1981), pp. 130–31.

[9] Orlando Salazar Mora, "La Comisión Permanente y la suspensión del orden constitucional," *Revista de Ciencias Jurídicas* (San José, Costa Rica), No. 44 (May–August 1981), pp. 19–48.

[10] O.s. no. 67 (21 July 1910), art. 5, *La Gaceta*, No. 23 (27 July 1910), p. 107. The original members of the Special Committee were Manuel Bejarano, Manuel Coto Fernández, Manuel de Jesús Jiménez, Pedro Pérez, and Tranquilino Sáenz. The first two and the fourth belonged to the PRf while the third and the last were PRj deputies. In early May 1911, the *civilista* Pérez resigned. Radical PRf Deputy Alfredo González replaced him. See o.s. no. 2 (2 May 1911), art. 6, *La Gaceta*, No. 97 (4 May 1911), p. 507.

Although they only held 31 percent of the legislative seats, they obtained 40 percent of the votes on the committee. The PR*j*, in contrast, saw its share of committee seats shrink to 40 percent from 48 percent of the chamber's seats the faction held.

The Special Committee was unable to issue an unanimous report. Two PR*f* and one PR*j* deputies wrote the majority report, which broadly endorsed the reforms. They argued in favor of the secret and direct franchise. Anticipating the criticism that the "masses" were unprepared to exercise this right, the deputies suggested that casting ballots in secret would be "a practical school where the people will be educated." Concerned with fragmenting public administration, they recommended against direct election of provincial and local authorities. Instead, the deputies suggested that citizens select slates of candidates from which the president could choose to name provincial and cantonal executives.[11]

The two minority reports opposed the most far-reaching reforms. Both PR*f* Deputy Manuel Bejarano and PR*j* Deputy Manuel de Jesús Jiménez (the president's brother) endorsed direct elections for the presidency. Deputy Jiménez advocated the elimination of two-stage elections for deputies while Bejarano did not. Representative Bejarano backed the direct election of district administrators. Deputy Jiménez criticized the effort to democratize local government because he believed the republic was small enough to dispense with this reform. Both deputies stood behind direct elections for certain officials to protect the rights of the citizenry and because they would more efficiently register the preferences of voters.

The minority reports also differed on how to implement the direct ballot. PR*f* Deputy Bejarano believed that citizens did not have enough information to vote intelligently for deputies and municipal councilmen elected in multimember districts. Citizens were, however, informed about the affairs of their province as a whole to select their governor. Given the alleged ignorance of voters, only electors would have the qualifications necessary to promote "the formation of a government with persons that unite the personal capacities it demands and reflects with its individual spirit the dominant tendencies of public opinion."[12]

Appraisals of the qualifications voters held also led to rather different views regarding the secret franchise. Deputy Jiménez not only pointed out

---

[11] "Dictamen de la Comisión Especial (10 May 1911)," Ibid, No. 111 (20 May 1911), p. 569.
[12] "Dictamen del Diputado Manuel Bejarano (17 May 1911)," Ibid, No. 113 (23 May 1911), p. 581.

that privacy would improve the ability of electoral results to reflect public opinion, but claimed that "the Costa Rican people had already demonstrated its capacity to exercise the franchise."[13] PR*f* Representative Bejarano, in contrast, made a different set of claims by asserting, in the first place, that the secret franchise was not necessary in Costa Rica since it did not have a society "ruled by tyrants, fanaticism or by capital." He then argued "it cannot be concealed from anyone that the secret franchise . . . in which perhaps a majority of voters do not read or write, has to present numerous material difficulties and that, for this reason, it cannot be used to avoid fraud."

Uncertainty about the consequences of reform fueled the splits among Special Committee members. In a legislature split between PR*f* and PR*j* deputies, it was doubtful whether enough deputies would form a coalition to enact all these reforms. Waiting for midterm elections, however, promised to improve the success of enacting reform bills. Since indirect elections remained in effect, the 1909 electors – overwhelming supportive of Jiménez – would no doubt vote to increase the number of PR*j* deputies in Congress.

Midterm Elections, Legislative Alignments, and Reform Possibilities

Provincial Electoral Councils delivered a resounding victory for the president. Initial returns indicated that the PR*j* captured thirteen of the twenty-two seats subject to renewal. The PR*f* obtained eight and the PC was left with one seat. When combined with the nineteen deputies elected in 1910, the PR*j* held 56 percent of all legislative seats.[14]

At least for the progovernment *La República*, second-stage elections were a "disaster" for the PR*f* because it had failed to wrest control of Congress from the president. Factional alignments and institutional arrangements, this newspaper noted, made Deputy Fernández dependent upon pleasing the president. Unless a candidate obtained an absolute majority

---

[13] "Dictamen del Diputado Manuel de Jesús Jiménez (17 May 1911)," Ibid, No. 112 (21 May 1911), p. 573.

[14] Initial results appeared as "Resultado de las elecciones de Diputados," *La República*, No. 8445 (7 April 1912), p. 3. Almost a week later, the editorialist noted that fifteen PR*j* and seven PR*f* were elected. Apparently, progovernment forces picked up the PC deputy as well as one from the ranks of their Republican rivals. See "Tribuna libre: el desastre del fernandismo," Ibid, No. 8452 (16 April 1912), p. 1. The quotation in the next paragraph also stems from this article.

in the 1913 general elections, the new Congress would select a new president from among the two front runners. President Jiménez therefore only needed to win over seven of the new deputies to hold the majority necessary to choose his successor. Fernández, in contrast, needed to obtain fifteen or approximately 79 percent of them to be catapulted into the presidency in the run-off legislative race.

La República's forecast was a bit one-sided, even if it correctly noted how expectations about the 1913 elections were already shaping partisan alignments in Congress. It assumed that no deputy would defect from the president's contingent – an unrealistic assumption given the electoral cycle governing political competition. Then, as well as now, deputies evaluated policies in light of their impact on their future careers, especially as the end of the four-year presidential term approaches. Support of the successful presidential candidate would increase their chances of being reelected to Congress or named to an ambassadorship or to a lucrative position in the executive branch of government.[15] *La República's* central point, nevertheless, remained valid: Electoral politics was paramount. Given its legislative minority, the PR*f* would continue to "ponder all national problems in relation to its future plans and through the prism of its political interests, in all moments, of Fernández."

If office-seeking approaches are valid, the PR*f* should oppose reforms that increase uncertainty. It will back only reforms that are efficient – that is, that promise to augment its share of state power. This theory also predicts that all PR deputies will behave similarly because majorities possess an interest in conserving their share of state power. If a sociological approach is correct, PR*f* deputies will support reform because they better represent non-elite interests. Being less populist in orientation, PR*j* legislators will more likely oppose democratic reforms.

Partisanship, Roll-Call Votes, and the Constitutional Amendments

To put pressure on deputies, PR*j* Deputy Alberto Vargas got approval for a motion to take roll-call votes on each of the proposals submitted for

---

[15] This cycle appears to exist before and after 1949, when the Constituent Assembly banned deputies for running for consecutive reelection. Under current rules, deputies must wait a term before running for office and serve their terms concurrently with that of the executive. For the most systematic discussion of these issues, see John M. Carey, *Term Limits and Legislative Representation* (New York and London: Cambridge University Press, 1996), which assesses the implications of the Costa Rican case for legislative theory.

approval.[16] Not all congressional votes, then or now, were or are taken in this way. Deputies sometimes vote in secret. Most voting continues to take place through voice votes, where scribes simply total the numbers of votes in favor or against a measure. As Vargas and others pointed out, legislative votes taken in this manner shielded deputies from their constituents.

In rapid succession, representatives satisfied the two-thirds requirement to eliminate two-stage voting and to prevent individuals from running for the presidency if they had been ministers in the six months prior to election day.[17] Deputies overwhelmingly supported both measures. Virtually all parties had been victims of the intrigues hatched between the first- and second-stage elections whereby their electors had been harassed, jailed, and very likely bribed to vote against the wishes of the party leadership. Similarly, all parties had an interest in stripping high officials of the executive branch of any advantages they might have in political campaigns.

The debate on the secret franchise reignited in late May. Proponents repeated their arguments: Only privacy could insulate the mass of citizens from the pressures that landlords, *gamonales*, employers, and public officials placed on ordinary voters. Their arguments were (and are) widely known. How their rivals justified their opposition to this quintessentially democratic reform is much less well-known. Analyzing how they met the challenge of defending the status quo explains why enough deputies failed to enact this key democratic reform.

Adversaries of the secret franchise developed three arguments in defense of their position. The first was a clever reformulation of the facts governing electoral campaigns in an agriculturally based society concentrated in a relatively small geographic area. In the words of Claudio González, one of the most eloquent of the PRf deputies, the secret franchise was pointless where "it is, of course, publicly known which party citizens support." In Costa Rica, he added, "everyone clearly expresses his sympathies, either in an effort to attract adherents to his party or because

---

[16] O.s. no. 13 (22 May 1912), art. 8, *La Gaceta*, No. 121 (31 May 1912), p. 669. Vargas presented the motion in the prior session; see o.s. no. 12 (21 May 1912), art. 7, Ibid, No. 116 (25 May 1912), p. 637.

[17] The roll-call vote occurred during o.s. no. 21 (3 June 1912), art. 4, Ibid, No. 128 (9 June 1912), p. 667. Also, see "El voto directo," *El Republicano*, No. 119 (5 June 1912), p. 2. Though these were roll-call votes, not even the legislative transcript contains a list of how each deputy voted on the measure. According to this daily's reporter (and a newspaper sympathetic to Fernández), deputies unanimously approved both amendments.

of pride in his affiliation or even to win the sympathy of a candidate."[18] Privatizing the act of voting needlessly promised to complicate the process of selecting public officials.

The second and most fascinating of the reasons against the establishment of the secret franchise concerned its alleged moral evils. In one of the most trenchant of speeches on the topic, PRf Deputy Francisco Aguilar remarked that

darkness and secrecy lend themselves to the influence of the passions, that are blind and without judgment, and find refuge in the reform I impugn. The absence of sanctions, because of the distance from the stimulus of shame, that cover the other sentiments, allow voting to occur in highly undesirable conditions.[19]

Not only was the secret franchise unnecessary, but it was downright wicked. The alleged immorality of voting in private was, in fact, part of a broader liberal agenda seeking to create educated and "safe" citizens out of the unwashed (and potentially dangerous) lower orders.[20] The secret franchise would therefore spawn the development of a citizenry unable to stand on its convictions. As Claudio González put it, this reform would permit voters, "for reasons of personal convenience," to endorse a slate of candidates that, "if obligated to declare publicly, they would prefer to abandon in order to support the good conscientiously."

Deputy Fernández identified the third shortcoming of the secret franchise. If men were required to decipher and mark a paper ballot in the privacy of a voting booth, those who could not read or write would be unfairly deprived of their suffrage rights. Unscrupulous polling station officials and party militants would, in Fernández's words, "vote without their personal convictions and be open to being cheated"[21] "This would be improper in a country where 50 percent" of the citizens were illiterate, according to PRf Deputy Juan Alfaro.[22]

---

[18] González's defense of the status quo is not only part of the archival record of congressional sessions, but also appeared in *El Republicano* in the form of several spirited and frequently literary essays. The quotations stem from his "El voto secreto," Ibid, No. 106 (21 May 1912), p. 3.

[19] "Notas del Discurso pronunciado por el Diputado Aguilar Barquero, al discutirse los dictámenes acerca de reformas constitucionales," *La Gaceta*, No. 111 (19 May 1912), p. 608.

[20] On liberal worries of subaltern classes, see Iván Molina and Steven Palmer, eds., *El paso del cometa: estado, política social y culturas populares en Costa Rica, 1800–1950* (San José: Editorial Porvenir and Plumsock Mesoamerican Studies, 1994).

[21] O.s. no. 21 (3 June 1912), art. 4, *La Gaceta*, No. 128 (9 June 1912), p. 667.

[22] O.s. no. 12 (21 May 1912), art. 7, Ibid, No. 116 (25 May 1912), p. 637.

Table 2.1. *Roll-Call Vote on the Secret Franchise, 1912*

Vote on the Amendment[a]	Party Affiliation		
	PRf	PRj	Total
In favor	5	17	22[b]
Against	12	5	17
TOTAL	17	22	39

Notes:
[a] With 1 Degree of Freedom, the chi-square result is 8.934 (Asymp. Sig [2-sided] = .003).
[b] This does not include the one vote in favor cast by the lone PC deputy.
Sources: Party affiliations are from "Resultado de las elecciones de Diputados," *La República*, No. 8445 (7 April 1912), p. 3. Vote totals are from Ordinary Session No. 22 (4 June 1912), art. 5, *La Gaceta*, No. 131 (13 June 1912), p. 713.

Some of these charges are more persuasive than others. Though it might be the case that the secret franchise might promote venality, proponents of the public franchise did not explain why members of Congress rarely took roll-call votes on bills and amendments. That deputies typically favored using voice votes – in which the record showed only whether a majority had favored or opposed a measure – meant that their choices were hidden from their constituents. If landlords did not intimidate rural voters in Costa Rica, then it stands to reason that powerful social groups were even less likely to threaten deputies. Curiously, newspapers and the legislative transcript do not reveal that anyone ever confronted proponents of the public franchise with this contradiction.

Yet, not all of these charges can be easily dismissed. Designing a voting system for illiterates that upheld the privacy of the vote was a problem that bedeviled reformers for years. That 41 percent of the population ten years or older did not know how to read and write by the second decade of the twentieth century meant that perhaps one out of two males could potentially be deprived of his suffrage rights. Even if concern for illiterate males was a smoke screen to conceal class prejudices, it was an argument with more than a grain of truth to it.

Deputes cast their ballots on the secret franchise during the third and final debate on this matter on 4 June 1912. As reported in Table 2.1, those backing the secret franchise amassed a majority in favor of this measure, but not one sufficient to meet the two-thirds requirement. With twenty-three votes, they were six votes shy of the two-thirds majority of all deputies required of all constitutional amendments.

Sociological approaches argue that PRf deputies should have voted for this reform because they represented subaltern interests. The roll-call vote suggests that they overwhelmingly opposed this reform, even though virtually all PRf deputies represented core provinces. Chi-square tests indicate that the relationship between social structure and preferences on this measure is not very significant. With a chi-square value of 2.090, the relationship between province and opposition to the secret franchise is significant only at the 0.148 level. As Table 2.1 illustrates, the relationship between party affiliation and the vote on the secret franchise, however, is substantially more significant.

A rhetorical question PRf Deputy Claudio González asks provides an important clue why his faction overwhelmingly voted against this reform. In one of the articles he wrote for *El Republicano*, González asked "why, with the use of the secret franchise, do we want to protect disloyalty and shamelessness?" While the reference to "shamelessness" invoked the alleged danger of moral corruption and liberal fears of the popular sectors, the charge of "disloyalty" suggests that the PRf did not want to trust voters on election day. Eliminating the capacity of *gamonales* (local political machine bosses), public officials, and party hacks to monitor the behavior of citizens threatened to wreck existing ways of mobilizing the electorate. For a perennial aspirant to the presidency like Fernández, establishing the secret franchise promised to augment the uncertainty already associated with competitive electoral campaigns. Electoral self-interest, not class politics, therefore best explains how deputies cast ballots on this measure.

Congressional debate then shifted to the amendments concerning the direct election of governors and municipal executives. Increasingly radical and maverick PRf Deputy Alfredo González identified the principal defect of the executive appointment of these officials. In perhaps the single most evocative speech on institutional reform, he pointed out that, "in the existing centralized system, the voice of the majority has been most often drowned" and that governors and district administrators "have been active agents behind the official candidates with multiple resources to make them triumph." "In these conditions," González argued,

these positions have been occupied only by persons lacking all political culture or whose economic survival depends exclusively on the monies contained in the budget they receive for their services and which they would lose if they did not lend their efficacious help to the electoral farces prepared by the highest spheres of government.

For Alfredo González, the election of governors and district administrators promised "to reinforce the foundation upon which rests the edifice of the Republic and completely eliminate one of the means by which it is often falsified . . ."[23]

In a session where some PR legislators accused colleagues who opposed these measures of betraying the party platform, Alfredo González succeeded in gaining the support of the majority to declare Congress permanently in session until deputies settled these matters. A roll-call vote reveals that proponents of the direct election of district administrators were only one vote short of the two-thirds majority demanded of constitutional amendments. Amid howls of protest, an even larger majority defeated the measure of electing governors: Only twenty-two deputies supported it and seventeen opposed it. Deputies then argued whether the constitution required a vote of two-thirds of *all* deputies or simply of those present. A vote was taken and the truth known to all was affirmed: Two-thirds of all deputies must support measures to reform the constitution.[24]

As reported in Tables 2.2 and 2.3, the PR*f* was overwhelmingly in favor of the reforms. Even in the vote on governors, 76 percent of them endorsed the measure. The PR*j*, however, was deeply split: Almost as many voted in favor (twelve) as against (ten) the measure to elect district administrators. They did somewhat better on the bill to elect governors, where eight were in favor and thirteen were against this measure.

The reasons for this distribution of the partisan preferences appear to be intertwined. Unlike the secret franchise, these bills did not threaten existing ways of mobilizing the vote and therefore the interests of the PR*f*. Indeed, the tendered reforms promised to expand the reach of electoral politics. The PR*f* would be able to deploy its well-organized machine to send even more its members to elected office.

Both for principle and for expediency, the PR*j* opposed a set of measures that the president had endorsed. Some, like the president's brother,

---

[23] "Discurso del Representante González Alfredo al discutirse en tercer debate las reformas constitucionales (24 June 1912)," Ibid, No. 6 (7 July 1912), p. 33. It appears as if this wonderfully evocative speech was presented during o.s. no. 26. Its principal concern is the election of governors and *jefes políticos* (district administrators) and will be cited again in this chapter.

[24] O.s. no. 42 (2 July 1912), art. 6, Ibid, No. 8 (10 July 1912), pp. 45–6.

Table 2.2. *Roll-Call Vote on Direct Election of Governors,*
1912

Vote on the Amendment[a]	Party Affiliation		
	PR*f*	PR*j*	Total
In favor	13	8	21
Against	4	13	17
TOTAL	17	21	38

Note:
[a] With 2 Degrees of Freedom, the chi-square result is 5.596
(Asymp. Sig [2-sided] = .018).
Source: For party affiliations, see Table 2.1. Votes are from
Ordinary Session No. 42 (2 July 1912), art. 6, *La Gaceta*, No. 8
(10 July 1912), pp. 45–6.

Table 2.3. *Roll-Call Vote on Direct Election of Municipal*
Executives, 1912

Vote on the Amendment[a]	Party Affiliation		
	PR*f*	PR*j*	Total
In favor	15	12	27
Against	2	10	12
TOTAL	17	2	39

Note:
[a] With 2 Degrees of Freedom, the chi-square result is 5.110
(Asymp. Sig [2-sided] = .024).
Source: See Table 2.2.

fought a reform they genuinely believed would disrupt the administrative coherence of the state. Others resisted endorsing a measure out of dislike of Fernández. PR*j* Deputy Leonidas Briceño, for example, declared that "he [Briceño] came to the chamber elected by the province of Guanacaste, not through the efforts of a machine, but to seal a political pact signed two years earlier by a well-informed and free electorate." Not sparing any criticism of Fernández, Briceño added

that, for his part, he [Briceño] is free of any commitment with the PR, especially with the PR*f* faction, which had always struggled against his nomination, and that actually he does not have any other connection with this party that does not include his affection and support for President Jiménez.[25]

With these remarks, Briceño disclosed the reasons for the widening rupture within the party. Despite a common, though abstract, commitment to reform, the rivalry between PR*f* and PR*j* made collaboration difficult. The gap turned into a breach as the impending presidential elections, though still at least eighteen months away, became the central issue of political debate.

The Struggle to Enact a New Electoral Law

Reformers faced a hard set of choices. They could do nothing on the assumption that their partisan rivals would again block their efforts to enact the secret franchise. Alternatively, they could resubmit a package of reforms, but under a different guise. If the president sent Congress a project for a new electoral law, it only required the approval of an absolute majority of deputies present – a condition that the defeated amendments had met.

The Proposed Electoral Law

The new "Law of Elections" that President Jiménez sent Congress in May 1913 was the first attempt to replace the 1893 electoral law. It incorporated the reforms to prevailing law that the president and his Republican colleagues negotiated with President Cleto González between 1908 and 1909. And it went several steps further, even though the president admonished, in the preamble of the bill, that it did not represent a "thorough revision of the electoral law that contained the innovations adopted by most other countries."

Among its innovations numbered several proposals to augment confidence in electoral procedures. All polling stations and "electoral boards must contain representatives of all political groups competing at the time." The bill proposed that citizens could vote only at the polling station in the district where they were registered to vote. Only members of the armed forces, detainees, or prisoners were exempted from this

[25] O.s. no. 41 (1 July 1912), art. 12, Ibid, No. 5 (6 July 1912), p. 29.

requirement; these individuals could vote where they were stationed and their votes would be added to those of their home districts. By reducing the possibility of fraud, especially on the part of the government, both reforms promised to increase electoral safeguards for opposition parties. The bill also called for removing the judiciary from election administration. In line with the constitution, Congress should remain solely responsible for certifying election results.

The most far-reaching proposals of the reform bill included a "mixed-system" of voting and the use of the plurality system to elect deputies. Seeking to split the opposition to establishing the secret franchise, the "mixed-system" proposal called for the retention of the public franchise for illiterates and the use of the secret franchise for literate voters. The president also counseled replacing the use of proportional representation, then in use only when provinces sent three or more representatives to Congress, with that of the simple plurality rule.

Electoral Incentives, Committee Power, and the Reforms

The fortunes of electoral reform did not appear to brighten when Congress selected Fernández to be its president during Jiménez's last year in office. Indeed, deputies voted PRf representatives into all Directorate positions. To make the changes in the balance of power clearer still, outgoing Congressional President Ezequiel Gutiérrez declared himself to be a member of the PRf faction and was subsequently elected to be vice-president of the new legislative session. From possessing the loyalties of nineteen deputies, the PRf began the new legislative session with a comfortable majority of twenty-four seats. With these changes, a newspaper reporter asserted, the 1913 presidential campaign had begun.[26]

Issuing its report in late May, the Committee on Legislation applauded the president's effort to improve the electoral law, but expressed reservations about Jiménez's most innovative proposals. It welcomed the recommendation to select representatives through majority rule for logistical reasons. Under the system of "numerical proportional voting" used in Provincial Electoral Assemblies that sent three or more deputies

---

[26] "El Licdo. Don Máximo Fernández electo presidente del Congreso," *La República*, No. 8766 (3 May 1913), pp. 4–5. The balloting appears to have been secret, for only totals for candidates are recorded. See o.s. no. 1 (1 May 1913), art. 2, *La Gaceta*, No. 102 (7 May 1913), p. 505.

to Congress per election, electors cast ballots for candidates, even though citizens had cast ballots for parties.[27] Though the Committee recognized that plurality systems worked to the disadvantage of minorities, it claimed that "[proportional voting] is complicated to apply and difficult to practice."

The Committee rejected the president's "mixed-system" of voting. Establishing the secret franchise, it claimed, would promote dishonesty. The secret franchise was also unnecessary because "Costa Ricans do not possess the tendency to conceal their political proclivities." While conceding that some countries have privatized the act of voting, the Committee noted that such privatization had not eradicated venality from politics. "In the United States," for example, "the secret franchise is being implanted and it has always been said that the vote is a piece of merchandise there." It also pointed out that the secret franchise existed in Central America and rhetorically asked deputies to "judge what advantages these small nations have derived from it."

The report came very close to denying that "bribery" and "tyranny of the landlord" were problems in the country. It suggested that no one would "purchase" a vote because he could not "be sure of the vote of a perverse man." If "gratitude," the Committee claimed, "is the reason why the worker votes the way preferred by his boss, then safeguards for voters are not needed." On the other hand, "if the preceding case does not occur, and the boss with threats pretends to impose his political choices on his subalterns or workers," the secret franchise will offer scant protections, especially to those subalterns who are illiterate. The Committee then argued "that, in Costa Rica, we do not have such perversely motivated individuals . . . since we aspire to create a model republic."

The theme of Costa Rican exceptionalism ran throughout the report. The Committee noted that Athenians voted publicly and that Cicero argued that a principal cause of the fall of the Roman Republic was the secret franchise. Indeed, the report stated that

Costa Rica, like ancient Athens, has only practiced the public franchise, and the men who have presided over its destiny, because they are much, much better, in general, cannot be compared to those that have, on a majority of occasions, presided over our brothers in Central America.

---

[27] For an explanation of this provision, see República de Costa Rica, *Decretos relativos a elecciones, Instrucciones para practicar las de segundo grado, conforme al sistema de voto proporcional númerico y división territorial electoral* (San José: Tipografía Nacional, 1893), pp. 41–6.

So, even if the secret franchise was essential to protect the rights of citizens elsewhere, it was unnecessary in Costa Rica. Consequences that followed elsewhere did not occur in the country because Costa Rica, in a word, was different. In this way, antireform deputies deployed the ideology of Costa Rican uniqueness to limit the further democratization of the republic.

In line with office-seeking approaches, the Committee tacitly recognized that the reform bill only furnished literate voters with the secret franchise. Instead of claiming that illiteracy would prevent many citizens from benefiting from the secret franchise, it shifted to arguing that the intellectual inadequacies of most voters would not allow them to vote in secret. The report argued that "two-thirds of the people would be left without the vote" because of "clumsiness, on the one hand, nervousness and timidity, on the other."[28] Since ballots must not contain stray marks or stains to reveal the identity of their owners, the committee report asserted, large numbers of citizens would be accidently deprived of their suffrage rights.

The Committee report disclosed the apprehensions so many held about changing laws in an election year. Fernández was not only going to compete against PC leader Iglesias, but also against the PR*j* deputy, Dr. Carlos Durán. Though Fernández was the undisputed leader of the PR, his reputation had been sullied because he had lost the three campaigns in which he had participated. And the creation of direct elections only increased the importance of winning the presidential race in the first round. Unless he attracted an absolute majority of the vote, it would be the new Congress that would select the next president – a fact that added to pressures on the PR*f* and every other party to secure as many deputies as possible.

Remaining debates about reform became saturated with claims and counterclaims about the impact of change on electoral performance. In an otherwise perfunctory set of discussions in the sessions dedicated to approving the prior year's constitutional amendments, PR*j* Deputy Rafael Rodríguez pointed out that the elimination of indirect elections raised a question of whether election day should be held in December or in April. In the measures forwarded by the prior year's legislature, the wording continued to refer to elections being held in April – though, for what, remained unclear. PR*j* Deputy José Manuel Peralta accused the PR*f*

---

[28] "Dictamen de la Comisión de Legislación (20 June 1913)," *La Gaceta*, No. 146 (28 June 1913), p. 773. Its three members, all PR*f*, were Juan Rafael Arias Bonilla, Claudio González, and Juan Felipe Picado.

majority of surreptitiously advancing election day because time was unfavorable for PRf electoral interests.[29] In a decision the president backed, a majority voted in favor of dropping the reference, even though the new wording had not been approved by last year's legislature. Again, the PRj was split: Thirteen endorsed the unorthodox procedure, while eleven opposed it. All but one of the seventeen PRf deputies present backed the measure to delete the phrase about April from the constitution and instead to hold the elections in December.[30]

Elections incentives also prompted the formation of a coalition to strip the electoral law of another innovation. In the detailed discussion of this bill, Deputy PRf Juan Rafael Arias recommended against adopting the measure on plurality voting. In response, PRj Deputy Briceño suggested that the PRf majority was dropping its support because it was no longer sure it was going to win the 1913 general elections. Amid charges and countercharges, the PRf majority voted in favor of returning to using proportional representation if a province was sending three or more deputies to Congress.[31] A party focused on winning the next general election approved a new, if not revolutionary, Law of Elections.

Conclusions

In his penetrating remarks about the practice of republican politics, Deputy Alfredo González observed that his country "is in a moment of political transition." The arbitrary behavior of chief executives was a fresh memory; the election of a reform-minded president in 1910 was celebrated and recognized for the watershed event that it was. In such circumstances, it is not surprising, as Alfredo González noted, "that the heavy load of interests created on the back of what exists tries to reverse the generous impulses in ascension in the free exercise of our republican practices that motivate the President of the Republic."[32] This is as apt of a summary as

[29] O.s. no. 11 (15 May 1913), art. 6, Ibid, No. 114 (21 May 1913), pp. 605–6. Also, see Clotilde Obregón, *El proceso electoral y el Poder Ejecutivo en Costa Rica* (San José: EUCR, 2000), pp. 228, 238.

[30] Ibid. One deputy, whose affiliation is unknown, voted in favor of the change. Partisan affiliations are taken from the May 3 report of such matters.

[31] The quotations stem from o.s. no. 65 (1 August 1913), art. 4, *La Gaceta*, No. 34 (8 August 1913), p. 181. The approval of Arias motion occurs in o.s. no. 67 (6 August 1913), art. 2, Ibid, No. 37 (12 August 1913), p. 197. The Law of Elections is published in Ibid, No. 44 (21 August 1913), pp. 229–34.

[32] "Discurso del Representante González Alfredo al discutirse en tercer debate las reformas constitucionales (24 June 1912)."

any other about why reformers, despite controlling the executive and the legislature, did little more than eliminate two-stage elections and promulgate an electoral law stripped of its most far-reaching proposals. How do the approaches we outlined in the introduction explain the behavior of deputies during this first period of reform?

Sociological approaches do not seem to explain support or opposition to reform. PR*f* deputies, who belonged to the populist wing of the party, were as likely to represent the most socially stratified provinces as PR*j* deputies. It does not appear as if they were any less tied to landlord-dominated political networks. Contrary to sociological approaches, the PR*f* opposed the most democratic reforms Congress debated. The faction overwhelmingly voted against establishing the secret franchise.

Electoral considerations best explain the PR*f*'s behavior. By voting to retain the public franchise, the PR*f* cemented the role that parties played as mobilizers and monitors of the vote. By acting to limit changes, PR*f* reduced the uncertainty associated with increasingly competitive electoral races. They were also responsible for killing the president's electoral reform bill in committee in 1913 because, by the last year of Jiménez's term in office, they had gained the support of other PR deputies to wrest control of the Congressional presidency and of key committees from the faction loyal to the president. The possibility of standing for reelection, in fact, had driven some PR*j* deputies to abandon the incumbent ineligible for consecutive reelection and to vote in favor of an electoral law that implemented a number of "efficient" reforms.

Favoring the elimination of two-stage elections was also a reform in the interests of the PR*f* – and of every other party. All parties held an interest in getting rid of the time period between popular and second-stage elections that had allowed incumbents to jail or otherwise harass opposition electors. Furthermore, establishing direct elections promised to solve the principal-agent problem that all parties faced: namely, trying to maintain the loyalty of electors chosen every four years. In both general and especially in midterm elections, electors could increase political uncertainty by unexpectedly voting for candidates other than those endorsed by the party leadership and the electorate at large.[33]

Roll-call votes, however, suggest that not everyone in the PR voted in a narrowly self-interested manner. Though comprising the largest faction

---

[33] Iván Molina and Fabrice Lehoucq, *Urnas de lo inesperado: fraude electoral y lucha política en Costa Rica (1901–1948)* (San José: EUCR, 1999), pp. 33–6.

of the legislature, PR*j* voted in favor of the secret franchise and, curiously enough, split its vote on direct elections for public office. The behavior of PR*j* representatives on these measures suggests that they did not vote in their narrow, electoral self-interest. By voting to establish the secret franchise, they supported a reform that would increase political uncertainty and their ability to retain control of the state. And, by splitting their support on a measure that would eliminate electors from betraying the confidence of the people and of parties, the PR*j* again showed that it was not simply concerned with ensuring its ability to retain control of public office.

That President Jiménez was strongly in favor of electoral reform also does not make sense from an office-seeking perspective because, as the leader of the PR, he should have opposed any measure that might have lead to the electoral defeat of the PR. These results suggest that, even when faced with the decision of minimizing or maximizing uncertainty, some politicians override their interest in reelection to make counterintuitive choices. In line with sociological accounts, it is clear that the president held preferences not reducible to his short-term electoral interests. But, as an institutionalist perspective suggests, Jiménez could afford to have such preferences because the ban on consecutive reelection for presidents gave him the liberty to think of the long term. Simply put, he was out of a job at the end of his period in office, regardless of whether reform prospered or failed.

Our look at the politics of reform also suggests that the president and his supporters were unable to generate large-scale public pressure in support of the reforms. Nor did they even seem to be aware of the electoral benefits to be derived by wrapping themselves in the mantle of reform. Newspapers, whose pages are the only way of gauging the pulse of public opinion in a world before the advent of modern polling, do not suggest that citizens organized marches or sought to pressure their representatives to enact measures such as the secret franchise. These sources also do not disclose public debate about institutional reform. And, finally, newspapers do not chart the existence of a political crisis that the president could have exploited to sway undecided deputies that reform was preferable to instability.

3

Electoral Fraud during the Public Ballot, 1913–23

Introduction

Though parties did not overhaul the political architecture of the republic, they had amended the constitution so that citizens could directly elect presidents and deputies. They no longer had to struggle to maintain the loyalty of several hundred electors in the time period between popular and second-stage elections. With the establishment of direct elections, parties instead had to compete in a market for the support of an electorate rapidly expanding to include more than one hundred thousand men by the 1920s. How did this affect their efforts to stuff the ballot box?

In research Dana Munro conducted in the 1910s, he suggested that such changes had not fundamentally altered the relationship between parties and voters. "The representatives [that every party has] at the polls," he argued, "prevent fraudulent counting, but encourage corruption and the exercise of improper influence on the individual elector." Nevertheless, in comparison to other countries in Central America, Munro claimed "the amount of intimidation and coercion . . . is insignificant . . . , and attempts to influence voters by such means are generally condemned by public opinion."[1]

Munro's observations are both helpful and frustrating. On the one hand, they suggest that the establishment of direct elections had not decisively changed politics. On the other hand, Munro's remarks raise the question of whether these elections were meaningful political contests or elite-

---

[1] Dana G. Munro, *The Five Republics of Central America: Their Political and Economic Development and Their Relations with the United States*, 2ⁿᵈ edition (New York: Russell & Russell, 1967), p. 153.

dominated affairs. Simultaneously claiming that "corruption was practiced on a large scale" and that elections did not involve the widespread use of coercion seems to echo the conventional wisdom and to imply that these elections were genuinely competitive.

In this chapter, we show that most of the elections held between 1913 and 1923 were regularly contested. Furthermore, we show how dismantling two-stage elections had some rather dramatic effects on the relationship between parties and voters. It empowered an increasingly literate electorate to choose public officials every other year. It made elections more expensive and fueled the development of new parties. Because the public franchise allowed parties to keep a running tally of local races, parties also followed a carefully chosen mix of strategies to inflate and deflate vote totals. They, for example, coerced citizens, substituted ballots, and prevented opposition citizens from voting with the objective of staying ahead of their rivals.

Even with an increase in political competition, half of the charges contained in the petitions denounced procedural violations of electoral laws. Though fraud remained a low-key affair, direct elections did increase the worst types of fraud from 31 to 42 percent of all accusations parties made during this period. The intensification of political competition encouraged parties to use more blatant tactics to defeat their adversaries. The continuation of the public franchise, however, served to keep fraud in check because parties could easily monitor each other's behavior. By obligating voters to announce their choices in front of their peers, superiors, and subordinates, parties succeeded in deterring the worst types of fraud.

During this period, most accusations of fraud took place in the periphery, where only about a fifth of the electorate lived. Ballot-rigging continued to occur where greater numbers of voters were poor peasants and agricultural workers, illiterate, and ethnically discriminated against. Indeed, petitioners charged their rivals with committing the largest share of the worst types of fraud precisely where voters were least able to defend their political rights. Yet, we show that parties disproportionately complained about fraud in the periphery because politics was more competitive in outlying than in core provinces. Population densities made most races in the periphery one- or two-seat races, and laws awarded seats to plurality winners. That the distance separating winners from losers in these provinces was typically less than in the center, where proportional representation allocated most seats, meant that parties could more credibly claim that fraud had deprived them of legislative representation.

This chapter begins by analyzing the nature of political campaigns when voters directly and publicly choose presidents and legislators. It then overviews how the 1913 reforms fueled the growth of local parties, which took advantage of the fall in voter turnout rates in midterm elections to send their candidates to Congress. In the main sections of this chapter, we show how the 1913 reforms changed the ballot-rigging strategies of parties. We then show how, in the midst of a close election, the functional division of electoral governance failed to adjudicate competing claims about who really won the 1923 general elections.

Electoral Campaigns under Direct Voting

Along with an increasingly literate public, the expansion in the number of voters changed the environment in which parties struggled to obtain control of the state. Both trends made elections more expensive to run, as parties needed to hire writers, speakers, and organizers to spread their message throughout the largely rural districts of the republic. Competitive party politics also fomented the development of new parties, which struggled for the support of voters now capable of selecting public officials in general and midterm elections.

Political Instability

The first direct elections produced a deadlock in 1913. In an election that saw virtually the entire electorate turn out to vote, no party obtained an absolute majority of the vote. In the past, national leaders, deputies, and electors had typically used fraud or violence to resolve the stalemate. After months of intrigue, deals, and counterarrangements, deputies were unable to select one of the two front runners to be president. In an action many likened to a constitutional coup d'etat, outgoing President Ricardo Jiménez supported a coalition of PR and PC deputies to vote Radical PR Deputy Alfredo González – who had not run for this office – to the presidency.[2]

---

[2] Hugo Murillo Jiménez, *Tinoco y los Estados Unidos: génesis y caída de un régimen* (San José: EUNED, 1981), chap. 1. González's entry into the presidency produced a lively debate in the press. Some of the articles, including exchanges between President Jiménez and his

Presiding during an unprecedented economic and fiscal crisis (the Allied naval embargo of Germany during World War I wrecked Costa Rica's export markets), President González gained legislative approval for a series of radical financial reforms, including the establishment of an income tax. His critics also accused him of manipulating the 1915 midterm elections for partisan advantage. As we will see, accusations of fraud – almost all lodged against the president's followers – jumped dramatically in these elections. For the first time, rates of fraud in the center approximated the high rates more commonly found in the periphery. Two years later, virtually the entire political class backed a coup against González. Bankers, merchants, and coffee growers – both large and small – applauded Defense Minister Frederico Tinoco's seizure of power.[3]

During his rule, Tinoco convened elections for a Constituent Assembly. Containing distinguished jurists and politicians – including former PUN President Cleto González (1906–10) – delegates scrapped the existing constitution for one containing a bicameral legislature. Citizens then voted in 1917 and 1919 for senators and deputies from the president's own party, the "Peliquista" Party. Near the beginning of Tinoco's rule, some of his opponents had began an insurrection to overthrow his government. As military expenditures rose to confront the rebels, students and teachers led popular protests that led to the burning of the regime's mouthpiece, *La Información.*[4] Throughout this period, President-in-exile González led a successful effort to prevent U.S. recognition of Tinoco's government. After economic conditions failed to improve (diplomatic isolation meant no access to international loans) and the public grew tired of his increasingly authoritarian rule, Tinoco fled into exile after unknown assailants assassinated his brother.[5]

critics, appear in *Lo del 28 de abril: obsequio de El Imparcial a sus electores* (San José: Imprenta de "El Imparcial," 1915), *Una polémica memorable: obsequio de "La República" al Foro de Centro América* (San José: Imprenta Moderna, 1914).

[3] See Murillo Jiménez, *Tinoco y los Estados Unidos* as well as Eduardo Oconitrillo, *Los Tinoco, 1917–19* (San José: Editorial Costa Rica, 1980).

[4] Teachers and students from the female Colegio de Señoritas played a decisive role in these protests. See Steven Palmer and Gladys Rojas Chaves, "Educating Señorita: Teacher Training, Social Mobility, and the Birth of Costa Rican Feminism, 1885–1925," *Hispanic American Historical Review*, Vol. 78, No. 1 (February 1998), pp. 45–82.

[5] Two useful memoirs of this fascinating period are Tranquilino Chacón, *Proceso histórico* (San José: Imprenta y Libreria Falco y Borrasé, 1920) and *Proceso de la restauración o la intervención americana en Costa Rica* (San José: Imprenta, Libreria y Encuadernación Alsina, 1922).

Though electoral politics continued unabated, executive instability badly scarred the body politic. In an extraconstitutional compromise, a Committee of Notables named González's second designate to the presidency as interim president. Francisco Aguilar's consensus government scrapped Tinoco's constitution. It reinstated the 1871 constitution and called for general elections. With 89 percent of the popular vote (and a 59 percent turnout rate), citizens sent Julio Acosta of the Constitutional Party (PC*l*) to the presidency in 1920.[6]

Parties and Their Voters

With the dismantling of indirect elections, parties and their candidates campaigned directly in what was becoming a mass market for voters. Between 1897 and 1913, the number of voters increased from approximately fifty-six thousand to eighty thousand. Not only were more males registered to vote, but more of them were voting: Turnout went from 61 percent of the electorate between 1901 and 1912 to 71 percent between 1913 and 1923.

With a rapidly expanding electorate, parties went to great lengths to attract the support of voters. According to Munro, parties organized "committees and clubs . . . in each town and village," held "processions and serenades," printed newspapers, and even distributed free drinks "to arouse the interest of the voters." They made, he pointed out, "desperate efforts to secure the support of influential citizens who are not permanently affiliated with any party." The effect of such efforts, Munro claims, was to absorb the attention of the entire body politic. In his words,

as the contest progresses, feeling runs higher and higher among the politicians, and the voters become first interested and then excited. The meetings and ovations, the continual political arguments on the streets, resulting in an occasional riot, and the wholesale treating by the party workers in the drink-shops, distract the attention of the people from their ordinary occupations, and temporarily disorganizes the entire community.[7]

As political competition changed, so did society. Between 1892 and 1913, for example, literacy rates among individuals ten years or older had

---

[6] Eduardo Oconitrillo, *Julio Acosta García: el hombre de la providencia* (San José: Editorial Costa Rica, 1991). The election was held on 7 December 1919.

[7] Munro, p. 152. Also, see Patricia Fumero, "Cultura política y fiesta electoral en Costa Rica a inicios del siglo XX," *Revista de Ciencias Sociales* (San José, Costa Rica), No. 89 (2000), pp. 41–57.

increased from 45 and 36 percent to 59 and 51 percent in the center and periphery, respectively. And, increasing literacy rates were accompanied by the development of a mass culture. Between 1880 and 1914, more than 250 newspapers and magazines flooded the country. During these decades, twelve theaters and cinemas opened and at least thirty sports clubs were established. Electoral politics had become so intertwined with mass culture that newsreels between 1910 and 1915 included numerous scenes of electoral campaigning; speeches, parades and other methods of canvassing the vote had become indispensable ways for parties to mobilize voters.[8]

That more people could read a greater amount of information circulating about politics made election day, quite literally, that much more important and uncertain for parties. According the 1893 electoral law, popular elections were three-day affairs; in 1909, they were cut to two days. Monitoring a large and sophisticated electorate and attempting to control it now had to take place one day between 6:00 A.M. and 6:00 P.M. every two years for representatives and every four years for presidents.

As a result of these institutional and social changes, electoral campaigns became more expensive. The PUN, for example, spent 843 colones in the 1901 popular elections held in the Province of Alajuela.[9] If we assume the six other provinces spent equal amounts of money, the PUN invested 5,901 colones in this election. Mario Sancho, a leading critic, corroborates this figure. In 1935, he suggests that the 1901 presidential campaign cost a lot less than 10,000 colones – a figure that includes the sum the PUN and its much less important rivals spent in this election.[10] In the 1901 elections, the PUN spent 40 percent of its expenditures on orators, whose goals were to spread the party's message in the cantons (as municipalities are called) of the republic. Another 15 percent of its budget went toward paying for beasts of burden – horses, mules, oxen, and carts – to transport the party's publicists. In contrast, the costs associated with maintaining

---

[8] Iván Molina, "Explorando las bases de la cultura impresa en Costa Rica: la alfabetización popular (1821–1950)," in Patricia Vega, ed., *Comunicación y construcción de lo cotidiano* (San José: DEI, 1999), pp. 23–64, and Gilbert Acuña, et al., "Exhibiciones cinematográficas en Costa Rica, 1897–1950," unpub. Licentiate Thesis, School of History, University of Costa Rica, 1996, pp. 112, 127.

[9] "Detalle de los gastos de propaganda del Partido Nacional en Alajuela," Colección de Muestras de la Tipografía de Sibaja, 1901, The Juan Santamaría Cultural Historical Museum, Alajuela, Costa Rica. Though this flyer speaks of the National Party, it is clear that this label is being used as a shorthand term for the PUN.

[10] Mario Sancho, *Costa Rica: Suiza centroamericana* (San José: Tipografía "La Tribuna," 1935), p. 90.

an office and paying its personnel accounted for just 7 percent of the party's total costs.

Slightly more than two decades later, the Reformist Party (PfR) all by itself spent 57,541 colones on the 1923 presidential campaign of its candidate, General Jorge Volio – a rather striking sum considering the fact that no one expected him to win the election.[11] Another newspaper article reported that the PCI spent 70,000 colones in the two-month campaign to elect Acosta to the presidency in 1919. The same report also claimed that the PCI's rivals, the PR (Republican Party) and the PA (Agricultural Party), spent 150,000 and 170,000 colones, respectively, on their 1923 presidential campaigns.[12] The PfR spent 11 percent of this total on staff salaries and rental fees (which did not include office supplies). In even greater contrast to the 1901 data, 25 percent of the PfR's expenditures were spent on printing flyers, posters, and other written forms of publicity. By comparing these figures to those of 1901, it is clear that parties were spending more money to persuade an increasingly literate electorate.

Parties and Voter Turnout Rates

The turbulent years of 1917–9 gave birth to a new generation of parties. The establishment of direct elections in 1913 fueled the proliferation of a large number of exclusively local parties. Taking advantage of midterm elections, when voter turnout rates typically fell, provincial-level parties mobilized to capture legislative seats.

The PR, which had done so much to advance (and to delay) the cause of reform, continued to exist. Leading members had both supported and opposed Tinoco's coup against Alfredo González's reformist government in 1917. Tinoco himself had been a member of the PR since the early twentieth century. In the aftermath of the dictatorship, many in the political class united behind the PCI to support Acosta's compromise candidacy.

During this period, progressive politicians met with some short-term electoral success. The Independent Regional Party (PRI), the predecessor of the PfR, obtained 4 percent of the vote in the 1921 elections. Strongly supported in areas with large numbers of small and medium-sized peas-

[11] "El Tesorero General del Partido Reformista explica detalladamente las deudas contraidas por dicho Partido," *Diario de Costa Rica*, No. 1572 (5 October 1924), p. 9, and "La deuda reformista," *La Prensa*, No. 1748 (9 October 1924), pp. 1, 3.

[12] Ibid, p. 8.

ants, the PRI obtained 22 percent of the vote in Alajuela, the only province where it ran candidates.[13] A former priest who had briefly fought in Nicaragua in 1912 against the U.S. marines, Volio, led the P*f*R, which he established in 1923. After Volio was declared insane and interned in a sanatorium because of an aborted invasion of Nicaragua in September 1926, the P*f*R had all but fallen apart by the end of this decade. Its remaining deputies formed an alliance with the PUN, which returned to the political fray to support former President Cleto González's second (and successful) bid to become chief executive in the 1928 presidential elections.

After the establishment of direct elections in 1913, politicians created a large number of local parties. In the 1915 midterm elections, four out of the five parties fielded candidates only at the provincial level. In the 1919 general elections, ten of the twelve parties ran candidates for legislative office at the provincial level. In the 1921 midterm elections, thirty-two parties ran candidates at the local level; no party fielded a national slate of candidates in these midterm elections. In the 1919 general elections, the only of its kind where local parties competed, these parties won 7 percent of all Congressional seats. In contrast, local parties won approximately 15 percent of all legislative seats in midterm elections between 1921 and 1946.[14]

Between 1913 and 1923, turnout in general elections was an average of 71 percent or 10 percent higher than in the previous period. Turnout fell to 41 percent in the two midterm elections held during this period. Yet, as we have seen, the number of parties that participated in these elections boomeranged to: an average of 18.5 in the 1915 and 1921 midterm elections.[15]

What these trends reveal is that direct elections created an opportunity for local machines to compete for legislative seats. Even if dismantling indirect elections eliminated the principal-agent problem that national-level parties faced with controlling the behavior of electors over a four-year period, it complicated their negotiations with local-level interests, which, as their electoral performance improved, increased their capacity to bargain

---

[13] Iván Molina, "Estadísticas electorales de Costa Rica, 1897–1948: una contribución documental," *Revista Parlamentaria* (San José, Costa Rica), Vol. 9, No. 2 (August 2001), pp. 400–1.

[14] The difference between center and periphery was slight. In the center, 14.4 percent of all deputies belonged to provincial parties. In the periphery, provincial parties controlled 15.3 percent.

[15] We exclude the 1919 midterm elections because they were held during the height of the Tinoco dictatorship, when only his party fielded candidates for office.

over candidate selection and concrete policy benefits with national-level politicians. Such openings empowered local interests,which, in a fundamentally rural society, made the task of forming coalitions more complex for national-level politicians concerned with amassing votes and then gaining the support of stable legislative majorities to govern the republic.

Electoral Fraud in the Aftermath of Reform

How did electoral fraud change with direct elections for public offices? We shed light on this question by examining the impact of social structural conditions and institutional arrangements on ballot-rigging strategies. We also discuss how, despite the intensification of political competition, the continuation of the public franchise served to brake the spread of the most flagrant types of fraud.

The Nature and Spatial Basis of Electoral Fraud

Between 1913 and 1923, parties filed forty-four petitions to nullify electoral results that contained 373 individual accusations of fraud. Parties formulated another 105 charges – 22 percent of all accusations – during the tally of the vote that the Provincial Electoral Councils conducted. Table 3.1 reveals that, on average, parties filed eighty charges of fraud for every election between 1913 and 1923.

Again, a disproportionate share of the denunciation of fraud took place in outlying provinces. Table 3.1 indicates that 53 percent of all accusations were lodged against elections held in the periphery, even though it contained only a fifth of the electorate. That most fraud occurred in the periphery was only temporarily reversed in 1915, when parties filed petitions against elections in the central Provinces of San José and Alajuela. These elections generated 23 percent (111 of 478) of all accusations that parties made when voting was direct and public. Denunciations of fraud also took place against elections held in the center in 1917, when diverse factions of the Peliquista Party accused each other of committing acts of fraud.

Electoral laws, however, created a more competitive electoral environment in the periphery than in the center. In the periphery, 69 percent of Congressional seats went to parties that attracted relative majorities of the vote. In core provinces, in contrast, laws called for proportional representation to distribute 94 percent of the legislative seats. Because the distance between winners and losers was typically smaller than the "quotient"

Table 3.1. *Number of Accusations of Electoral Fraud, by Province and by General and Midterm Election, 1913–23*

Province	General 1913	Midterm 1915	General 1917	General 1919	Midterm 1921	General 1923	Total
Center							
San José	1	46	9	1		8	65
Alajuela	1	47	7		31	12	98
Cartago		15		14	7	9	45
Heredia	2	3	2	1		11	19
Periphery							
Guanacaste	5			26	35	38	104
Puntarenas	18				40	14	72
Limón	6				40	29	75
TOTAL	33	111	18	42	153	121	478

Source: La Gaceta (1913–23).

needed to obtain a seat in the center, parties faced powerful incentives to monitor and denounce the behavior of their rivals in outlying provinces. Fraud was therefore nearly four times more likely to occur in the peripheral than in the central parts of the republic. On average, there were 426 eligible voters per accusation of fraud in the periphery to 1,813 eligible voters per accusation in the center.

The geographic redistribution of fraud from the periphery to the center in 1915 helps to make the point that rates of denunciation stemmed from differing levels of political competitiveness. That the stakes of political competition were higher in the 1915 midterm elections – when a reformist government was increasing taxes amid a severe economic crisis and needed to increase its share of legislative seats – helps to explain why rates of denunciation increased to 592 voters per accusation in the center. Again, the number and nature of accusations of electoral fraud were not simply a function of the fact that large numbers of poor, landless, and illiterate voters made for a society less able to defend its political rights. The very nature of political competition could not only redistribute acts of fraud, but encourage parties to mobilize networks of observers to document and then petition Congress about violations of electoral law.

Once we control for the size of the electorate, in general elections there were 13,070 eligible voters per party in the center and 6,477 in the periphery. In midterm elections there were 4,425 eligible voters per party in the center and 2,967 in the periphery. The reduction in numbers was a product of the formation of local parties in midterm races: twenty-five parties in the center and nine in the periphery. Proportionally, however, there were 1.4 local parties in the periphery for every one local party in the center. Institutional incentives explain why politicians created more parties where civil society was ostensibly weak, and under the control of large-scale plantation owners and cattle ranchers, and fewer parties where society was more dense and vibrant. Different party formation rates demonstrate why political competitiveness was more important than social structure in shaping the strategies and rhythm of ballot-rigging.

A disproportionate share of the worst cases of fraud also occurred in outlying provinces. Table 3.2 reveals that 89 percent (forty-four of forty-nine) of the charges of official coercion against voters between 1913 and 1923 took place in the periphery. And such accusations account for 19 percent (44 of 251) of the complaints in the periphery during this period. Parties also accused the authorities of displaying favoritism toward what they called "official" candidates. According to Table 3.2, petitioners also complained about the purchase of votes. These charges comprised 6 percent (27 of 478) of all accusations made between 1913 and 1923.

The worst types of fraud added up to 15 percent (57 of 360) of all accusations lodged against polling stations. According to Table 3.3, parties accused public officials of striking the names of their supporters from the electoral registry, of preventing them from voting, or of simply not accepting their votes. Petitioners also charged officials with committing more egregious violations of electoral law, including the expulsion or intimidation of opposition poll watchers.

The petition filed against the polling station in the Village of San Vicente in the Province of San José after the 1915 midterm elections shows how blatant fraud could get. According to opposition poll watchers,

From 6:00 a.m., when the polling station was opened to vote for deputies, we noted the strong pressure that the police exercised against the citizens, forcing them to vote for the government ballot, especially since they were responsible for distributing the ballots [submitted that morning by each party].

Not only did the police abrogate the right to distribute ballots to voters, but they also threatened opposition voters. Later that afternoon,

Citizen Florentino Umaña Sancho went to deposit his vote for the Fusion [the opposition coalition], but his vote was rejected by the police, which had

Table 3.2. *Accusations of Electoral Fraud, by Province, 1913–23*

Accusation	Category of Fraud	Center				Periphery			Total
		San José	Alajuela	Cartago	Heredia	Guanacaste	Puntarenas	Limón	
Against polling stations[a]	1	59	74	45	16	93	39	34	360
Electoral census not taken	1							1	1
Official favoritism toward a party	2		6			1	7	3	17
Liquor distributed on election day	2							5	5
Auxiliary polling station not opened	2						1		1
Purchase of votes	3							10	10
Provincial electoral council acted illegally	3		2		1			2	5
Official intimidation against voters	3					1		1	2
Nonofficial intimidation against voters	3						1		1
Official coercion against voters	4	3	1		1	8	18	18	49
Official coercion against polling stations	4	1					3		4
Nonofficial coercion against voters	4						1		1
Person elected not qualified for post[b]			1		1	1	2	1	6
Others[b]		2	1						3
Unspecified[b]			13						13
TOTAL		65	98	45	19	104	72	75	478

Notes:
[a] See Table 3.3.
[b] These cases did not apply in our classification.

Source: La Gaceta (1913–23).

Table 3.3. *Accusations against Polling Stations, 1913–23*

Accusation	Category of Fraud	Center				Periphery			Total
		San José	Alajuela	Cartago	Heredia	Guanacaste	Puntarenas	Limón	
Technical or legal defects	1	53	53	41	13	29	16	11	216
Polling station officials arrived tardy	1							1	1
Voting booth in inappropriate place	2					4	5	1	10
Election held off schedule	2	1		1		2	2	4	10
No voting held	2					2	1		3
Voters did not meet requirements	3	3	13	3	3	18	1	2	43
Party representative excluded or threatened	3	1	1			25	2		29
Voters excluded inappropriately	3					4	1	7	12
Permitted substitution of voters	3		1			3	6		10
Voters cast multiple ballots	3						2	8	10
Number of votes was inflated	3		4			4			8
Voters prevented from casting ballots	3		1				3		4
Votes not received	3					2			2
Number of ballots exceeds number of voters	3	1	1						2
TOTAL		59	74	45	16	93	39	34	360

Source: La Gaceta (1913–23).

an order to prevent votes for being cast against the government. Other citizens also presented themselves to vote for the same ticket and ran against the same obstacles.

When asked, the municipal executive confirmed that he had issued this order. Opposition poll watchers concluded that "our presence at the polling station was useless, [as a result], we abandoned our posts and the polling station was comprised by its president and his alternate (both of whom were pro-government) and with the presence of any poll watchers."[16]

Parties also accused polling station officials of substituting pro- for antigovernment votes or of receiving votes from individuals not meeting suffrage requirements because they were too young, foreign, dead, under indictment, or lacked a permanent residence. Again, almost three-quarters of the worst types of fraud were concentrated in the periphery. Furthermore, these accusations represent 54 percent (89 of 166) of the total number of charges lodged against polling stations in outlying areas of the republic.

Table 3.4 indicates that the most serious charges of ballot-rigging increased with time. Both the purchase of votes and the use of coercion against voters climbed to 16 percent of all accusations between 1913 and 1923. Though the purchase of voters and the use of force account for just 11 percent of all accusations made between 1913 and 1923, this share represents almost twice the proportion of such charges made when elections were indirect – between 1901 and 1912, they comprised just 6 percent of all accusations. The least serious charges, however, slowly declined in importance. Parties abandoned impugning the qualifications of elected officials. They gradually stopped claiming that local authorities had failed to produce accurate lists of voters. Parties also quit accusing electoral officials of locating auxiliary polling stations in inaccessible places.

What does remain relatively constant throughout this period is the proportion of all accusations lodged against polling stations. These represent 75 percent of all accusations made between 1913 and 1923. Table 3.5 reveals that parties spilled a great deal of ink documenting procedural

---

[16] "Demanda de nulidad (5 December 1915)," *La Gaceta*, No. 2 (5 January 1916). The Provincial Electoral Council did not annul these votes. The Credentials Committee did not explicitly refer to this petition, but seemingly condoned such acts by claiming that most of the accusations were without legal basis or, if accepted, would not change election results. See "Dictamen de la Comisión de Credenciales y Renuncias (28 April 1916)," *La Gaceta*, No. 98 (30 April 1916), p. 493.

Table 3.4. *Accusations of Electoral Fraud, by General and Midterm Election, 1913–23*

Accusation	Category of Fraud	General 1913	Midterm 1915	General 1917	General 1919	Midterm 1921	General 1923	Total
Against polling stations[a]	1	22	92	12	37	109	88	360
Electoral census not taken	2					1		1
Official favoritism toward a party	2			6		8	3	17
Liquor distributed on election day	2					4	1	5
Auxiliary polling station not opened	2	1						1
Purchase of votes	3					1	9	10
Provincial electoral council acted illegally	3	2				1	2	5
Official intimidation against voters	3					2		2
Nonofficial intimidation against voters	3						1	1
Official coercion against voters	4		5		4	24	16	49
Official coercion against polling stations	4					3	1	4
Nonofficial coercion against voters	4	1						1
Person elected not qualified for post[b]		6						6
Others[b]		1	1		1			3
Unspecified[b]			13					13
TOTAL		33	111	18	42	153	121	478

Notes:
[a] See Table 3.5.
[b] These cases did not apply in our classification.

Source: La Gaceta (1913–23).

Table 3.5. *Accusations against Polling Stations, 1913–23, by General and Midterm Election, 1913–23*

Accusation	Category of Fraud	General 1913	Midterm 1915	General 1917	General 1919	Midterm 1921	General 1923	Total
Technical or legal defects	1	9	77	9	14	60	47	216
Polling station officials arrived tardy	1					1		1
Voting booth in inappropriate place	2	4			2	1	3	10
Election held off schedule	2		1			6	3	10
No voting held	2		1				2	3
Voters did not meet requirements	3	4	9	1	4	12	13	43
Party representative expelled or threatened	3	1	1		16	10	1	29
Voters excluded inappropriately	3	1			1	4	6	12
Permitted substitution of voters	3	2				6	2	10
Voters cast multiple ballots	3	1				6	3	10
Number of votes was inflated	3		3			2	3	8
Voters prevented from casting ballots	3			1			3	4
Votes not received	3			1			2	2
Number of ballots exceeds number of voters	3					1		2
TOTAL		22	92	12	37	109	88	360

Source: La Gaceta (1913–23).

violations of the law. Such infractions account for 60 percent (216 of 360) of all accusations made against polling stations between 1913 and 1923. Three of the worst types of fraud, in contrast, comprise 14 percent (51 of 360) of all such charges. Perhaps the most serious charges involved parties accusing their rivals of preventing "their" followers from voting. These accusations also included the illegal substitution of votes and the exclusion of poll watchers from supervising polling station operations.

These findings suggest that there are good reasons to accept Munro's claim that "the amount of intimidation and coercion . . . is insignificant."[17] Even though the most blatant types of fraud were gradually on the rise during the 1910s, most accusations denounced procedural violations of electoral laws. His observations, moreover, accurately portray politics in the Central Valley, where almost 80 percent of the electorate resided. In line with his observations, the petitions suggest that most blatant types of fraud were "generally condemned by public opinion" and disproportionately occurred in the periphery.

The petitions also disclose that decreasing the opposition's vote totals was just as important as increasing one's own at polling stations on election day. According to Table 3.6, parties accused their rivals of fraudulently inflating their vote totals on 107 occasions. Petitioners also charge opponents with deflating their own totals on 105 occasions between 1913 and 1923. That parties tried to increase their vote totals as often as they tried to decrease those of their rivals makes sense: With the public franchise, it was easy for parties to gauge each other's performance at the local level. Though local party sections communicated with the national party leadership, it was difficult to determine which party was winning across the country. Especially in tight races, parties sought to fabricate majorities in any way they could at every polling station.

Who was committing these acts of fraud? According to standard images of Latin American politics, rural oligarchs used gamonales (rural machine bosses) to mobilize captive peasants to support their candidates. In 1923, for example, *La Noticia* reported

that the consciousness of the citizenry has been pressured in particular places of the capital: owners or administrators of farms appeared on their property in the early hours of Sunday morning to pressure their workers to renounce their political beliefs and to vote for the ballot supported by the owner.[18]

---

[17] Munro, *The Five Republics of Central America*, p. 153.
[18] "Después de la batalla," *La Noticia*, No. 374 (5 December 1923), p. 1.

Table 3.6. *Accusations of Fraud, Classified by Whether They Increased or Decreased Vote Totals, 1913–23*

Province	+	−	Election	+	−	Impugned Votes	+	−
Center								
San José	4	4	1913	7	9	1–9	24	5
Alajuela	20	17	1915	12	8	10–49	10	8
Cartago	3	1	1917	2	1	50–99	6	3
Heredia	3	2	1919	7	4	100–499	6	4
			1921	45	45	500+		2
			1923	34	38			
Periphery								
Guanacaste	29	19						
Puntarenas	15	35						
Limón	33	27						
TOTAL	107	105	TOTAL	107	105	TOTAL[a]	46	22

Note:
[a] The totals are not equivalent because accusations did not always indicate the number of impugned votes.
Source: La Gaceta (1913–23).

Yet, the petitions typically accused public authorities – and not land-lords – of using force on election day. The only exception to this finding dates to December 1913, when a PR observer noted that

The election practiced in Unión Mine, sixth district (in the Province of Puntare-nas) is null because Republican voters were prevented from entering the polling station by the very leaders of the Company, who used coercion against the citizens by threatening them and demanding that they vote for the Civil Party.[19]

It is significant that we only found two such denunciations after search-ing newspapers for such reports. The absence of any more information about such cases suggests that subordinates had more room for maneuver

---

[19] "El acta de escrutinio de elecciones (14 December 1913)," *La Gaceta*, No. 148 (23 Decem-ber 1913), p. 851. This mine, apparently owned by the Cañas Syndicate Company, a firm most likely of U.S. parentage, was located in the heart of the periphery. Carlos Araya Pochet, "El segundo ciclo minero de Costa Rica (1890–1930)," *Avances de Investigación: Proyecto de Historia Social y Económica de Costa Rica, 1821–1940* (San José, No. 3, 1976), p. 7. This source indicates that the mine was owned by the Cañas Syndicate Company in 1907. We are not sure who owned it in the mid-1920s. The PC was the party led by Rafael Iglesias (1894–1902), the dictator whose political career and party were dying.

than commonly thought. Indeed, another article we found claims that progressive and "haughty" peasants actually defied social pressure to vote in favor of the PfR – the sort of reform party that landlords and capitalists dislike. None other than *La Prensa*, a newspaper known for its support of the PfR, noted that

> Despite all of the money spent by our political enemies to buy votes, despite all of their betrayals of democracy and justice, and despite the shameful pressure of some landlords against haughty peasants, the Reformists knew how to comply with their obligations.[20]

This should not come as too much a surprise. Coercing employees to vote in certain ways could prove to be more problematic than beneficial. Such actions could politicize labor relations. Attempts to shape the voting preferences of workers also raised the possibility that employers, once the electoral season was complete, could become subject to reprisals, especially if their party lost the elections.

The Intensity and Magnitude of Fraud

It is not possible to assess the overall effects of vote deflation and inflation. Though the petitions do not always specify numbers of fraudulent ballots, we can nevertheless get a sense of the magnitude of these activities by assuming that all votes cast at these polling stations were fraudulent. At the very least, this assumption allows us to determine the extent of fraud by erring on the side of the victim on the thirteen occasions when petitioners accused parties of vote inflation or deflation. Only one of the five parties accused of such behavior in the center had a vote margin less than the percentage of impugned polling stations. In the periphery, however, the exact opposite holds: Six of the eight parties charged with vote inflation or deflation had vote margins over their nearest rivals less than the percentage of tainted polling stations. Indeed, in these races, the difference between the share of impugned polling stations and the margin of victory range from nearly 5 to 64 percentage points. To the extent that all votes at these polling stations were fraudulent, it appears as if vote inflation and deflation were again more successful in the periphery than in the center.

---

[20] "El legítimo triunfo de nuestro partido," *La Prensa*, No. 1245 (5 December 1923), p. 1.

Table 3.7. *Questioned Polling Stations, 1913–23*

Election Year	Percent Questioned	Victor's Lead	Percentage Difference
1913	3.1	11.3	8.2
1915	14.6	38.7	24.1
1917	2.5	99.2	96.7
1919	4.9	78.4	73.5
1921	14.5	14.2	–0.3
1923	10.7	4.6	–6.1

Source: *La Gaceta* (1913–23), and Iván Molina, "Estadísticas electorales de Costa Rica (1897–1948). Una contribución documental," *Revista Parlamentaria* (San José, Costa Rica), Vol. 9, No. 2 (August 2001), pp. 388–403.

By placing each accusation of fraud within one of four categories, we also discover that efforts to stuff the ballot box became more blatant with time. During the period when elections for executives and legislators were direct and public, category three and four infractions – which are blatant efforts to stuff the ballot box – accounted for 42 percent of all accusations – up from 31 percent of all accusations reported between 1901 and 1912. This finding is in line with the trend we discovered that the seriousness of charges increase, election by election, between 1913 and 1923.

Again, the deterioration in the nature of fraud was concentrated in the periphery. While the category three and four accusations that took place in the center account for 19 percent of all infractions, the worst two types of fraud in the periphery represent 62 percent of all accusations parties made between 1913 and 1923. Even by controlling for region, parties denounced increasingly blatant acts in outlying areas. Between 1913 and 1923, the worst two types of fraud went from 26 to 62 percent of all accusations made in the periphery. In contrast, the worst two types of fraud in the center actually declined by about half – from 35 to 19 percent.

That fraud became worse raises the question of whether its impact on electoral outcomes was any more decisive between 1913 and 1923 than during the prior period. According to the petitions, only 3 percent (20 of 645), 2 percent (15 of 671), and 5 percent (33 of 671) of the polling stations were impugned in the 1917, 1919, and 1923 presidential elections. The rate of questioned polling stations increased during midterm elections when the petitions denounced fraudulent acts in 15 percent (94 of 643) of the polling stations in 1915 and 15 percent (97 of 671) of the polling stations in 1921. Table 3.7 summarizes this information.

Table 3.7 also presents the margin of votes that separated the party that won from the first runner-up in these elections. On the basis of these figures, it is clear that only the outcomes of the 1921 midterm and the 1923 general elections could have been the product of fraud. Yet, the difference between the margin of votes the victorious party obtained and the percentage of impugned polling stations – less than a third of a percentage point – becomes insignificant because a third of the accusations in the petitions charge other parties with electoral misconduct. It does not appear as if the progovernment party stole the 1921 midterm elections because it was not the only party accused of rigging the ballot box.

For similar reasons, it is not at all clear that the PR robbed the 1923 election from the PA. If we subtract 1 percentage point from the total of impugned polling stations that make the PA the perpetrator of fraud, the share of polling stations with questionable results is still not sufficient to sway the election in favor of the PA. If we add all of these votes to those won by the PA, the PA still is short of an absolute majority of the popular vote by at least 3 percentage points. As we will see, however, fraud was responsible for the PR's presidential victory in 1923 because two Provincial Electoral Councils tallied votes in such a way as to create a bare majority for a PR-led coalition in Congress.

Institutional Failure and Political Crisis

Splitting election administration between the executive and legislative branches of government seemed to distribute state power fairly most of the time. On most occasions, the magnitude of fraud was not typically large enough to throw most elections. Yet, the invalidation of votes, the inflation or deflation of vote totals, and the incorrect tally of the vote could become an issue of enormous contention because it could affect the balance of power in Congress and therefore the governability of the republic. Furthermore, when election results were close, the partisan control of election administration could ignite a crisis threatening political stability.

Institutional Controls and the Separation of Powers

As in the preceding period, Provincial Electoral Councils annulled votes during their tally of the vote. Between 1913 and 1923, the Councils ruled in favor of a third (33 of 105) of the requests to nullify votes that party observers made during the tally of the vote. Again, their approval rate varied regionally: while the Councils approved 75 percent of the requests made in the center, they endorsed only 39 percent of the changes made in the periphery. Whether the Councils could, however, make these judgments became a highly controversial issue, one with enormously important constitutional consequences.

The behavior of the 1913 Credentials Committee suggests why the seemingly small matter of whether Councils could annul votes was a serious matter. During the 1913 elections, a PR petitioner claimed that the Provincial Electoral Council of Limón did not tally almost a hundred votes for his party in the community of La Estrella. He accused the Council of annulling votes to help its president, a PC legislative candidate in the province. Apparently, election officials and poll watchers in Estrella could not agree on where to place the polling station. The Council of Limón tabulated only the votes at the polling station that PC officials organized; it ignored the votes cast at the rival polling station in La Estrella. Before Congress convened in early May of 1914, the Credentials Committee, which the PR dominated, concluded that

There does not exist any legal precept that authorizes Provincial Councils to annul votes, and much less to do so as officiously as the Council of Limón by assuming authority it lacks. The powers of the Provincial Electoral Councils emanate from article nine of the [electoral] law, and regarding the elections of the President of the Republic and of deputies, it does not concede them the authority to declare any type of nullification. The Councils do not possess any attributes other than to count votes in light of the poll books. The authority to decide nullifications in deputy elections corresponds only and exclusively to Congress.[21]

Two things make this decision noteworthy. First, the Committee's opinion reveals that partisan majorities found it very difficult to avoid ruling in their own interest. Between 1913 and 1923, the Credentials Committee endorsed only two of forty-four petitions. It divided its opinion on another seven petitions, that is, when more than one party had a representative on this three-person Committee. The Committee therefore rejected 79.5 percent of the formal complaints parties filed with the legislature. The behavior of Congress was even less partial. It only approved the Credentials Committee's two unanimous decisions. It, in other words, dismissed 93 percent of all the petitions that parties submitted between 1913 and 1923.

---

[21] "Dictamen de la Comisión de Credenciales (28 April 1914)," *La Gaceta*, No. 95 (30 April 1914), p. 449. Two of the PR deputies on this Committee belonged to the *fernandista* faction and one belonged to the *jimenista* wing of the party.

Second, this decision illustrates that the Credentials Committee and Congress as a whole always took great pains to justify their behavior. The Credentials Committee often claimed that petitioners had failed to prove their charges.[22] It argued that it could not accept evidence that party personnel furnished because it was "partisan." The Committee also dismissed petitions because they lacked what it said were "practical consequences." In the aftermath of the 1915 midterm elections, for example, the Credentials Committee rejected the opposition petitions filed against results in the Provinces of Alajuela and San José. In this complaint, the opposition claimed that the PR had unfairly deprived it of several Congressional seats. According to the opposition alliance known as the Fusion, the government party had packed polling stations with its partisans, artificially inflated its number of votes, and even tried coercing citizens to vote for its candidates. The PR-dominated Credentials Committee upheld the election of these deputies. It argued that

> If we accept the complaints . . . the most that could be obtained would be to take away a few votes from the two candidates who were elected . . . If, by chance, we detained ourselves to consider, one by one, . . . the charges to nullify that are made, it would be a speculative . . . [and] . . . without any practical consequences. The majority of such charges are lacking legality and, even if admissible, in absolutely no way do they change the election.[23]

But, in 1914, the Credentials Committee offered a justification that make it clear how it viewed the separation of powers. As executive bodies, it claimed, Councils could do nothing more than tabulate votes found in poll books. The constitution reserved the faculty of certifying election results exclusively with Congress. If annulling votes was part of tallying, and tallying was part of certification, then Congress created a precedent about how the functional division of election administration worked.

A Crisis of Political Succession

The defects of the functional division of election governance became manifest in 1923. In an election that the PR, the PA, and PfR contested, no

---

[22] This section draws upon Iván Molina, "La Comisión de Credenciales y Renuncias del Congreso: Un capítulo olvidado de la política costarricense (1902–1948)," in Ronny Viales, ed., *Memoria del IV Simposio Panamericano de Historia* (Mexico: Instituto Panamericano de Geografía e Historia, 2001), pp. 113–31.

[23] "Dictamen de la Comisión de Credenciales (28 April 1916)."

presidential candidate obtained the constitutionally required 50 percent of the popular vote. Jiménez of the PR attracted the support of 42 percent of the electorate. Alberto Echandi of the PA got 38 percent of the vote. Jorge Volio of the PfR came in a distant third with 20 percent of the vote.

In the absence of a clear victor, Congress became responsible for selecting the next president. Initial returns indicated that the PA had won the presidency. When added to the twelve PA deputies elected in 1921, the ten seats the party was going to win allowed it to assemble a bare majority of 51 percent (twenty-two deputies) to elect its candidate to the presidency.

During the official tally of the votes that the Provincial Electoral Councils in Alajuela and Heredia conducted, however, the PA lost two legislative seats, allegedly because of faulty electoral registries. These Electoral Councils then reallocated these seats, one to the PR and the other to the PfR, which had formed an alliance known as the Fusion to thwart the PA's presidential aspirations.

The unexpected reallocation of legislative seats among contending parties posed a threat to political stability. Newspaper reports indicated that dissatisfied elements of the PA and the PR were separately planning revolts to prevent their adversaries' candidates from winning the presidency. The PA began to attack the president for not having overturned the verdicts the Electoral Juntas of Alajuela and Heredia reached. President Acosta placed the police and army on alert as he restructured both to ensure that both held equal numbers of PA an PR followers. As rumors circulated that PR deputies with controversial claims to their seats were going to be kidnapped to deny Jiménez enough votes to be elected president, the PR interned its deputies in safe houses under armed guard.[24]

---

[24] All of these events were staple items of the newspapers between December 1923 and May 1924. The organization of one insurrection is reported in "Los graves rumores que circularon ayer: se hablaba de un levantamiento jimenista contra el gobierno, en connivencia con el de Cambronero," *Diario del Comercio*, No. 974 (11 December 1923), p. 1; "Sensacionales declaraciones sobre el levantamiento de Cambronero," Ibid, No. 979 (16 December 1923), p. 1; and "Reportaje celebrado con la mujer del alzado Lorenzo Cambronero," Ibid, No. 989 (29 December 1923), p. 1; of another, see "La revolución de anoche," *Diario de Costa Rica*, No. 1414 (29 March 1924), p. 1; and yet another in "Los sucesos políticos de Cartago," Ibid, No. 1431 (22 April 1924), p. 1. This last report also describes a threatened mutiny by the Cartago army barracks to prevent Jiménez from becoming president. Acosta's efforts to balance rival parties' affiliates in the army are

The President's Dilemma

Amid rumors of insurrection and the safeguarding of deputies, the president proposed that the three candidates name a Committee of Honor consisting of fifteen citizens. Each party would name a third of its members. The Committee would judge whether the Alajuelan and Heredian Provincial Electoral Councils' decisions were "was in accordance or not with the law." On behalf of the PA, Alberto Echandi accepted the proposed arbitration on the condition that the Fusion jointly nominate five members of the Committee. The PR candidate requested that the Committee not only investigate Council behavior in the central Provinces of Alajuela and Heredia, but reexamine the Congressional rulings on the petitions submitted after the 1921 midterm elections – most of which were leveled against the president's party.

The president's proposal sank once Volio, the PfR candidate, rejected it. Volio too reminded the president of the 1921 elections when he recommended that parties should not

> . . . substitute the two institutions that the constitution said should review this issue, that is, the Tribunals of Justice, if criminal mistakes had been committed, and the Constitutional Congress, the only body called to declare whether the declaration of Congressional results has been well or badly made. . . . When, two years ago, I was a victim of egregious mistake made by a Provincial Council that stole two deputies from me . . . no one thought of forming a Committee of Honorables, no one spent time thinking about the event, and neither did I think that I would have disturbed the peace at the heart of the republic [because this Congressional verdict]; Congress simply resolved the case.[25]

When both Jiménez and Volio referred to the 1921 midterm elections, they were pointing to the fact that most of the petitions – 63 percent of all accusations (97 of 153) – filed in the aftermath of this election accused the PC*l* of rigging the results of the ballot box. Yet, when the Credentials Committee and Congress – dominated by the PC*l* – reviewed these alle-

---

discussed in "El movimiento de ayer en las esferas militares: se están equilibrando las fuerzas echandistas y jimenistas," Ibid, No. 1417 (2 April 1924), p. 1. The possible kidnapping of deputies is reported in "Existía el plan de secuestrar a tres diputados," Ibid, No. 1415 (30 March 1924), p. 1, "Los sucesos políticos de Cartago," and "La clausura de diputados amenazados de secuestro," Ibid, No. 1431 (22 April 1924), p. 7.

[25] "Presidencia de la República (17 December 1923)," *La Gaceta*, No. 289 (20 December 1923), p. 1592. Both this citation and the information in this paragraph stem from this source.

gations in May 1922, they rejected them. The Committee, in fact, concluded "that all of them are invalid because if, in some cases, some can be reasons to [impugn] some votes, this would not alter the final result."[26]

This conclusion did not serve the interests of the PRI, the PfR's predecessor. It also violated the Congressional precedent that Electoral Councils not be allowed to nullify votes. The PCI's opponents had accused the Provincial Electoral Council of Alajuela, which the president's party dominated, of having inappropriately excluded enough votes to cost the PRI two Congressional seats. Reminding the president of what had transpired in 1921 was doubly embarrassing because it was his brother, Raúl Acosta, who led the progovernment forces in these elections.

Should – or could – the president have reversed the Councils's decisions? As the PA reminded the public, the 1913 electoral law endowed the president with "disciplinary authority" in electoral matters. If he had sacked the Alajuelan and Heredian Councils, the PA might have regained its two "lost" seats. In response, the Fusion would have filed petitions in Congress to override the results of his decision. Even if the PA would have prevailed, the PR and the PfR would have rendered President Acosta – so concerned with staying above the partisan fray – unable to escape the charge that he had helped one side in a hotly contested election.

By refusing to intervene, however, the president perhaps hoped to encourage parties to settle their disputes in a mutually acceptable way. Leaving things the way they were created a stalemate. Even with their two additional deputies, the PR and the PfR did not hold a two-thirds quorum necessary to convene Congress. Even with a bare majority in Congress, they would not have been able to meet to make Jiménez president. Perhaps Acosta's decision to do nothing was actually in the best interests of the PA and of the republic as a whole. Remaining above the fray forced the PA, PR, and the PfR to negotiate – unless, of course, a coalition wished to step outside of the constitution to resolve this dispute in its favor.

What was constitutional, however, was not entirely clear. There was no precedent for the situation in which the country found itself. The law did empower the president to supervise the election process, and the Councils were creatures of the executive. A higher body of law – the constitution itself – did empower Congress to certify election results. To the extent that the decision to annul votes was a component of certification – which

---

[26] "Dictamen de la Comisión de Credenciales (21 April 1922)," *La Gaceta*, No. 108 (14 May 1922), p. 520.

Congress had jealously guarded and no one had contested – the existing institutional architecture of the republic failed to generate a legitimate way of resolving this conflict. In the context of an indecisive presidential election and an evenly balanced set of forces in Congress, the rather small matter of whether a Provincial Electoral Council could annul votes became the fulcrum of a constitutional and political crisis.

Congress, Partisanship, and the Classical Theory of Electoral Governance

PA representatives struggled to negotiate a pact with the PR and PfR around the selection of a compromise candidate. The PA proposed that twenty-one deputies from each of the two parties attend the inaugural session of Congress to decide whether to accept the petitions to nullify the verdicts made by the Electoral Councils of Alajuela and Heredia. If such a Congress accepted these juntas' legitimacy, then Echandi would choose from a slate of three candidates proposed by Jiménez; if it rejected the petitions, the PR chief would choose from a list submitted by his rival.

The plan, however, to catapult a third candidate into the presidency did not prosper. The PR candidate believed it was based on too many imponderables to succeed. Jiménez also refused to endorse the pact once General Volio declared he would not support a deal that did not result in the election of one of the two runners-up. For, if the two largest parties could reach a mutually beneficial agreement, neither would need to negotiate with the PfR to form a government. In response, PA deputies announced that they planned to boycott the 1 May session to prevent the formation of a two-thirds quorum (twenty-eight out of forty-three deputies) required to hold the inaugural session of Congress. Through the use of this parliamentary ruse, they aimed to block Jiménez's election to the presidency.[27]

---

[27] The first list of names submitted by the *echandistas* consisted of Carlos María Jiménez (Ricardo Jiménez's nephew), Arturo Volio, and Carlos Brenes ("La proposición del Partido Agrícola al Licdo. Don Ricardo Jiménez," *Diario de Costa Rica*, No. 1435 [26 April 1924], p. 1). The Reformist chief issues a statement published in "El Gral. Volio declara que no acepta ninguna otra combinación política," Ibid, No. 1436 (27 April 1924), p. 1. Jiménez's skepticism is discussed in "El Partido Agrícola amplía sus proposiciones al Licdo. Jiménez," Ibid, p. 6. Another list, containing the names of Alfredo Jiménez, Arturo Volio, and Oscar Rohrmoser, was disclosed in "Las novedades políticas de ayer," Ibid, No. 1438 (30 April 1924), p. 5. The public declaration of the PA not to attend the inaugural session is "Manifiesto de la Diputación del Partido Agrícola al País," Ibid, No. 1439 (1 May 1924), p. 8.

The Fusion nevertheless succeeded in assembling a quorum to conduct legislative business. The Fusion relied upon the presence of one PA deputy alternate to achieve a coalition of twenty-eight PR deputies and their alternates – itself a questionable act because alternates could not typically substitute deputies unless unusual circumstances existed and the Congressional presidency approved the substitutions. With this out of the way, the Credentials Committee, composed of a deputy representing each of these parties, accepted practically all of the decisions the Provincial Electoral Councils of Alajuela and Heredia made. The Committee concluded that

The law says that polling stations, as soon the election is complete, should submit the ballots, one poll book, and the other documents relative to the election to the Provincial Council; and, in another place, it adds that the Provincial Councils should verify the tally of the vote as soon as they have received the documents and poll books. . . . The law stipulates that the validity of the election needs to be approved by two bodies: the Provincial Council and the Congress. The Provincial Council tallies, but to tally is not a simple revision of the totals reached by the District Councils. To tally, according to the *Dictionary of the Royal Spanish Academy*, is the examination and exact and diligent investigation that is done to something to know what it is and to form an opinion of it.[28]

Curiously basing itself on a definition from what remains the authoritative dictionary of the Spanish language, the Committee endorsed the right of Provincial Electoral Councils to nullify votes by ignoring the very precedent it had set. With this decision, the Credentials Committee contributed to the collapse of existing ways of arbitrating conflicting interpretations of electoral law. In the midst of a hotly contested election, the nullification of a few votes had altered the balance of power in Congress, stripped the president of his "disciplinary authority in matters electoral," and set the stage for the controversial election of a new president.

With the dirtiest work out of the way, Congress then turned its attention to selecting a new president. Casting a pointless ballot for Echandi, PA Deputy Gerardo Zúñiga justified his behavior by claiming that he was constitutionally required to attend the inaugural session of Congress and that the failure to elect a president would only plunge the republic into civil war and dictatorship.[29] In return for the PfR's support, PR deputies

[28] "Dictamen de mayoría de la Comisión de Credenciales (30 April 1924)," *La Gaceta*, No. 107 (18 May 1924), p. 509.
[29] "La Nota política," *Diario de Costa Rica*, No. 1394 (4 March 1924), p. 1, presents the alternative way of determining how to meet a legislative quorum. On the events of 1 May, see

voted to make Volio second designate to the presidency and promised to enact portions of P*f*R's social reformist program.[30]

Conclusion

As in the first decade of the twentieth century, elections remained highly competitive between 1913 and 1923. Candidates organized campaigns. Parties deployed networks of publicists and activists to solidify the support of the loyal and to persuade the undecided. All sought the backing of an increasingly literate male electorate that included virtually all men twenty years or older.

Though the PR had largely failed to live up to its campaign pledges to reform the electoral laws of the republic, it did overcome factional disagreement to dismantle indirect elections for public offices. The 1913 general elections were, in fact, the first in which citizens (81 percent of whom turned out to vote) directly chose their president and one-half of all deputies. Two years later, voters selected the other half of Congress in the first popular midterm elections held in the history of the country. In a pattern set during these elections, turnout rates typically fell and enabled large numbers of local parties to field candidates to contest national parties for control of legislative seats.

Again, the periphery was responsible for a disproportionate share of the denunciations of electoral fraud. Though it only contained about a fifth of the electorate, parties lodged slightly more than half of their accusations against elections held in the outlying provinces of the republic. Three-quarters of the worst types of fraud also occurred in the provinces with the largest share of voters who were poor and illiterate peasants and agricultural workers. And, even in the periphery, slightly more than half of all accusations claimed that parties and the authorities used coercion against voters, allowed citizens not satisfying suffrage requirements to vote, and committed other such egregious acts of fraud.

"Los diputados que concurrirán hoy a la sesión," and "El Congeso declaró electo Presidente de la República al Lic. Ricardo Jiménez," Ibid, No. 1439 (1 May 1924), p. 5, and No. 1440 (2 May 1924), pp. 1, 4. The renegade deputy justified his behavior in "Carta del Diputado señor Zúñiga Montúfar," Ibid, No. 1454 (18 May 1924), p. 6.

[30] Victoria Ramírez A., *Jorge Volio y la revolución viviente* (San José: Ediciones Guayacán, 1989), pp. 112–46; Marina Volio, *Jorge Volio y el Partido Reformista* (San José: EUNED, 1973), pp. 174–230. The latter author is a daughter of the late Volio.

Conclusion

Social structure helps to explain why infractions of electoral law were disproportionately concentrated in the periphery. Unlike in the Central Valley, agricultural workers labored on large cattle ranches and banana plantations in the periphery. In central areas, in contrast, large numbers of small and medium-sized peasants lived in closely linked communities that could better defend their political rights. Large numbers of poor, economically dependent, and uneducated voters in the periphery thus made for a civil society less able to defend itself against assaults on its civil liberties.

Yet, it is misleading to overestimate the impact of social conditions on decisions to stuff the ballot box. The most vulnerable voters were also located in the most politically competitive provinces. Unlike in the center, most races in the periphery involved one or two legislative seats, which went to plurality winners. Because the distance separating winners from losers was usually less than the number of votes needed to satisfy a "quotient" in core areas where proportional representation allocated seats, parties faced more incentives to denounce fraud in outlying areas.

Though social structural and institutional arguments are consistent with the spatial distribution of fraud, only the latter can explain why rates of party formation are greater in the periphery than in the center. Once we control for the size of the electorate, there were more eligible voters per party and more local parties in outlying than in core areas. Sociological theories cannot account for why the most socially stratified parts of the country produced more parties than those with a denser, more vibrant civil society. Only an approach that incorporates the effects of institutional arrangements on political behavior can really explain geographic variations in ballot-rigging and party formation.

Between 1913 and 1923, procedural violations committed by polling station officials still accounted for nearly half (216 of 478) of all accusations of electoral fraud. In large part, the predominance of the mildest forms of fraud was a product of the fact that citizens still voted publicly. Though this voting system stripped citizens (especially the poorest and least educated ones) of the anonymity necessary to vote according to their preferences, the public franchise did facilitate the ability of parties to monitor the behavior of their rivals. In an atmosphere where parties could detect and denounce egregious violations of electoral law, officials attempted to manipulate outcomes by continuing to open polling stations behind schedule, to record votes in poll books unfairly favoring progovernment candidates, and to commit other such infractions of electoral law. That such acts may have stemmed more from carelessness than from dishonesty suggests that, at the very least, petitioners went to great lengths to observe the behavior of public officials and, of course, their partisan rivals.

Nevertheless, the most flagrant types of fraud increased in frequency after the establishment of direct elections for all public offices. Though they accounted for less than a fifth of all denunciations of electoral fraud between 1913 and 1923, the petitions contain twice as many charges of the use of coercion against voters than between 1901 and 1912. Our own classification of the accusations indicates that the two worst categories of fraud increased to 42 percent of the total, an increase of 11 percentage points from the preceding period. The growth in the number of the most blatant types of fraud reflects the fact that progovernment parties had to poll more votes than their rivals in popular elections to retain control of the presidency; no longer could they reverse a defeat at the polls by manipulating second-stage elections. Uncertainty about election results therefore increased competitiveness and the corresponding willingness of parties to risk detection by committing the most blatant acts of fraud during popular elections.

Not only did the public franchise help stem the growth of the worst types of fraud, but the incentives generated by this voting system also explain why parties spent as much time inflating their own vote totals as they did deflating those of their adversaries. The public franchise allowed their local affiliates to keep a running tally of the vote during election day. As a result, parties could deflate opposition vote totals and/or inflate their own at each polling station to ensure that they kept ahead of their rivals in what were typically competitive elections. Analysis of the petitions confirms this prediction: By counting up the accusations that indicate whether adversaries illegally increased or decreased vote totals, we discover that parties spent as much pursuing one activity as the other.

Even if we interpret the magnitude of fraud very liberally, misconduct was not responsible for most election outcomes. The victor's margin of votes was typically greater than the share of polling stations with impugned votes. In the 1921 midterm election, when the vote difference between the triumphant party and the first runner-up was smaller than the proportion of questioned votes, we can only assume that fraud delivered a victory for the incumbent party because a third of the charges complained about the behavior of nonofficial parties. So, even if fraud could have swung election results in 1921, it was not responsible for a government victory because, simply put, parties did not argue that official forces had stolen enough votes to win this election.

As in the preceding period, both the Credentials Committee and Congress as a whole rejected most petitions to nullify electoral results. It argued that allegations of fraud were insufficiently documented or that accepting them would not have altered election outcomes. Entrusting the legislative majority with the responsibility of certifying election results seemed to have worked most of the time, even if Congress could not quite escape the charge that it had become a "grand elector."

When an election was close, however, fraud could unhinge the stability of the republic. An essentially adversarial system of electoral justice was unable to deliver impartial judgments. When no candidate won an outright victory at the polls in the 1923 presidential election, two Electoral Councils annulled enough votes to allow the PR to pick up additional legislative seats and thereby hold a bare majority in Congress. Through some rather dubious constitutional maneuvers, the Credentials Committee and Congress as a whole – which the PR and the P*f*R dominated – rejected their opponents' petitions that the Electoral Councils had inappropriately nullified votes. Amid protests and rumors of civil disturbances, the PR and the P*f*R succeeded in sending none other than a well-known democratic reformer, Jiménez, to the presidency.

4

Institutional Change, Electoral Cycles,
and Partisanship, 1924–8

Introduction

This chapter explores an important puzzle of institutional reform. It explains why a president got deputies to approve two far-reaching reform bills. The first established the secret franchise, a voter registry, and an electoral tribunal to adjudicate conflicting claims about election results. The second eliminated the ability of parties to distribute ballots on election day. With this reform bill, only the secretariat of the interior could furnish voters with paper ballots. Both sets of reforms strengthened safeguards for opposition parties as well as for voters. Both also increased the uncertainty of political competition.

In line with office-seeking approaches, most deputies did not want to liberate voters from their control. Winning elections was difficult enough. Increasing the number of voters over which they had no information only promised to augment political uncertainty. Indeed, short-term electoral considerations combined with sociological factors to make representatives unwilling to safeguard voters' privacy rights. Even if class was not a central issue in politics, middle-class deputies did not want to make their future even more dependent upon the voting behavior of a largely rural (and one-third illiterate) electorate.

Institutionalist perspectives begin to resolve the puzzle of reform. In the first place, they suggest that the president was likely to back electoral reform to repair the damage done to his reputation. Though no one accused Ricardo Jiménez for ordering Provincial Electoral Councils to tally votes in controversial ways, many blamed him for the fraud that allowed the PR and PfR to send him to the presidency. As opposition Deputy León Cortés declared, "Señor Jiménez, with his own hand, was responsible for having burned his own prestige."[1] That he could run again for high office – though he could not serve consecutive terms – encouraged Jiménez to focus on his long-term political reputation. Revitilizing his commitment to democratic reform would be an ideal way to construct the image of a fair, publicly spirited statesman.

In the second place, institutionalist approaches suggest that the president could capitalize on public support for cleaner government and use his veto power to fashion a coalition in favor of reform. Opposition deputies, for example, would be interested in changing electoral laws because they wished to facilitate their access to state power. Progovernment reformers, especially if they represented a populist constituency, might be interested in spearheading democratic reform. The constitutional fact that representatives needed to assemble a two-thirds majority to override a presidential veto convinced enough deputies to support a set of reforms more extensive than even opposition legislators wanted. As we shall see, that the president could veto bills he disliked transformed a standoff between pro- and antireform parties into propitious territory for far-reaching institutional changes.

This chapter begins by showing why partisan alignments in Congress created opportunities for reform. Using office-seeking theories of reform, it then shows why the opposition presented a rather modest bill of electoral reforms. Most importantly, the chapter contributes to institutionalist accounts of political change by explaining how constitutional-level rules can empower a president to pivot between pro- and antigovernment forces to get a reluctant Congress to back fundamental changes in electoral law. The conclusion places our findings about the politics of the 1925 and 1927 electoral laws in the context of theories of institutional reform outlined in the introduction to this book.

The Struggle to Reform Institutions

Amid the opposition boycott of the inaugural session of Congress, the new president issued a call for reform.[2] Jiménez's actions threatened to reduce

---

[1] "Discursos pronunciados y leídos en la sesión verificada el día 13 de mayo corriente por los Diputados del 'Partido Agrícola,' referentes a la elección de Presidente de la República y declaratoria de Diputados electos (13 May 1924)," *La Gaceta*, No. 111 (23 May 1924), p. 547. This was the fourth ordinary session of the year.

[2] "Mensaje de don Ricardo Jiménez, Presidente de la República, al Congreso Constitucional (8 May 1924)," in Carlos Meléndez Chaverri, ed., *Mensajes presidenciales, 1918–28*, Vol. V (San José: Academia de Geografía e Historia de Costa Rica, 1985), pp. 141–2.

the governing coalition's slim Congressional majority. Seeking to test the president's commitment to institutional change, the PA submitted a reform bill to Congress.

Legislative Alignments and Reform

In line with office-seeking perspectives, the opposition recommended changes just extensive enough to prevent the sort of actions that had just deprived it of the presidency. The first of their two key recommendations included the creation of a National Electoral Council. Deputies of each of the seven provinces would chose the Council's members to supervise the tally of the vote that the Provincial Electoral Councils' conducted. Their bill also contained an extensive set of recommendations attempting to regulate the inclusion and exclusion of names in and from electoral registries.[3]

Two PR deputies wrote the report for the Committee on Legislation. They welcomed the call to reform electoral laws while sarcastically rejecting the tendered bill. "When it was announced that a number of sincere devotees of republican liberties and practices within this chamber had presented a project to reform the current electoral law," the Committee wrote, "our curiosity, full of anticipation, ran to read the bill. Oh!, it was said: Here must be a wise proposal to introduce the secret ballot. . . . But, that reading did not find the secret vote. . . ." Nor did it find "an article or group of articles that established, regulated and guaranteed female suffrage" or an effort to reduce the uncertainty and tension that the Congressional run-off system produced. Instead, the Committee pointed out, the bill opted "to create a new apparatus for the electoral machinery of the state called an Electoral Tribunal," which it labeled as "some sort of an enlargement of the Provincial Electoral Councils, which already cost, among other details, secretaries, scribes, janitors, etc., that is, 175 colones a session."[4]

Undeterred, the opposition asked the president in mid-October to include its bill on the agenda that he was developing for the extraordinary

---

[3] "Proyecto (16 June 1924)," *La Gaceta*, No. 142 (29 June 1924), pp. 765–8. Almost a month later, León Cortés, rapidly emerging as one of the most vocal PA deputies, submitted a revised version of this project. See "Proyecto (14 July 1924)," Ibid, No. 164 (24 July 1924), pp. 918–21.

[4] "Dictamen de la Comisión de Legislación (28 July 1924)," Ibid, No. 168 (31 July 1924), pp. 949–50.

sessions of Congress. According to the constitution, only the president can set the legislative agenda during extraordinary sessions of the legislature. Further postponing consideration of such a bill, PA deputies pointed out, would only destroy "the rightness of the cause and the serenity" indispensable for reform "because, by the end of next year, elections to renovate Congress must be practiced." Without such conditions, they implied that "the ill-feeling that all parties experienced" in the last elections would repeat itself.[5]

Even after the PR's rejection of its bill, the PA did not give up on the cause of reform. As the party of the opposition, the PA possessed an interest in loosening up access to state power. Fairer elections might only further reduce the PR's tenuous control of Congress. What office-seeking approaches cannot explain is why the opposition blatantly appealed to the president. Why did the PA do this?

Institutional Configurations and Reform Possibilities

Two reasons explain why the PA was appealing to its political enemy. First, the end of ordinary sessions turned the executive into the legislative agenda-setter. According to the 1871 constitution, Congress set its own priorities for only three months of the year. Only with the return of ordinary sessions in May of the following year could the PA even try to assemble a coalition in favor of change. Second, the partisan distribution of power endowed every party with a veto on the passage of legislation. Though the PA was the largest single party in Congress, it held 49 percent of the seats – frustratingly less than a majority. The PR held 37 percent (sixteen of forty-three) of all deputies.[6] When the only PA deputy to attend the 1 May session that elected Jiménez to the presidency became a P*f*R deputy, the P*f*R increased its numbers from five to six deputies. The Fusion, as PR and P*f*R alliance called itself, held a bare majority – 51 percent of the legislative seats.

The PA was powerless to enact legislation on its own. In line with sociological approaches, the P*f*R would support institutional change if

---

[5] "El memorial de la Diputación Agrícola, presentado ayer al señor Presidente de la República (18 October 1924)," *La Tribuna*, No. 1343 (25 October 1924), p. 5.

[6] "Los diputados que concurrirán hoy a la sesión," and "La nota política," *Diario de Costa Rica*, No. 1439 (1 May 1924), p. 5.

its rhetoric of reform on behalf of urban artisans and peasants was sincere. Even if the opposition persuaded some of rivals to cross the partisan divide in Congress, however, it still had to gain the president's support to enact legislation. Unless the PA amassed a two-thirds majority, the president could veto its bill. That the PR's reception was chilly indicated that it was not going to back just any reform bill the PA put on the agenda.

Institutional arrangements and the Congressional balance of power therefore turned the president into a pivotal player in politics. Without his support, deputies would fail to enact bills into laws. Recognizing the president's crucial role also had an additional, partisan benefit. By working with the president, the PA could also isolate the president from his party and make him more dependent upon currying their support to enact legislation. How would the president react?

The President's Response

Later that month, President Jiménez responded to the opposition's request. In a deft maneuver to placate the pro- and antigovernment forces, he issued a pronouncement that simultaneously took the middle ground and pushed for a set of more radical institutional changes.

In a letter addressed to PA deputies, the president declared that he could only support a reform bill that created voter identification cards so that each citizen could "prove his identity" before casting his ballot. Similarly, he called for the adoption of a permanent civic registry of voters "with the aim of avoiding inclusions and exclusions from electoral rolls that occur at the last minute and are resolved in an atmosphere of inflamed partisan passions." He also recommended extending the right to vote to women and adopting the "Australian ballot." "The system of secret voting," he noted, "was in effect in all advanced democracies," and, "it is the most secure way of averting the purchasing of votes that eliminates all dignity and prestige from popular elections."

The president also indirectly supported the opposition's call for the formation of an electoral tribunal. He recommended "the cessation of the faculty the president now has to interpret dark passages of electoral law." This, he claimed, would prevent the president from becoming "a grand elector, whom parties illegitimately attempt to persuade to interfere in the electoral process or to attack when they fail to enlist the president as an instrument of their interests." And, in the only allusion to his own election, the president also called for removing Congress from the business of selecting chief executives.[7]

By championing the cause of reform, Jiménez circumvented the limitations that minority government posed. His declarations informed the PR and PfR that he would side with their opponents unless they backed enough of his legislative program. By mid-year, for example, the president had lost several votes, even as the PR gained another deputy for its congressional ranks.[8] His positive response to the PA's invitation was therefore a diplomatic way of telling the party that it could not take him for granted: With a razor-thin Congressional majority, it was natural that progovernment deputies would make excessive demands on the president. His announcement also put his opponents on notice that he was not going to switch sides unless they backed far-reaching reforms. He, in other words, was not going to sell out his ostensible supporters for a meager set of reforms.

Striking a deal with his nominal opponents also protected reform from progovernment attacks. Indeed, his proposal tacitly recognized that, in line with office-seeking theories of political change, the PR was unlikely to back reforms that facilitated the opposition's return to power. Though the PA also opposed reforms that increased the uncertainty of political competition, the legislative balance of power forced it to choose between settling for no reform or for supporting the president's far-reaching reforms. Unless pro- or antigovernment legislators could form a two-thirds majority to override a presidential veto, each was forced to support a large number of the president's proposals to advance their own partisan goals. The laws governing the production of laws, along with the distribution of partisan preferences, therefore created as it safeguarded a reform-oriented coalition.

With his support of reform, President Jiménez therefore began to revitalize his commitment to democratic reform. That he could not run for consecutive reelection, as institutionalist theories suggest, empowered him to think about the long-term interests of the body politic. The structure of executive-legislative relations, and the Congressional balance of power, allowed him to become the pivotal player in political competition.

---

[7] "Importante carta del Presidente de la República acerca de la reforma de la Ley Electoral," Ibid, No. 1592 (29 October 1924), p. 1.
[8] "La novedades políticas: La difícil situación del Gobierno en el Congreso," Ibid, No. 1495 (6 July 1924), p. 6.

Institutional arrangements, in other words, allowed Jiménez to transform a strategic weakness into a political advantage.

Political Threats and Committee Reports

Less than a week later, Deputy Cortés launched a motion to form a Special Committee to study the president's proposals. After a few minutes of recess, a legislative majority selected its representatives in line with the partisan balance of power in Congress: The PA and the PR each obtained two committee seats while the PfR got the fifth.[9]

It took some time for a Congressional Committee to issue its report on the executive's proposals. Some members of the opposition interpreted a lack of progress as evidence that a plot was afoot to ensure that midterm elections were held with the same Provincial Electoral Juntas that had deprived their candidate of the presidency. Should the electoral law not be reformed, they recommended that the PA abstain from participating in the December elections. By early February, after a meeting of the PA Executive Committee, the opposition stopped just short of the threat advocated by hardliners. "According to the course taken by the reform of the Electoral Law in Congress," the statement read, "the PA will decide whether it takes part in the [midterm] elections for deputies."[10]

Amid an increase in political tensions, the Special Committee issued its judgment on a draft electoral reform bill on the same day that the PA published its threat.[11] As part of its report, the Congressional Committee included a draft of an new electoral law containing the PA and president's suggestions. The first of the three principal innovations the bill called for was the creation of an electoral tribunal to resolve conflicts of interpreta-

---

[9] E.s. no. 33 (3 November 1924), art. 4, *La Gaceta*, No. 263 (22 November 1924), p. 1666. The two PR deputies were Manuel Coto and Horacio Castro. The two PA representatives were Cortés and Francisco Cordero. The PfR was was Enrique Fonseca.

[10] "El Partido agrícola se abstiene de ocuparse en las próximas elecciones de diputados (2 February 1925)," *La Tribuna*, No. 1425 (3 February 1925), p. 1. This article was also published as "Declaraciones del Comité Ejecutivo del Partido Agrícola (2 February 1925)," *Diario de Costa Rica*, No. 1669 (3 February 1925), p. 5. The statements issued by hardliners appeared several days earlier as "La nota política: el Partido Agrícola no irá a las elecciones de diputados si no se reforma la Ley Electoral," *La Tribuna*, No. 1416 (23 January 1925), p. 5.

[11] The two PA deputies supported the proposed reforms. The PR and PfR deputies also endorsed the bill, but reserved the right to introduce amendments during the debate on the bill on topics not discussed in the preamble of the bill.

tion regarding the application of the law. Establishing the secret franchise was the second. And the third was the creation of a Civic Registry containing a comprehensive listing of men qualified to vote and entrusted with distributing personal identification cards to them.[12]

Several months later, fourteen PA, one PR, and one PfR deputies floated a bill recommending the candidate with a plurality and at least a third of the popular vote be elected president. Should no candidate satisfy these requirements, the presidency should be awarded to the candidate with a plurality of votes in a run-off restricted to the two runners-up. In a transparent reference to the events of the prior year, they also suggested that alternates be allowed to help fill a quorum in inaugural Congressional sessions. Finally, they recommended moving the popular election from the second Sunday of December to the same day in February in the year that the new president should assume control of office.[13]

The Dilemmas Posed by Female Suffrage Rights

Though the Committee's report acknowledged that, "in recent times, a select group of Costa Rican women has been acquiring the recognized elements of culture," it did not endorse "this novel reform of our electoral practices." Given the president's commitment to meaningful change, why did the Committee refuse to extend suffrage rights to women?

One answer to this question is that deputies could not bring themselves to institutionalize equal political rights for women. As the cognitive expression of a male-dominated social structure, sexist attitudes would hold back democratic reform. Another response would focus upon the electoral impact of doubling the size of the electorate. As a "redistributive" reform, parties would oppose a measure that promised to increase the uncertainty of political competition.

Debate on female suffrage rights was therefore more than just a referendum on the progressiveness of Costa Rican males. It was part of a larger debate about the impact of legal change on the partisan distribution of power. This is why the president of Congress allowed the debate to rage on before letting deputies begin formal debate on the reform bill as a whole. Though, as opposition leader Cortés noted, this procedure was

---

[12] "Dictamen de la Comisión Especial," *Proyecto de modificaciones a la Ley Electoral vigente* (2 February 1925), (San José: Imprenta Nacional, 1925).
[13] "Proyecto (22 May 1925)," *La Gaceta*, No. 117 (24 May 1925), p. 845.

"new, but not irregular."[14] This unusual change in procedure was indispensable to prevent a sufficiently large number of pro- and antigovernment deputies from coalescing to sink the reform bill because of opposition to the extending suffrage rights to women.

Newspaper debates on the political topic of the day were one-sided and polemical: Columnists, intellectuals, and feminists supplied arguments in favor of extending the vote to women much more often than their opponents provided counterarguments. In a series of passionately argued essays, Pedro Pérez, a distinguished jurist, pointed out that it was time to extend suffrage rights to "our mothers, wives, daughters, and sisters." For, doing so, he added, "is as natural, necessary, and legitimate as it is for their husbands, sons, fathers, and brothers: it is a human right given, without restrictions of any kind, to men and women, by the Creator. Not recognizing this is a crime against humanity. And this crime can only be explained by a lack of education and culture." Echoing the sentiments of the Boston tea party, Pérez also took his theoretical arguments to their logical conclusion. He argued that it was a violation of natural rights "to demand that Costa Rican women pay taxes of any type, when they are excluded from parliamentary representation."

Pérez also confronted the antisufragists with an empirical fact. Implicitly referring to the fact that illiterate males were participating in politics, he pointed out that

within our undeniable smallness, we can count upon hundreds and thousands of ladies educated in almost all branches of knowledge, including doctors of medicine, surgery, dentistry, and pharmacy; professors of languages, music, voice, drawing, painting, obstetrics; nurses, scribes, accountants, typists, stenographers, cashiers, retail assistants, dramatic actresses, archivists, clothes designers, florists, hatters, athletes, seamstresses, detectives, orators, writers, etc.

This large list, he added, "does not include the more than one thousand degree-holding educators of the more than forty thousand pupils of the elementary schools of the nation." On another occasion, Pérez estimated that the total number of educated women in the country could be as high as ten thousand.[15]

---

[14] "Dictamen de la Comisión Especial."
[15] The estimate is from his "VOTO FEMENINO: el dictamen de la Comisión," *La Tribuna*, No. 1430 (8 February 1925), p. 11. All other citations are from "El Licenciado Pérez Zeledón y el voto femenino," Ibid, No. 1395 (28 December 1924), p. 3. Approximately a third of these women were school teachers and therefore state employees.

The Struggle to Reform Institutions

From the moment the president recommended extending voting rights to women in October 1924, his words activated an embryonic feminist movement that consisted of middle-class educators.[16] Feminists waged a journalistic war in support of their cause and led a petition drive to collect the names of distinguished women and men in support of female suffrage rights. In her contributions to this public debate, Señora Sara Casal v. (widow of) de Quirós referred to the large number of distinguished citizens, many by name and constituting the equivalent of a *Who's Who in Costa Rica*, who had signed the petition. She called for an extensive Congressional debate on the matter so that "the names of the adversaries of this reform are left to history." In a plea directed at those deputies who believed that extending voting rights to women would only debase "the fair sex," she stated that

I respect your opinion since you can oblige your wives and daughters, within your homes, to be as passive as you demand. But, by being deputies, you do not have the right to impose your will on other homes or on those independent women, whether because they are widows, separated from their husbands, or simply abandoned by them, as occurs on a majority of occasions, nor on unmarried women. No one has conceded you the right to assume such power.[17]

As PfR delegation chief Jorge Volio noted, opponents of suffrage rights for women really did not confront these arguments. Opponents of equal rights for women used three lines of reasoning to deflect these criticisms. The first was moral: Many deputies wanted the "the fair sex" (or, more evocatively, "*el bello sexo*") not to experience the "evils that characterize our politics." For, "by becoming a suffragists, forming legions in the streets, losing the rhythm of her elegant and alluring ways...," this polemicist suggested, "she would lose the secrecy of her femininity."[18] The

---

[16] See Steven Palmer and Gladys Rojas Chaves, "Educating Señorita: Teacher Training, Social Mobility, and the Birth of Costa Rican Feminism, 1885–1925," *Hispanic American Historical Review*, Vol. 78, No. 1 (February 1998), pp. 45–82. Also, for description of some of the issues at stake, see Macarena Barahona Riera, *Las sufragistas de Costa Rica* (San José: EUCR, 1994), especially pp. 74–97.

[17] "VOTO FEMENINO," *La Tribuna*, No. 1431 (10 February 1925), p. 3. The report on the lack of interest sparked by this reform, even on the part of women, is "La campaña feminista no prospera," Ibid, No. 1353 (6 November 1924), p. 2.

[18] With the exception of phrase about the "fair sex," all other quotations stem from "El perfil del día: el voto femenino," *La Tribuna*, No. 1348 (31 October 1924), p. 4. The first phrase was commonly used by defenders of the status quo. Like other published opinions against female voting rights, the author of this piece is identified by a pseudonym, in this case as the White Lieutenant ("El Teniente Blanco"). Also, see "El diputado Mayorga Rivas propone el voto femenino: se plantea la tesis de la inconstitucionalidad," *Diario de Costa Rica*, No. 1687 (24 February 1925), p. 4.

second was practical: Endowing women with the right to vote required a constitutional amendment. Unless deputies separated this reform from others, it could bog down the entire reform bill into a debate about the constitutionality of this measure and delay in the enactment of a new electoral law. Since the PA had publicly announced that it would reconsider its decision to participate in the 1925 midterm elections should a new electoral law not be enacted, approval of female franchise rights threatened to unleash a chain of events that might very well plunge the republic into the political uncertainty and violence from which it had only recently escaped.

Finally, many deputies appeared to have found suffragists' arguments beyond the pale of rational debate. Deputy Cortés, for example, could do little more than point to what he believed to be an unacceptable consequence of extending voting rights to women: that they would then be eligible for holding public office. This, for Cortés, seemed so patently absurd that it required little defense and elaboration.[19] On 24 February, a majority of twenty-four to fifteen voted to kill this reform.

Judging from the relative silence that met feminist arguments, hostility to new ideas about the place of women in society helps to explain the defeat of this measure. As in all countries with republican systems of government, debates about extending voting rights to women pitted proponents of gender equality against "defenders" of the "fair sex," whose members they defined principally by their relation to men, especially in their capacity as nurturing, protective, and virtuous mothers. In a society that was predominantly rural, unabashedly patriarchical, and proudly bound by tradition, extending voting rights to women threatened to disrupt male hegemony.[20]

Yet, sexist attitudes cannot completely explain the failure of suffrage reform. In stark contrast to countries that had or were extending the franchise to women, Costa Rica did not have a broad-based feminist move-

---

[19] "Falta seriedad en el Congreso," *La Tribuna*, No. 1447 (1 March 1925), p. 1. The second reporter wrote, "the debate about female franchise rights was made on the basis of laughter and malicious jokes. Don León Cortés said that women were nothing. Another deputy bent over (se volcó)." Volio's speech is reprinted as "Discursos . . . : Volio Don Jorge," *La Gaceta*, No. 77 (3 April 1925), pp. 547–8.

[20] For a discussion of this issue, see Eugenia Rodríguez, "Nicolasa, ¿Habráse visto cosa igual? . . . Los discursos sobre mujeres y participación política en Costa Rica (1910–1949)," *Revista Parlamentaria*, Vol. 7, No. 1 (April 1999), pp. 85–122.

ment that could pressure politicians into doing so. Working-class women were largely excluded from the embryonic movement, for whom emulating the bourgeois ideal of feminine virtue and domestic bliss was unattainable. Casals de Quirós, for example, openly expressed her preference that "the female franchise be restricted: that only those with a basic diploma, married women with various children that have a great deal of experience, widows, and others who, in effect, have a certain amount of preparation be given to right to vote." Furthermore, even many middle and upper-class women had failed to sign the petition that Casals de Quirós circulated, either out of indifference, fear, or both. As Casals de Quirós noted, with anger and shame, "many, many [women] interested in the reform would not sign it out of fear of their husbands."[21]

Her feminist, though class-bound, stance on suffrage reform may have very well been a strategic choice. Like her North American counterparts who abandoned equal rights for African American women in order not to alienate white, Southern politicians whose votes were necessary to reform the U.S. constitution, Casals de Quirós may have sought to ameliorate the fears men held of female emancipation by excluding the mass of women that so frightened middle- and upper-class Costa Ricans.

However, it was partisan concerns about the distribution of state power that ultimately defeated the effort to enfranchise women. Though chi-square results indicate that the relationship between partisanship and vote on the measure is statistically significant at the .16 level for all parties, the level of significance improves to .06 if we drop the PR from the test. Despite the fact that its leader was the chief sponsor of this reform and the president, the PR split its vote on the measure even as the PfR, the junior partner of the governing alliance, largely supported it. Like many opposition deputies, over half of the PR representatives could not bring themselves to support a measure that would double the size of the electorate and dramatically increase the uncertainty of electoral outcomes. That over 70 percent of the PA opposed this bill suggests that the struggle for female suffrage rights was doomed once it became identified as benefiting one side in what was ultimately a partisan dispute about the distribution of state power. Table 4.1 analyzes the results of this measure's roll-call vote.

[21] "Campaña a favor del voto femenino," *La Tribuna*, No. 1356 (9 November 1924), p. 4.

Table 4.1. *Roll-Call Vote on Female Suffrage Rights, 1925*

Vote on the Amendment[a]	Party Affiliation			Total
	PA	PR	P*f*R	
In favor	5	7	3	15
Against	14	9	1	24
TOTAL	19	16	4	39

Note:
[a] With 2 degrees of freedom, the chi-square result is 3.630 (Asymp. Sig [2-sided] = .163). Two cells have expected counts of less than 5 (the minimum expected count is 1.54). When the PR is dropped, the Chi-Square is 3.45 (Asymp. Sig [2-sided] = .063) with 1 degree of freedom.

Sources: For party affiliations, see *Diario de Costa Rica*, 1 May 1924. Votes are from "Extraordinary Session No. 96 (24 February 1925), art. 2," *La Gaceta*, 54 (6 March 1925), p. 402.

Institutional Design and Strategic Interplay: Electoral Tribunals

Debate on institutional design was inherently strategic because so many of its provisions promised to increase the uncertainty of electoral competition. Pro- and antigovernment forces pushed for what was possible, not necessarily for what they wanted. Compromise was defined, on the one hand, by placating a reformist president and, on the other, by preventing the formation of a veto-proof majority. In line with institutionalist models, the give and take surrounding the National Electoral Council – which promised to reduce the president's authority in electoral matters – underscore the importance of constitutional arrangements and the partisan distribution of power in structuring the possibilities for reform.

Both opposition and progovernment deputies responded in ways consistent with office-seeking perspectives on far-reaching reforms. The PA wanted to create a body truly above the partisan fray to facilitate its access to power. In the words of Deputy Cortés, the Special Committee had striven "to create an electoral institution that is above all political influences, a body composed of the most honorable and qualified persons who inspire absolute confidence and who will guarantee the interests of all political groups."

Progovernment deputies, in contrast, preferred the status quo because the tribunal's decisions might very well be less advantageous than a presidential verdict. Jiménez, after all, was the leader of Fusion. Though deputies wanted to reduce the executive's discretionary authority, many deputies were uncertain about the political implications of erecting an institution whose verdicts on matters electoral, for all intents and purposes, would be final. If the National Electoral Council supervised the tally of the vote, some representatives argued, it would take on powers that the constitution delegated exclusively to Congress. Without a constitutional reform, only Congress could validate the election of its members. Other deputies claimed that the tribunal would usurp the authority to settle disputes about the interpretation of electoral law best left in the hands of the president.[22] To assuage the opposition's concerns, the PfR leader argued that all parties were better off relying upon the president's interpretations because few "held the moral conditions" Jiménez possessed.[23]

Wishing to avoid open disagreements with the governing coalition, the PA supported a PR amendment that empowered the president to name the members of the National Electoral Council to eight-year terms.[24] Even at the cost of allowing "the members of the Council to be named by the president, our political enemy," the PA Congressional leader announced, the opposition accepted this compromise to ensure that the "cause of reform would prosper." Why did the opposition endorse a compromise that was not in its short-term electoral interests?

Like so much of the debate about electoral reform, the structure of executive-legislative relations in an evenly split Congress put the PA in the position of having to accept what it did really want. Unless the opposition

---

[22] E.s. no. 110 (16 March 1925), art. 6, *La Gaceta*, No. 75 (1 April 1925), p. 535.

[23] All quotations in this paragraph appeared in e.s. no. 110 (16 March 1925), art. 6

[24] E.s. no. 113 (20 March 1925), art. 2, *La Gaceta*, No. 80 (7 April 1925), p. 566. Also, see "Discurso del Diputado León Herrera en que da las razones que lo hicieron proponer moción a fin de que el nombramiento de las Juntas Provinciales quede a cargo del Consejo Electoral," Ibid. Though roll-call votes were not taken on these measures, the *Diario de Costa Rica* does report that only some PR deputies while the entire "PA delegation" voted for the first compromise bill. This and other sources also indicate that, of the twelve deputies who spoke during debate on the matter, nine were from the PR and two were from the PfR, and all contested the committee report. The nine PR deputies were Juan Rafael Arias, Ramón Castro, Manuel Coto, Carlos Leiva, Santos León, Emiliano Odio, José Joaquín Ortiz, Ernesto Ortiz and Pablo Mercedes Rodríguez. The two PfR were Enrique Fonseca and Jorge Volio. The only deputy who spoke in favor of the committee report was, of course, Cortés. Their statements appear in e.s. nos. 110–3 (16–8, and 20 March 1925), arts. 2, 5, and 6 and *La Gaceta*, Nos. 75, 79, and 80 (1, 1, 5, and 7 April 1925), pp. 535–6, 560, and 565. The newspaper report of the partisan affiliation of legislators during this vote is "Se aprobó la creación del Consejo Electoral formado por 3 miembros nombrados por el Presidente," *Diario de Costa Rica*, No. 1708 (21 March 1925), p. 4.

conceded ground to its rivals, it might not amass the votes necessary to enact the reform bill and to protect it from a presidential veto. Ever the political realist, Cortés added that "the fear we have that [an adverse] amendment would motivate an executive veto has obliged me to vote in the negative, as on many occasions I have been compelled to act against my most intimate views . . ."[25] So, in the effort to restructure the electoral machinery of the state, the opposition was forced to take decisions that simultaneously discouraged a presidential veto and withstood the onslaught of reform opponents.

Parties and Voters: Maintaining the Links That Bind?

Both transcripts of Congressional debates and newspaper reports indicate that, unlike in the early 1910s, no one spoke out against the secret franchise in the mid-1920s. Indeed, Congress quickly passed it in a voice vote soon after it quashed the effort to enfranchise women. Why?

The secret franchise was in no one's electoral or class interests. Dismantling the public franchise would only make parties and their middle-class leadership dependent upon satisfying the preferences of a male electorate, many of whose members were illiterate. Though ethnic and social conflicts did not divide Costa Ricans politically, the middle- and upper-classes held a profound disdain for the lower orders.[26] So, if office-seeking and sociological approaches are valid, deputies would never have approved this reform. Perhaps, however, support for the secret franchise stemmed from the power the constitution gave the president. An institutionalist approach suggests that deputies would vote for this reform only because they did not want the executive to veto any of their policies.

Evaluating the ability of these hypotheses requires analyzing several ostensibly arcane issues of electoral law. Establishing the secret franchise was certainly a move in the direction of the president's preferences; support for three related measures determined whether the franchise would indeed be secret. The first revolved around the organization of the Civic Registry. The second consisted of the production, distribution, and use of paper

---

[25] Along with the quotations, all of these events occurred during e.s. 113 (20 March 1925), art. 2, *La Gaceta*. Newspaper reports of this session indicate that Volio's amendment obtained five votes. See "Se aprobó la creación del Consejo Electoral . . ."

[26] Iván Molina and Steven Palmer, eds., *El paso del cometa: estado, política social y culturas populares en Costa Rica, 1800–1950* (San José: Editorial Porvenir and Plumsock Mesoamerican Studies, 1994).

ballots. And, the third was whether citizens should be required to present identification cards before voting.[27]

Consensus existed among pro- and antigovernment deputies that the current system of registering voters gave too much discretionary authority to local political authorities. What divided them was whether this institution should be housed in San José, as the majority recommended, or whether, as the PfR leader proposed, its functions should be decentralized among the seven provinces of the republic "to prevent the use of connections and traps by one person during electoral periods." Though deputies defeated the PfR chief's amendment, his effort to shift some of the authority for registering citizens from one office in San José did succeed in "establishing a Civic Registry in the capital and as many auxiliary provincial Registries as provinces exist as well as two for the second judicial circuits of Alajuela and Guanacaste."[28]

Agreement on the use of paper ballots, however, conceals the resistance of parties to safeguard the privacy rights of voters. Though Congress approved Deputy Cortés's amendment "that paper ballots all be white, and that party differences be made by painting the edges with a color adopted by each party or, in its absence, a portrait of its candidates," deputies never got around to debating how voters could keep their ballot choices secret.[29] Under existing practice – and in no way did the reform bill contravene – parties supplied citizens with ballots on election day. Even PfR Deputy Volio, perhaps the most reformist of all representatives, did not trust voters enough to prevent poll watchers from observing which ballot citizens chose on election day. According to Volio, citizens should still be required to ". . . to take a ballot of their liking . . . at the locale where the ballots can be found" – and in full view of polling station officials.[30]

Representatives had a more difficult time deciding whether identification cards were indeed required of those who voted on election day. Many deputies were unsure that the Civic Registry could set up shop and

---

[27] The transcript of e.s. no. 101 (3 March 1925), art. 6, Ibid, barely refers to this vote. It is given somewhat greater prominence by "Se rechazó la idea del voto obligatorio y se aceptó el secreto y directo," *Diario de Costa Rica*, No. 1694 (4 March 1925), p. 4.

[28] E.s. no. 104 (6 March 1925), art. 4, *La Gaceta*, No. 64 (18 March 1925), pp. 475–6. Deputies agreed to furnish Alajuela and Guanacaste, the provinces with the most dispersed populations, with sufficient registrars so that citizens would not be deterred from registering to vote.

[29] E.s. no. 123 (3 April 1925), art. 3, Ibid, No. 94 (26 April 1925), p. 653.

[30] E.s. no. 126 (15 April 1925), art. 2, Ibid, No. 97 (30 April 1925), p. 673.

distribute proper identification for an electorate numbering approximately one hundred thousand voters. At least several deputies noted that the Civil Registry, created in 1881 to catalog births and deaths in the republic, was not free of errors. Individuals, they claimed, could be found who were lawful citizens, but were not registered as having been born in the national territory. Despite these objections, Congress approved a motion of Cortés's that "only to the Chief of the Civic Registry corresponds the task of emitting personal identification cards and certifications that can be seen as authentic in electoral matters."[31]

The absence of a comprehensive electoral registry, oddly enough, made mandatory identification easier for critics to accept. For, without a comprehensive registry, identification cards could not be made available to all citizens. The logistical constraints of assembling a national registry of voters and of distributing identification cards made delays inevitable and excusable; they also made the reforms that much more acceptable to their opponents. So, the PfR chief proposed a motion that final word on who could vote would depend upon approving a law of personal identification. And, the PfR also endorsed the amendment to rewrite article 35 so that citizens without identification cards could still vote if two "notoriously well-known witnesses" or a poll watcher vouched for such individuals.[32]

It is tough to determine how much class prejudice contributed to political calculations about the effects of liberating voters from the gaze of polling station officials. It is reasonable to assume that middle- and upper-class deputies, like their class counterparts, did not hold a largely rural and partially illiterate electorate in high esteem. Yet, we find no accounts in newspapers, legislative transcripts or U.S. State Department files that class interests figured in their decision making. It is clearer that the uncertain effects of establishing the safeguards necessary to maintain the secrecy of the franchise unhinged political calculations. No less than the PfR chief, surprisingly enough, did not argue in favor of centralizing ballot distribution on election day. Furthermore, deputies settled for creating the secret franchise without centralizing ballot distribution probably to avoid offending voters and public opinion as a whole. In a society with universal manhood suffrage rights, no party wanted to go on record as opposing a quintessentially democratic reform.

---

[31] E.s. no. 127 (16 April 1925), art. 3, Ibid, No. 99 (3 May 1925), p. 694.
[32] E.s. no. 126 (15 April 1925), art. 2, Ibid, No. 97 (30 April 1925), p. 673.

Final Debates

As the bill wound its way through debate, progovernment deputies succeeded in passing amendments to cripple it. During its third debate, PR Deputy León Herrera tried to organize a coalition to repeal the measure establishing an National Electoral Council. Though a majority did not support his original amendment, deputies did pass an amendment that stripped the proposed body of "disciplinary authority over all public officials who intervene, in an official manner, in electoral operations."[33] With this action, Congress left the president with ultimate, though reduced, control of the electoral machinery of the state. After debate on its most controversial matters came to a close, Congress approved the reform bill in third and final debate on 22 April.

The coalition in favor of reform remained intact during the detailed discussion of the bill. It demonstrated its ability to resist large-scale changes to the bill by electing Cortés to the presidency of Congress at the beginning of the 1925 ordinary sessions. The coalition foiled PR Deputy Carlos Leiva's motion to drop the provision requiring voters to exhibit their identification cards on election day. And, it defeated efforts to convert the detailed discussion into a new and full-fledged debate on the reform bill. Speaking on behalf of Congress, Cortés declared that deputies finally approved the reform bill on 22 June.[34]

After a year of struggle, the republic had a new Law of Elections. It created a new tribunal (whose members, however, the president appointed). The republic established the secret franchise (though it was not clear how much privacy voters would have). It also called for the use

---

[33] E.s. no. 128 (17 April 1925), art. 2, Ibid, No. 99 (3 May 1925), p. 695. Also, see "Discurso del Representante León Herrera, leído en la sesión del día 17 de abril al discutirse el artículo 103 del proyecto de reformas a la Ley de Elecciones vigente," Ibid, pp. 695–6, made during this session.

[34] O.s. no. 36 (22 June 1925), art. 6, Ibid, No. 148 (1 July 1925), p. 1073. Along with Leiva, Deputies Arias and Rodríguez – both members of the PR – argued in favor of repealing the requirement that voters show identification before voting. See o.s. no. 32 (16 June 1925), art. 6, Ibid, No. 145 (27 June 1925), pp. 1059–60. By obtaining the support of twenty-one of the twenty-two members of his delegation and the support of his brother (Claudio Cortés Castro), a PR member, León Cortés became president of Congress for the 1925 sessions. His closest rival, Arturo Volio, obtained twenty-one votes, but failed to vote for himself. If he had done so and if one PfR deputy not present had attended the inaugural session, Volio would have remained president of Congress. See o.s. no. 1 (1 May 1925), art. 1, Ibid, No. 105 (10 May 1925), p. 747.

of identification on election day (but created exceptions for citizens not possessing this document).

Veto Games and Political Coalitions

A day after Congress completed the reform bill, President Jiménez vetoed it. The president's veto was a bit of a shock to his contemporaries. No less than a reporter for *La Tribuna*, a newspaper known for its Republican leanings, had claimed that Jiménez would "in all probability" approve the bill. In late June, the opposition *La Opinión* had editorialized that he would support the bill "because President Jiménez is ready to cooperate, in all relevant matters, to ensure the openness and order of the elections necessary to hold during his term in office."[35]

Even though he noted that the electoral law "contained reforms that are an undeniable improvement," Jiménez returned it to Congress with a number of what he called "retouches." He pointed out that the law did not specify whether the state or voters would furnish the opaque envelopes within which citizens would place their ballots. "If the latter were permitted," the president noted, "the secret franchise would not exist because the parties that wished to buy votes would select envelopes possessing an identifiable color or form." He then shifted to criticizing the loopholes that would allow parties to manipulate the Civic Registry. It was not clear to him whether the central office or district polling stations were ultimately responsible arbitrating conflicts about the inclusion and exclusion of names on the electoral rolls. Unless deputies resolved this ambiguity, polling stations could modify the electoral rolls "at the last hour." The president also contended that the proposed electoral law had failed to regulate the "excessive amount of power possessed by the president in the electoral process." Though the draft law made the chief executive responsible for ensuring that all public officials obeyed the law, it did not "define the nature and extent of the jurisdictional authority exercised by the president." Neither did the proposed law delineate the responsibilities of the members of the Grand Electoral Council or of Provincial Electoral Councils.[36]

---

[35] "Nota Editorial: No habrá veto," *La Opinión*, No. 1424 (25 June 1925), p. 4. The prior citation is from "El Señor Presidente estudia la nueva Ley Electoral," *La Tribuna*, No. 1546 (2 July 1925), p. 1.

[36] "El veto del señor Presidente a la Ley de Elecciones (3 July 1925)," *Diario de Costa Rica*, No. 1794 (4 July 1925), p. 3. The president's veto was also published in *La Gaceta*, No. 151 (4 July 1925), p. 1089.

The president's implicit threat to veto a law he found unacceptable had become real, even if he proved willing to compromise on matters of principle. He did not object, for example, that deputies had killed the proposal to enfranchise women or that they had not drastically curtailed the executive's discretionary authority. Nor did he criticize the bill for allowing citizens without identification cards to vote as long as they could have two others vouch for their identity. Noting how easy it would be to take advantage of this loophole, Jiménez sarcastically added that he had no doubts that parties could provide, "if necessary, the six most loyal and unscrupulous friends to testify, even if falsely," for each of their supporters. Yet, the president was unwilling to support a bill that did not go substantially beyond the minimal set of reforms PA deputies initially endorsed.

Despite the Congressional president's misgivings, the committee that had edited the bill issued a report suggesting that Congress adopt the executive's suggestions. It recommended limiting the ability of polling stations to include or exclude names from local list of voters. But, it did little more than reiterate that the president was responsible for disciplining virtually all public officials to ensure that elections were free and fair. After a failed attempt to attach a rider that municipal elections be held in December and congressional elections be held in February, deputies quickly approved, in three debates, the amendments to the electoral law.[37] After receiving the president's signature on 16 July, the republic obtained a new Law of Elections.

Once again, office-seeking approaches explain why the PR Congressional delegation did not take a strong stand in favor of reform. As the largest progovernment party, it had an interest in maximizing its share of state power. Indeed, to the extent that the bill safeguarded the rights of voters and guaranteed transparent elections, short-term electoral considerations and class prejudices shaped the behavior of most deputies. Empowering citizens to vote their conscience was simply too risky for the PA and the PR. Most representatives, after all, agreed to dilute the scope of reforms – which is why the president vetoed the bill.

---

[37] The Committee's report was published in Ibid, No. 161 (16 July 1925), p. 1158. Its members were Juan Rafael Arias, Francisco Mayorga, and Arturo Volio. The rider was separated from the Committee's response to the president during o.s. no. 52 (14 July 1925), art. 4, Ibid, No. 169 (25 July 1925), p. 1214. The changes referred to in this paragraph are to articles 25 and 102, respectively. See "Decreto No. 75 (23 July 1925)," *Colección de Leyes y Decretos, Año 1925* (San José: Imprenta Nacional, 1926), pp. 131–68.

Sociological approaches do help explain some things. They, for example, correctly predict the behavior of PfR deputies. As a party trying to build a constituency among urban artisans and peasants, the PfR supported democratic reform to prove that it wanted to help ordinary voters. Voting in favor of institutional change therefore meant that the party too could benefit electorally from the promulgation of the reform bill. Furthermore, sociological approaches do help explain why most deputies could enact the secret franchise in name only: Fear of the lower orders may have kept them from centralizing ballot distribution to safeguard citizen's privacy rights. Class-oriented perspectives also help explain why no one less than PfR chief Jorge Volio went on record to oppose this measure. Even if he was the leader of a reformist party, Volio did belong to a socially prominent family.

Only institutionalist approaches can explain why the PA collaborated with the president. Because the rules governing access to high office had helped deprive the PA of the presidency in 1924, the PA's strategic interests changed as it became an opposition party. Institutions converted the long-term interests all parties may have held in democratic reform into the PA's short-term political project. Even if some of the president's pet reforms promised to increase the uncertainty of election results, a reform bill that strengthened safeguards for the opposition was better than no reform at all. The very modest nature of the president's requests, along with his willingness to concede on other points of disagreement, ensured that the bill was supported by opposition and small parties that were potential targets of officially sponsored fraud. Once Alberto Echandi, the titular leader of the PA, found Jiménez's objections to possess merit, the probability that the opposition would cooperate with the president only increased.[38] This is why, to quote a PfR deputy, the coalition in support of "the law will include twenty-one PA and five PfR deputies" – a particularly revealing remark since representatives rarely agreed to use roll-call votes during deliberation on the reform bill.[39]

---

[38] "El Señor Presidente Jiménez y el candidato Señor Echandi nos declaran su maerce de penscer sobre la ley de Elecciones y el veto opuesto por el Poder Eiecutivo," *La Tribuna*, No. 1550 (7 July 1925), p. 4.
[39] "Los Diputados Reformistas están con el resello de la Ley Electoral," *La Tribuna*, No. 1550 (7 July 1925), p. 7.

Finally, only institutionalist approaches can account for why President Jiménez was so committed to democratic reform. Because he could not stand for consecutive reelection, he could think of the long-term benefits of electoral reform. Unlike most other politicians, he could afford to think about building a reputation as a reformer because, simply put, he was out of a job at the end of his four-year term. And it was the structure of constitutional relations between the executive and legislative branches of government that allowed him to take advantage of his position as a pivot to build coalitions of pro- and antigovernment forces to advance his agenda.

Constitutional Reform and Double-Ballot Elections

Unlike so much of the debate on electoral reform, the discussion to eliminate Congress's role in selecting presidents remained uncontroversial. As a quintessential efficient reform – one that promised to reduce uncertainty on election day – deputies debated the merits of several ways of accomplishing this objective. No one ever seriously argued in favor of maintaining, in some way, the Congressional role in selecting a president should no candidate attract the support of a majority of voters.

Like all other matters Congress debated, however, partisanship played a central role in the outcome of this measure. PR Deputy (and former Congressional President) Arturo Volio's report failed to obtain the two-thirds of all votes required of constitutional amendments because only 20 percent of PA deputies endorsed it. The distribution of the vote was even more partisan when PA Deputy Francisco Mayorga's report received absolutely no support from the PfR and only 36 percent of the PR delegation. That results of both roll-call votes are statistically significant indicates that partisanship was a central consideration for deputies casting ballots. These results are reported on Table 4.2.

With thirty-three in favor and five against, deputies finally settled on approving PR Deputy Arias's majority-plurality proposal. Like Mayorga's report, Arias's bill called for holding a run-off election. It, however, dropped Arturo Volio's suggestion that candidates needed to attract the support of two-thirds of the voters in the run-off election. Unlike the votes on the two earlier proposals, the party identification of legislators is not related to their votes on the compromise bill. With a significance level of .71, these results indicate that partisanship was no longer motivating the behavior of deputies. Indeed, these results suggest that PA deputies voted

139

Table 4.2. *Roll-Call Votes on Double Ballot Elections, 1925*

Vote	Volio's Amendment[a]			Total
	Party Affiliation			
	PA	PR	P*f*R	
In favor	4	10	3	17
Against	16	4	1	21
TOTAL	20	14	4	38

Vote	Mayorga's Amendment[b]			Total
	Party Affiliation			
	PA	PR	P*f*R	
In favor	20	5	0	25
Against	0	9	4	1
TOTAL	20	14	4	38

Vote	Arias's Amendment[c]			Total
	Party Affiliation			
	PA	PR	P*f*R	
In favor	17	12	4	33
Against	3	2	0	5
TOTAL	20	14	4	38

Notes:
[a] The chi-square result is 10.466 (Asymp. Sig [2-sided] = .005). Two cells have expected counts of less than 5 (the minimum expected count is 1.79).
[b] The chi-square result is 23.719 (Asymp. Sig [2-sided] = .000). Three cells have expected counts of less than 5. The minimum expected count is 1.37.
[c] The chi-square result is .681 (Asymp. Sig [2-sided] = .711). Four cells have expected counts of less than 5. The minimum expected count is .53.

Sources: For party affiliations, see Table 4.1. Votes are from Ordinary Session No. 70 (7 August 1925), art. 9, *La Gaceta*, No. 54 (21 August 1925), p. 1372.

strategically: They compromised around a set of changes that were closest to their own. The supramajority required by a constitution to change its articles had succeeded in compelling both sides of Congress to endorse a bill both found tolerable.[40]

Following the guidelines for amending the constitution, Congress sent the president a proposal calling for awarding the presidency to the runner-up who obtained a plurality of the votes in the run-off among the two candidates who attracted the most votes in the first-round elections. Meeting in an extraordinary session on 1 March, Congress would convene the run-off if no candidate obtained an absolute majority of the popular vote. The constitutional reform bill also transferred election day from the first Sunday of December in the year before the new president assumed responsibilities to the second Sunday of February. And, the bill recommended that Congressional alternates be allowed to substitute for principals if the latter were not present either on 1 March or on 1 May, the date on which presidents were inaugurated.[41] In his 1926 Message to Congress, the president notified Congress that its recommendations met with his wholehearted approval. By late May, Congress endorsed the reforms by more than the required two-thirds of all deputies in three separate debates.[42]

---

[40] O.s. no. 70 (7 August 1925), art. 9, *La Gaceta*, No. 191 (21 August 1925), p. 1372. The minutes incorrectly characterize Arias's proposal as a majority-majority bill. Both the initial committee reports and the document sent to the president confirm this.

[41] See the letter sent to the president via the "Señor Secretario de Estado en el Despacho de Gobernación," 17 August 1925, from the first and second secretaries of the Congress. The actual date on which Congress approved these measures is 13 August 1925. They are reprinted in Ibid, No. 190 (20 August 1925), pp. 1363–4.

[42] "Mensaje de don Ricardo Jiménez, Presidente de la República al Congreso Constitucional (1 May 1926)," in Meléndez Chaverri, ed., *Mensajes Presidenciales, 1918–1928* (San José: Academia de Geografía e Historia de Costa Rica, 1981), pp. 172–8. The committee report was published as "Dictamen de la Comisión de Constitución y Legislación sobre la reforma constitucional en cuanto a elección de Presidentes de la República (10 May 1926)," *La Gaceta*, No. 108 (14 May 1926), p. 615. The committee's members were Alejandro Alvarado, Carlos Brenes, and Manuel Coto. The report was approved in third debate during o.s. no. 16 (20 May 1926), art. 10, Ibid, No. 128 (3 June 1926), pp. 755–6. In 1936, Congress reformed this law. Since 1936, candidates who obtain a plurality and at least 40 percent of the vote win the presidency outright. No presidential run-off election has ever been held. See Fabrice Lehoucq, *Lucha electoral y sistema político en Costa Rica, 1948–1998* (San José: Editorial Porvenir, 1997), pp. 23–4. For an argument of the merits of "the double complement rule," see Matthew Shugart and Rein Taagepera, "Plurality vs. Majority Election of Presidents: A Proposal for a Double Complement Rule," *Comparative Political Studies*, Vol. 27, No. 3 (October 1994), pp. 323–48.

The Reform of Electoral Laws (II)

Less than a year before his term was due to expire, President Jiménez sent Congress another reform bill. The president was careful not to criticize the recently passed law. Indeed, he praised the law "as a happy effort." The president, however, pointed out that "no one should have expected" the effort to reform electoral laws to have been "finished in the way that the Goddess Minerva emerged armed and perfect from the head of Jupiter."[43]

A month before the 1925 midterm elections, Congress amended the electoral law to allow voters to bring their own ballots into polling stations. As Deputy Cortés (now an affiliated member of the opposition) explained, voters lost their privacy rights because everyone seemed to be supplying citizens with the envelopes within which ballots were inserted, even though "the spirit of the law was that the government would exclusively furnish them, along with the poll book and other items necessary for the act of voting."[44] Both facts, Cortés suggested, permitted parties to mark ballots and related paraphernalia in such a way to keep track of the behavior of their voters. Or, to quote from a sarcastic report in the *Diario de Costa Rica*, the last-minute reform meant that the country was "simply going to try a caricature of the secret ballot" because "it will be known beforehand how each citizen will vote."[45] This and related shortcomings kept the issue of reform very much alive.

Institutionalist approaches suggest why the president continued to reform electoral laws. Regardless of his actions, he was out of a job within a year. The constitutional prohibition on the consecutive reelection of presidents liberated Jiménez from thinking about short-term electoral

---

[43] All of the references to the president's project in this and subsequent paragraphs stem from the letter, dated 5 March 1927, that he enclosed with the reform bill he sent Congress and published in Ibid, No. 54 (6 March 1927), p. 378. It was also reprinted as "El señor Presidente de la República envía al Congreso un interesante proyecto de reformas a la Ley Electoral," *Diario de Costa Rica*, No. 2299 (6 March 1927), p. 9.

[44] E.s. no. 108 (8 March 1927), art. 4, *La Gaceta*, No. 61 (15 March 1927), p. 430. Information on Cortés's lack of a partisan identity stems from "De última hora," *La Tribuna*, No. 2145 (20 July 1927), p. 1. This report refers to his neutrality, which we take to mean that he was wavering in his commitment to Cleto González, to whom the *Diario de Costa Rica* claimed Cortés was loyal in April of 1926. Despite his comments, Cortés was not in favor of the secret franchise. Like many other deputies, he believed that illiterates would lose their suffrage rights if the franchise were really made secret.

[45] "Del momento político: la situación del próximo Congreso," Ibid, No. 1915 (26 November 1925), p. 4. The amendment to article 34 of the electoral law that undermined the secrecy of the franchise is "Decreto No. 29 (6 November 1925)," *Colección*, p. 657.

considerations. Eliminating the loopholes that remained promised to solidify his image as a democratic reformer and promoted his long-term career prospects. No longer was the president focused on retaining the loyalty of legislative deputies; indeed, most deputies were openly identifying themselves with one of several presidential candidates in efforts to secure a lucrative public post in the next administration.

Why deputies would even consider a reform bill in an election year is the issue we now address. As office-seeking theories suggest, deputies would be especially loath to increase the uncertainty of electoral competition in an election year. How the president got them to sign a bill they did not want to approve is the central puzzle of this section. Before examining legislative politics however, we discuss the president's project.

The President's Bill

The president recommended that local polling stations be stripped of the capacity to include or to exclude the names of individuals on the lists of voters that the Civic Registry prepared. Even though the 1925 law made the Registry "the competent authority to register citizens and to cancel such registrations," it "maintained the old practice of letting polling stations, at the last hour, rule on requests to include or to exclude citizens in the definitive list for the election in question." He suggested that polling stations be restricted to receiving and counting votes.

The president also advocated overhauling the distribution and use of identification cards. "Experience has demonstrated," he pointed out, "that identification cards do not remedy the shortcoming that needs repairing. . . . As the identification card neither possesses the affiliation, the photograph nor other references of its owner, it is easy for those who are not its legitimate owners to use." Asking for witnesses was pointless because "it is known how easy it is to find compliant and false witnesses." And, under these conditions, he added, "heartless politicians" would continue "to purchase electoral identification cards from citizens of ill-repute and have surrogates use them." To prevent this from occurring, Jiménez recommended that electoral identification cards contain the signatures and photographs of their owners.

Finally, the president suggested that the government supply citizens with ballots on election day. "Ballots taken to polling stations," the president argued, "can be identified in some way and, additionally, do not guarantee the sanctity of the vote, a result which obtains if the voter alone selects the ballot of his choosing in the voting booth." To help voters, especially illiterate ones, distinguish among parties and candidates, Jiménez recommended that the proposed ballots display the colors and photographs as well as the names of the candidates and parties competing for the presidency.

Partisan Alignments and Election Year Politics

Initial reception to the president's bill was chilly. Newspaper reports indicate that, in line with office-seeking approaches, a majority of deputies opposed changes that would effectively guarantee the secrecy of the franchise. This time around, not even the opposition was in favor of reform. After the opposition campaign manager, Manuel Castro, expressed his dislike of the bill, Jiménez noted that his bill was unlikely to pass because of the hostility of the opposition. Indeed, the president was particularly blunt when he suggested that "the eternal struggle of the past against the present and, second, the interests of parties" were the reasons why deputies were likely to oppose his bill.[46] Examining political alignments reveals why election year politics might turn deputies into opponents of institutional change.

Though the PR had won 62 percent (or thirteen of twenty-one) of the seats in the 1925 midterm elections, the PR had split into two factions. Arturo Volio (a nephew of Jiménez's and president of Congress between 1926 and 1929) led one faction vying for the PR presidential nomination. Carlos María Jiménez (another nephew of the president's and his campaign manager in 1924) led the other. By 1926, the PR was split between eleven "carlistas," as supporters of Carlos María were known, and thirteen independents or governmental supporters.[47]

[46] "Ante la negativa del Partido Unión Nacional para aceptar el voto secreto en las próximas elecciones el Señor Presidente de la República declara que la discusión es inútil porque ese partido tiene mayoría en el Congreso," *La Tribuna*, No. 2036 (10 March 1927), p. 1. The discussions between Castro and the president are mentioned in "La entrevista del Jefe de Acción del Partido Nacional con el Presidente de la República," Ibid, No. 2037 (sic) (11 March 1927), p. 1.

[47] The source of partisan affiliation of legislators is from "Situación en que va a quedar el próximo Congreso de mayo con relación a los partidos políticos," *Diario de Costa Rica*, No. 2201 (9 April 1926), p. 1. Background on the pressures placed on Jiménez is discussed in Despatch No. 651 (23 September 1925), Roy T. Davis to the Secretary of State, U.S. National Archives (hereafter cited as USNA), 818.00/1128, especially pp. 4–5.

The 1925 midterm elections finished the PA. Capturing only five seats, the PA had only twelve deputies left in Congress. In January of the next year, Echandi resigned his position as party chief. No one expected the party to survive until the next presidential election. PA deputies, in fact, were negotiating with the seven PfR deputies to form a coalition to gain control of the 1926–7 Congressional Directorate. Both factions were also in contact with Cleto González, elder statesman and former president (1906–10), who was rumored to be reactivating his National Union Party (PUN) in a bid for the presidency in 1928.[48]

Despite efforts to overcome discord, presidential ambitions split the PR and cost it the Congressional Directorate. On 1 May, after the new deputies were sworn in, the coalition of nineteen PA and PfR deputies put forth a slate of candidates that included Arturo Volio as Congressional president. Playing upon factional antagonisms among Republicans, the coalition attracted the support of Volio and two other PR independents to deliver the president with his first postelection defeat.[49] The effect of the opposition victory was to trigger the start of the 1928 presidential campaign.

As office-seeking approaches suggest, no party wanted reform. Both PR factions opposed changes that would increase the uncertainty of winning the 1928 general elections. The factional struggle, along with the race against the PUN, compounded both factions' opposition to electoral reform. With enactment of the 1925 law, the PUN was no longer interested in institutional change. Like the PR, it did not want to make the race for the presidency any harder than it was going to be. Pivoting between pro- and antigovernment was therefore not going to allow the president to advance his own political agenda.

Committee Responses

Nearly a month after the president had sent his bill to Congress, the Committee on Legislation issued its report. Unexpectedly, it did not reject the

---

[48] "General Conditions Prevailing in Costa Rica in the Period from December 26, 1925 to January 8, 1926," Despatch No. 701G (8 January 1926), Roy T. Davis to the Secretary of State, USNA, 818.00/1135, pp. 7–8. With Echandi's resignation, Alejandro Alvarado, a member of the Directorate, became its temporary leader.

[49] "La coalición de los Agrícolas, Reformistas y Republicanos Independientes ganó el Directorio," *Diario de Costa Rica*, No. 2041 (2 May 1926), p. 5.

president's proposals. Representing the *carlista* faction of the PR, Carlos Brenes did nothing more than endorse the bill in its entirety. The two other members – one from the independent faction of this party, the other from the PA – backed most of the president's proposals, modified others, and extensively discussed all of them.

Both the PR independent, Manuel Coto, and the PA deputy, Alejandro Alvarado, concurred that local polling stations be stripped of their ability to add or remove names from the electoral registry. Only the Electoral Registry in the capital, they agreed, should possess this responsibility. The independent and PA deputies also agreed that identification cards should contain photographs of their owners. They wondered, however, whether it was a practical suggestion given "the difficulties that parties would have, especially in remote places, to execute this requisite because of the implied costs. . . ." To avoid these logistical nightmares, they recommended that this measure be postponed until the 1930 midterm elections.

Surprisingly, the Committee majority supported the centralization of ballot production, despite expressing concern that illiterate voters might be unable to use a single, government-supplied ballot. Nevertheless, it claimed "that it was worth trying, borrowing from the experience of other advanced nations . . ." Hopefully, they added, ". . . the percentage of inevitable errors would decrease over time."[50]

Not only did the Committee endorse the reform bill, but so did Congress. Despite the explosive nature of the issues raised by the majority report, the bill went unopposed through the three debates required of all bills. However, once the detailed discussion of the bill began on 13 May, it met veiled resistance as deputies began to raise objections or simply neglected to finish discussing it. Six weeks later, only 46 articles of 176 that existed had been discussed. As *La Tribuna* noted, these articles concerned the less controversial issues the project raised.[51]

Delay, Opposition, and Public Opinion

Throughout legislative proceedings, no one ever publicly attacked the reform bill. Indeed, after the president's declarations about his meeting

---

[50] "Dictamen acerca del proyecto de Ley de Elecciones (1 April 1927)," *La Gaceta*, No. 80 (7 April 1927), pp. 569–70.
[51] "El Congreso parece haberse olvidado de la discusión de la Electoral," *La Tribuna*, No. 2128 (30 June 1927), p. 3.

with the opposition campaign manager, leading opposition party members, like Cortés, announced their support for the bill, even as they believed that a government-supplied ballot would confuse illiterate and barely literate voters. Others, including ex-President González, wished to read it carefully before speaking on the issue. Several reports appeared that deputies were in favor of the bill, but only dissented on the nature of the procedures for depositing votes into ballot boxes – a rather peculiar claim given the centrality of individual privacy in discussions about reform. But, as politicians of every stripe and hue refused to criticize the bill, enough deputies claimed that it was too long and complex to review quickly.[52]

Those who detested reform applauded the delays even as if they could not come out publicly against reform. Judging from newspaper editorials and reports, widespread public (if diffuse) support existed for the president's bill. The need to obtain the support of electoral majorities conflicted with the efforts of presidential candidates to consolidate support within their parties. By mid-1927, Carlos María Jiménez and González were struggling for advantage and could ill afford to antagonize party activists and the electorate as a whole, regardless of how the candidates may have personally felt about reform. The first was reorganizing the PR in the face of his uncle's refusal to use state resources for his advantage; the second was reviving the PUN, which had not fielded a candidate since the 1910s. As the uncertainty of who would win the race increased with the proximity of the election, parties became increasingly reluctant to liberate citizens from the gaze of party observers. Given the reluctance of party leaders to attack measures that aimed to safeguard the rights of voters, antireform deputies channeled their hostility into parliamentary ruses that postponed debate on the bill.

In early June, for example, Congress stumbled across a series of difficulties related to the functioning of the Civic Registry. Cortés argued that the bill never referred to its creation or even operation, even though the proposed legislation hinged upon the existence of such an agency. When the bill was again brought up for discussion nearly a month later, Cortés reiterated his charges and pointed out that a backlog of amendments existed that, if adopted, would destroy the overall harmony of the bill. PUN deputies Alvarado (formerly of the PA) and Jorge Ortiz (formerly of the PR) motioned that a Special Committee, consisting of equal numbers

---

[52] "La Ley Electoral tiene medio locos a los diputados," Ibid, No. 2115 (15 June 1927), p. 3.

of PR and PUN deputies, be formed to produce a new draft bill. Congress selected Arias, Bernardo Benavides, Luis Castaing, and Cortés to sit on the committee, signaling that campaign dynamics were dominating the partisan allegiances of deputies. By this point, the first three had left the block of independent and progovernment backers to become, in the case of Arias, affiliated with the PUN. Benavides and Castaing shifted their allegiance to Carlos María Jiménez, the PR standard-bearer becoming increasingly estranged from the president. Cortés remained unaffiliated.[53]

Reports published on the eve of the bill's publication in *La Gaceta* suggest that the Special Committee could not bring itself to echo the president's recommendations. Interviewed by *La Tribuna*, Deputy Castaing identified, with an undisguised amount of pride, three innovations made by the Committee. First, it suggested that campaigning in the street be reduced to two months. Second, it transferred the responsibility of distributing electoral identification from the police and other authorities of the secretary of the interior to the principal polling stations of each district. Finally, PR Deputy Castaing was most excited by the solution to the difficulty of establishing the secret ballot without confusing illiterate voters. Devised by PR Deputy Benavides, it called for the use of one ballot, printed by the secretary or interior, that voters would deposit in one of several ballot boxes, each of which would display the name and banner of each political party. To ensure the secrecy of the vote, the Committee required local polling stations to place ballot boxes in a concealed area.[54]

The very next day, the president denounced the Committee's recommendations. He lambasted the Committee for, instead of following the example of other democracies, creating what he scornfully called a "creole invention." The use of multiple ballot boxes in a secret room, Jiménez claimed, furnished voters with the chance to tamper with ballot boxes. He reiterated the need for photographic identification to ensure each citizen only voted once. And, through the use of what Cortés called the "pre-

---

[53] Doubts about the Civic Registry begin during o.s. no. 24 (2 June 1927), art. 6, *La Gaceta*, No. 136 (15 June 1927), p. 917. It was during o.s. no. 48 (5 July 1927), art. 8, Ibid, No. 175 (31 July 1927), p. 1206, that the Special Committee was formed. This document claims that Ortiz developed the idea for such a committee. The notes published in "Una comisión especial estudiará la nueva Ley de Elecciones," *Diario de Costa Rica*, No. 2398 (6 July 1927), p. 5, mention Alvarado as the author of this idea, which Ortiz subsequently modified. All other details are consistent between both accounts. Data on the partisan affiliation of legislators are from "De última hora."

[54] "De última hora." We have rearranged the order of the innovations presented in the article.

emptive veto," the president threatened to torpedo the bill if his proposals were not adopted.[55]

In response, the Special Committee submitted its collective resignation to Congress. Speaking on behalf of the Committee, Cortés angrily refuted each of the president's charges and claimed that the Committee had only acted out of concern for the public interest. On the central issue of the secret franchise, he argued that the president's proposals were no better than theirs. According to Cortés, putting ballot boxes within sight of polling station officials and party observers, along with permitting voters to call upon the observer of their choice for assistance, made the president's bill a mixed system of voting. Literate voters would benefit from the secret franchise while illiterate ones could remain under the sway of parties. In his most pointed set of remarks, he claimed that the president was hardly in a position to offer critical comments on a bill whose details he had only read about in preliminary newspaper reports. He also reminded his colleagues that the president's bill was packed with contradictions, suggesting that the president also had not read his own bill.[56]

The secret franchise remained a highly controversial issue. Ostensibly, debate on the issue revolved around the logistics of safeguarding the privacy rights of a male electorate that, according to the 1927 population census, was one-third illiterate. But, as the president noted during initial consideration of the bill, there were several ways to solve this problem. Legislators, for example, could pass a law that required ballots to have the portraits of candidates and the colors of parties. In support of this suggestion, the president pointed out that "it is not possible to give [illiterates] a 5 colón bill in place of a 100 colón note." Even peasants who did not know how to read or write could remember enough to vote their preferences. What kept the issue alive and polemical was that parties did not want to lose their ability to control the behavior of "their" voters.

---

[55] The president's denunciations were published on 21 July in *La Tribuna*. Unfortunately, this issue is missing from the Newspaper Room of the National Library. We have been unable to find other copies of this issue. Other newspapers refer to the president's remarks, but none report them. This reconstruction is based upon reports of Congressional reactions to his declarations summarized in minutes of Congressional sessions and newspaper reports where Cortés reacted to the president's denunciations. See e.s. no. 4 (21 July 1927), art. 4, *La Gaceta*, No. 186 (13 August 1927), p. 1263, and especially "Incidente alrededor de un reportaje del señor presidente: renuncia colectiva de la Comisión Especial," *Diario de Costa Rica*, No. 2412 (21 July 1927), p. 5.

[56] Ibid.

Congress did not accept the Committee's resignation. As the chief presiding officer of Congress, PR Deputy and presidential candidate Volio accepted PUN Deputy Arias's suggestion that the ensuing debate revolve around eight issues, the first of which consisted of whether deputies would indeed safeguard the privacy of voters. In a series of wide-ranging debates, Congress largely sided with the president. On 11 August, it endorsed Jiménez's request that ballot boxes be within sight of polling station officials and party observers. A day later, Congress approved the centralization of ballot production. Two days later, it backed a series of measures, one of which prevented party observers from helping voters having difficulty marking paper ballots – itself an action voted on by Congress. In a key defeat for the president, it postponed the use of photographic identification for the forthcoming elections, even as it legislated that voters should be required to present such documents.[57]

The votes on these measures offer an important clue as to why Congress, ever focused on the 1928 elections, sided with the president. With one exception, the legislative transcript does not even record the number of deputies voting in favor of proposals. That no deputy motioned to hold a roll-call vote and that newspapers did not describe the behavior of factions suggests that a consensus existed around most measures. Enough deputies apparently understood that the president would veto a bill that many of them, given the shortcomings of the 1925 law, wished to have in effect for the forthcoming elections. No party wanted to be blamed for provoking the president's veto. In an election year, parties had to court public opinion. Sabotaging reform would not sit well with the electorate, and the president demonstrated that he was more than willing to act as the public's spokesperson. Though the president had been impartial during the 1925 midterm elections, failure to support his bill might very well encourage him to punish obstructionists during the forthcoming general election.

The only measure that did receive a clear vote was postponing the use of photographic identification for the 1928 elections. As the *Diario de Costa Rica* noted, Congress unanimously approved this measure on 16 August.

---

[57] Arias's eight points were presented during e.s. no. 18 (10 August 1927), art. 4, *La Gaceta*, No. 197 (27 August 1927), p. 1320. The location of ballot boxes is passed during e.s. no. 19 (11 August 1927), art. 4, Ibid, No. 198 (28 August 1927), p. 1328. The subsequent measures were voted on during e.s. 20 and 21 (12 and 16 August 1927), arts. 5 and 4, Ibid, Nos. 200 and 201 (31 August and 1 September 1927), pp. 51, 1337.

And, a day later, when Deputy Brenes Ortiz called for a motion of revision to reopen debate on the matter, a majority of undisclosed size killed his effort. Speaking on behalf of a majority, the measure's opponents argued that the time and expense required to produce identification cards containing the portraits of their owners would effectively disenfranchise many voters in the next election.[58]

The concerns did not bother the president. In a speech littered with the caustic wit for which he was famous, Jiménez asked how the country could have recently afforded to conduct a census of the entire population when it could not allegedly pay for a census of the electorate, one that could also furnish voters with reliable forms of identification. "The census had cost more than 100,000 colones," he reminded everyone, but "portraits [of each citizen] would cost about 25 cents and, since there are about 92,760 voters in the Republic, the cost would be 23,190 colones." In these and other declarations, he implied that photographs were not indispensable. There was plenty of time to produce well-drawn portraits of citizens. Such portraits would suffice because "there is no need to produce oil paintings to adorn the galleries of the Louvre or the Prado."[59] His efforts, however, proved to be of no avail.

Discussion of the central items identified by Deputy Arias was completed on 17 August, when Congress also approved the entire bill during first debate. A day later, the bill was approved in a third debate. Two weeks later, it passed its second and final detailed discussion.

Despite the clause postponing the use of photographic identification, the president endorsed the bill for very much the same sort of reasons that Congress accepted most of his recommendations. Congress was dragged into approving such a bill largely because a highly competitive race for the presidency made parties interested in eliminating loopholes that might deprive them of a victory in 1928. Enough legislators swallowed the bitter pill of establishing the secret franchise, once and for all, because the consequences of liberating voters from their control were worse than the alternatives. If legislators did not approve a bill that the president could support, they would get no new bill whatsoever.

---

[58] E.s. no. 22 (17 August 1927), art. 2, Ibid, No. 203 (3 September 1927), p. 1366.

[59] Except for the last, all quotations stem from "El Señor Presidente de la República dice que si los partidos no quieren gastar para las cédulas personales de votación, el Estado debe pagar el gasto," *La Tribuna*, No. 2150 (26 July 1927), p. 1. The last is from "Ante la negativa del Partido Unión Nacional . . ."

The bill became more palatable for enough legislators once Congress unanimously approved, against the president's wishes, a delay in the use of photographic identification. By creating such a loophole, the uncertainty associated with a reform that threatened to shrink the size of the electorate was brought under some control. That the opposition PUN wanted as many guarantees as possible and was grateful for Jiménez's probity in electoral matters convinced enough of them to support the compromise bill. And, as the ostensibly progovernment party, the PR endorsed a new law for many of the same reasons, especially since the president refused to campaign actively for their candidates.

The president accepted these changes because the power his veto conferred was not boundless. If deputies unanimously approved of a measure he disliked, the bill's opponents might succeed in rounding up the two-thirds majority needed to override his veto. When confronted with the choice between the bill approved by Congress and the one he wanted, he chose to play it safe. In the end, the rules governing the relations between the executive and legislative branches of government meant that parties unwilling to compromise ran the danger of getting nothing of what they wanted. On 29 September, the much debated reform bill became the new law of the land.[60]

Conclusions

After several decades of struggle, reformers succeeded in establishing the secret franchise. Even though deputies voted to repeal the public ballot in 1925, only two years later they supported additional reforms to make the secret franchise effective. Chief among these was the centralization of ballot production; as several deputies and newspapers noted, citizens would have little privacy to vote if parties were handing them paper ballots on election day. Why did the deputies enact this reform? And, why did they successfully oppose other important electoral reforms and the extension of suffrage rights to women?

Arguing that parties are fundamentally driven by reelection incentives, office-seeking theories accurately predict the behavior of parties on some of these measures. First, such approaches explain why the PA called for reform in the aftermath of the 1923 general elections. Having just been deprived of the presidency, the party possessed an interest in institutional

[60] See "Ley de Elecciones," *Alcance a La Gaceta*, No. 224 (29 September 1927), pp. 1–9.

change. Exactly as a narrow focus on electoral interests suggests, the PA only recommended reforms extensive enough to prevent another one of its candidate from being cheated of a presidential victory.

Second, office-seeking theories explain why Congress opposed the establishment of suffrage rights for women. Doubling the size of the electorate simply injected too much uncertainty into political calculations. That the PA voted overwhelming against this measure also indicates that it did not want to enfranchise a sector of the population that might very well vote, out of gratitude, disproportionately for the PR. Third, they could get away with creating the secret franchise because, as we noted, they retained the right to distribute paper ballots to voters. Parties typically instructed followers to show their ballots to party observers upon entering the building where they voted.

Parties, however, made a number of decisions that confound office-seeking perspectives. First, President Jiménez endorsed the PA's call for reform in 1925. It made no sense for the president, as leader of the PR, to decrease his party's ability to retain control of the executive and legislative branches of government. Even more confounding was the president's decision to endorse a radical set of changes, including the establishment of the secret franchise and suffrage rights for women. Indeed, the president kept reaffirming his commitment to reform by vetoing bills that Congress passed because they did not contain enough of his proposed innovations.

That a majority of deputies approved the president's bills is perhaps the most puzzling outcome from an office-seeking perspective. Indeed, what makes the politics of the 1927 electoral law so fascinating is that deputies ended up voting for a law they did not want. Curiously enough, they did not attack the president or his proposals, even when Jiménez threatened to veto the bill initially passed by Congress. Along with the president's decision to continue reforming electoral laws, the behavior of the legislative majority clashes with the interests that both the president and the legislators have in maximizing their control over state offices. Why did they do this?

Barbara Geddes's institutionalist theory suggests that a necessary condition of redistributive reforms is the existence of a balance of power in the legislature.[61] If the larger parties all have equal access to patronage and

---

[61] Barbara Geddes, *Politician's Dilemma: Building State Capacity in Latin America* (Berkeley, CA: University of California Press, 1994).

power, she argues, institutional reforms will help each of them. In line with these predictions, pro- and antigovernment forces were evenly balanced in the legislatures the president faced. The PR and the P*f*R, in a coalition known as the Fusion, held a slight majority of seats in 1925. The opposition PA held the plurality that was just shy of an absolute majority. Two years later, when the centralization of ballot production and other measures made the secret ballot effective, the distribution of power was split among four factions. In the aftermath of the 1926 elections, the PR split into two wings as the strength of the PA dropped. The P*f*R remained the smallest party in Congress in 1927.

While access to the trough of state no doubt helped the cause of reform, it was the incentives that the executive-legislative structure unleashed that pushed deputies to endorse reforms many of them did not really want. Not belonging to a party with majority support in Congress actually frees them from taking a partisan line. For wily politicians, such apparently unfavorable circumstances empower them to pivot between pro- and antigovernment forces to build majority coalitions in favor of far-reaching reforms. Reforming electoral laws invites the support of the opposition because it has an interest in facilitating access to state offices. Reform also appeals to smaller numbers of progovernment and independent deputies not as dependent upon the maintenance of the status quo to return to public office. The political stalemate in Congress also magnified the power of the executive because no party or faction could single-handedly assemble a two-thirds coalition to override a presidential veto. As the president's acceptance of the defeat of the amendment to enfranchise women illustrates, he understood that jettisoning certain proposals was crucial for preventing the opponents of reform from amassing a large enough majority to override his vetoes.

The effort to reform electoral laws also succeeded because the president had begun to court public opinion. In the early 1910s, Jiménez did not appeal to public opinion to overcome the resistance of legislative opponents. The newspapers are barren of his declarations about this topic. By the mid-1920s, however, the president had become widely quoted in the press about the necessity of reform. When initial reactions from Congress and other political leaders were unfavorable, he came very close to attacking them. The unwillingness of reelection-minded legislators and presidential candidates to criticize his proposals indicates that no party wanted to go on record for opposing changes that strengthened safeguards for voters.

Conclusions

What this chapter therefore demonstrates is the importance of institutional incentives in creating the very possibility of reform. As in most presidential systems, Costa Rican chief executives were constitutionally prohibited from holding office for consecutive terms, even if they could launch bids after spending a term away from the highest office in the republic.[62] This rule, we argue, created an opportunity for the occupant of a national office to appeal to the common interests of the entire electorate – something unimaginable to locally minded legislators. They alone possessed an interest in spearheading the democratization of electoral politics, largely because they could again run for the presidency. Indeed, reformers, especially successful ones, had a ready-made set of issues to overcome the tensions between self-interest and national interests; they could credibly claim that they were concerned with common interests, an incredibly useful weapon to vanquish rivals on the road to the presidency.

[62] Since 1969, they have been unable to stand for reelection at all.

5

Electoral Fraud during the Secret Ballot, 1925–48

Introduction

Despite the resistance of Congress, the secret franchise had become the law of the land. Reform had also stripped parties of the ability to furnish voters with paper ballots on election day. The new law required parties to submit the names of their candidates to the secretary of the interior a month before election day. The secretariat of the interior then printed ballots containing the names, colors, and portraits of presidential candidates. The parties' ability to distort the will of an electorate that, by the late 1920s, consisted of approximately one hundred thousand voters had abruptly diminished. Public opinion had become a force that parties had to reckon with and one that complicated their political calculations. Or had it?

With one exception, legal denunciations of fraud accompanied every election year; in some years, defeated parties also resorted to the use of violence to gain control of the state. Even after the reforms of the mid-1920s, political folklore suggests that presidents regularly and predictably stuffed the ballot box. In his novel *Mamita Yunai*, leftist writer and activist Carlos Luis Fallas described how the "official" party handed ID cards to indigenous peoples in the outlying Province of Limón while herding them to a polling station staffed by relatives of the local police chief.[1] Others argue that reformist governments took the

---

[1] Carlos Luis Fallas, *Mamita Yunai*. These events appear on pp. 51–9 in the second edition published by the Editorial Costa Rica in San José in 1986. The title is local parlance for the United Fruit Company; "Mommy United" is the literal translation. Though Fallas's novel is about United Fruit's abuse of the local workforce, he does not implicate the company in violations of electoral law.

fabrication of votes to new heights during the 1940s. Indeed, opposition-tinged accounts of this decade argue that governments, in alliance with the Communist Party, used the powers of the presidency for partisan advantage.[2]

Our findings indicate that there is some truth to these portraits. According to the petitions to nullify electoral results, parties accused their rivals of increasingly blatant acts of fraud after the establishment of the secret franchise. The use of coercion, the stealing of ballot boxes, and similar charges began to climb as a share of all accusations after the mid-1920s. No longer able to monitor the behavior of voters closely, parties had no choice, we suggest, but to resort to more flagrant violations of the law to win highly competitive elections. Yet, our analysis of the petitions reveals that electoral reform, paradoxically enough, actually reduced overall rates of fraud. In relation to the size of the electorate, fraud fell by nearly 50 percent after the elimination of the public franchise. It went from 1,083 eligible voters per accusation between 1901 and 1925 to 1,990 eligible voters per accusation between 1928 and 1946. Indeed, only by factoring in the effects of institutional change on political competition can we explain perhaps the most important finding discussed in this chapter: the geographic redistribution of accusations of electoral fraud from the periphery to the center by the mid-1940s.

This chapter assesses the impact of institutional arrangements and social structural accounts on electoral competition after the mid-1920s. It begins by reviewing the principal changes wrought by the 1927 law to make sense of the incentives that institutional arrangements generated. It examines changes in the party system and in voter turnout rates. This chapter then analyzes the impact of reform on the nature, spatial distribution, and magnitude of electoral fraud from the late 1920s to the 1940s. And, following the pattern established in earlier chapters, it explores the largely partisan reasons why the Credentials Committee and Congress as a whole rejected most of the petitions to nullify electoral results. This chapter ends by identifying the sources of the political polarization of the 1940s and how the fraud-tainted 1944 elections threatened the stability of the republic.

---

[2] See, in particular, Alberto F. Cañas, *Los ocho años* (San José: EUNED, 1982).

Political Competition under the Secret Franchise

Parties Lose Control

What happened to a rural machine boss after the 1928 election is typical of the surprises that greeted parties after the establishment of the secret franchise. Upon discovering that the PUN had won the local election, a rural machine boss exploded because he had lost 2,000 colones in a bet that "his" canton would vote for the PR's candidate, Carlos María Jiménez, in the 1928 presidential election. Once he realized that the PR had lost by more than 250 votes, he lambasted "his" voters as "sons of a bitch, spoilers, with my beast of burden, and the blue banner, they voted for don Cleto [González]," the PUN's candidate.[3]

The 1928 election results also surprised the PR leadership. In its aftermath, the PR issued a polemic entitled *Manifesto of the Republican Party to All Costa Ricans*. The *Manifesto* argued that the secret franchise had become "the new weapon put in the hands of those that have offered gold for votes." It claimed that its rivals had bribed voters. The *Manifesto* accused polling station officials of having given electoral identification cards to rival voters and thereby deprived their rightful owners of their suffrage rights. Only fraud, it alleged, could have prevented the PR – the party in power – from winning these elections. The PR also called for the reinstatement of the public ballot because it ". . . at least offers the opportunity to show the bravery and moral highness of those who honorably exercise [the franchise]."[4]

As reform increased uncertainty over election outcomes, society itself was becoming more literate. In 1927, 68 and 61 percent of the population nine years or older knew how to read and write in the center and periphery, respectively. And, in 1950, 83 percent of the population ten years or older was literate in the center – a good ten percentage points more than in the periphery. Throughout this period, the population remained

---

[3] Cited in Jaime Cerdas Mora, *La otra vanguardia* (San José: EUNED, 1993), p. 42.
[4] Partido Republicano, *Manifiesto del Partido Republicano a los costarricenses* (San José: Imprenta "La Tribuna," 1928), p. 16. For analysis of this document, see Iván Molina, "'Destacen ustedes dos:' práctica e ideología del fraude electoral en Costa Rica de 1928," in Margarita Vannini and Frances Kinloch, eds., *Polítca, cultura, y sociedad: Centroamérica, Siglos XVIII, XIX, y XX* (Managua: Instituto de Historia de Nicaragua y Centroamérica, 1998), pp. 95–107.

largely rural. Even by 1950, only 33 percent of all Costa Ricans lived in villages and cities.[5]

Both institutional and social change led to increasingly expensive campaigns. Not only did prospective candidates have to travel the length of Central Valley with their entourages, but they had to maintain headquarters in important towns and cities. Parties also had to broadcast their speeches over the radio and then pay to have them reprinted in newspapers whose daily runs had reached about twenty thousand by the 1940s. Parties also used newspapers as the medium to publicize their activities, to denounce their adversaries, and, most curiously, to publish long lists of the names of their supporters. Indeed, by the 1940s, the boasting so typical of political campaigns expressed itself as a series of wagers that individuals and parties published under the heading of paid announcements.

Running for presidential office was costing approximately half a million colones by the mid-1930s.[6] A U.S. diplomatic report indicates that the 1948 elections were going to cost approximately 6 million colones. According to this report, the National Republican Party (PRN) was going to spend 3.5 million colones to reelect Rafael Ángel Calderón Guardia to the presidency. The opposition Party of National Union (PUN) was going to spend another 2.5 million colones. State Department officials also estimated that the administrative costs of the election would add another 1.5 million colones to this total. As a result, the despatch noted, these were going to be "probably the costliest [elections] in the country's history." This, the report acutely observed, meant that they were going to cost "ten colones or approximately $1.80 at the current rate of exchange for every man, woman, and child in the country." Since the constitution restricted voting to men above twenty (or eighteen if they were married or "professors of some science"), parties were going to spend approximately 36 colones per eligible voter. With a 1948 average minimum daily wage rate of 5.20 colones for workers on coffee plantations, parties spent 61 colones

---

[5] In the 1927 population census, only the population of the principal cities of the republic were considered urban areas. Villages were classified as rural areas. With the way that the data are presented, it is not possible to identify the population of villages exactly.

[6] The first reference to this cost is from Mario Sancho, *Costa Rica: Suiza Centroamericana* (San José: Tipografía "La Tribuna," 1935), p. 56. The exact reference reads as "the presidencies of don Cleto [González] and don Ricardo [Jiménez] have cost around half a million each one. . . ." The first was president for the second and last time between 1928–32 and the latter succeeded him for his third and final term.

or the equivalent of twelve days of labor for each ballot cast in what remains perhaps the most hotly contested elections of the twentieth century.[7]

Parties and Voter Turnout Rates

After the reforms of the 1920s, the first of three changes to the party system consisted of the formal appearance of an avowedly Marxist party. Established in 1931, the Communist Party became the most important minor party during the 1930s and 1940s. The second important systemic change was the development of a hegemonic party by the late 1930s. Finally, the number of local parties fielding candidates did begin to decline by the 1940s.

Even before its first campaign for municipal office in 1932, the Communist Party became the target of persecution. It was unable to get itself registered to field candidates and, as a result, did not run in the 1932 general elections. Between 1934 and 1942, the newly named Workers and Peasants Bloc (BOC) obtained 12 percent of the vote in midterm elections. It received 5 and 10 percent of the presidential vote in 1936 and 1940, respectively. The Communist Party retained this name until 1943, when it publicly moderated its policies and became the Popular Vanguard Party (PVP) to form a successful alliance with the PRN known as the Victory Bloc. In the 1948 elections, the PVP ran its own legislative candidates and captured 13 percent of the Congressional vote.

The PR split by the end of the 1920s. The PRN, its most successful offshoot, backed Ricardo Jiménez in 1932 in his third bid for the presidency. He ran against Manuel Castro of the PUR (Republican Union Party) and Carlos María Jiménez of what was left of the PR. When none obtained an absolute majority of the popular vote, the constitution called upon Congress to convene a run-off election between Jiménez, who had attracted 47 percent of the vote, and Castro, who had the support of 29 percent of the voters. Believing that the PUN government would be partial to the PRN, Castro launched a coup, known as the "Bellavistazo," less than

---

[7] The figures for the 1948 race are from "Current Political Situation," Despatch No. 402 (December 18, 1947)," From [unknown] to Secretary of State, U.S. National Archives (hereafter cited as USNA) DS 818.00/12-1847, p. 3. According to this report, 4 million colones had been spent and 2 million more were going to be spent in the last two months of the campaign. Wage data are from Samuel Z. Stone, *La dinastía de los conquistadores* (San José: EDUCA, 1975), p. 136.

twelve hours after the closing of the polls.[8] After several days of shooting and negotiations, the PUR surrendered control of the Bellavista barracks. And, having resigned his position as second runner-up, Castro left Congress in a quandary. It seemed pointless to convene a run-off with only Jiménez left in the race. On 1 May, when the new Congress convened for this first time, deputies voted Jiménez as first designate to the presidency who, because of the absence of a popularly elected executive, became president.[9] With Jimenez's assumption of the presidency, the PRN came to dominate politics well until the 1940s.

The explosive growth in local-level parties began to slow down, especially by the 1940s. Between 1925 and 1948, an average of nine parties fielded candidates; for the six midterm elections held during this period, the average was fifteen. By splitting these periods, we discover that the overall average fell from twelve in the 1930s to five in the 1940s. And, differences between general and midterm elections continued to exist. Between 1925 and 1938, three and nineteen parties participated in general and midterm elections, respectively. And, during the 1940s, these figures became four and seven, respectively. The downward trend reflects both the fact that local-level political networks were becoming consolidated, especially since Congress created only one canton between 1940 and 1947.

Seventy-six percent of the electorate turned out to vote in general elections between 1925 and 1948. Turnout rates fell to 55 percent in midterm elections during this time. Unlike the previous period, however, turnout was higher in the center than in the periphery – 68 and 57 percent, respectively, over all elections. And, this is a pattern that holds by controlling for election type. In the center, the average turnout rate in general elections was 80 percent, exactly 18 points higher than in the periphery. During midterm elections, this pattern remained in effect, even if it became rather small: Turnout was an average of 56 percent in the center, only 5 points higher than in the periphery.

Because turnout rates typically fell during midterm elections, parties that attracted few votes had a better chance of electing deputies because

---

[8] The only discussion of the coup remains Eduardo Oconitrillo García, *El Bellavistazo* (San José: Editorial Costa Rica, 1989).

[9] On the legal manueverings that led to Jiménez's third presidency, see Fabrice Lehoucq, "The Origins of Democracy in Costa Rica in Comparative Perspective," unpub. Ph.D. Dissertation, Duke University, 1992, p. 69.

their share of provincial vote totals expanded as turnout fell. This trend was particularly favorable for the Communist Party, which could depend upon a gradual but increasing amount of electoral support. In the Province of San José, one of its most consistently predictable bases of support, the Communist Party's average share of the vote went from 10 percent in general to 16 percent in midterm elections. In its other long-term electoral fortress, the Province of Limón, such figures went from 9 to 26 percent in general and midterm elections, respectively.[10]

Mainstream parties succeeded in passing compulsory voting laws in 1936 to stem the fall in turnout and thwart the success of the Communist Party.[11] Mandatory voting laws, in fact, did coincide with an increase in turnout rates. Between 1936 and 1948, turnout averaged 74 percent of eligible voters. In contrast, it was 56 percent between 1897 and 1934. This difference holds even if we control for election type: Turnout went from 38 before to 68 percent after this reform in midterm elections, and from 66 to 77 percent in general elections. And, compulsory voting still affected turnout rates throughout the period when the secret franchise was in effect. Turnout went from being 37 percent of the electorate between 1925 and 1934 to 68 percent between 1938 and 1946.

Electoral Fraud, 1925–38

Electoral laws and social structure still made the periphery the site of a disproportionate amount of fraud. Precisely where voters were the poorest, the least literate, and the most rural, institutional arrangements generated incentives for parties to commit – and to denounce – the greatest number of fraudulent acts. Institutional change also left its foot-

---

[10] See Iván Molina and Fabrice Lehoucq, *Urnas de lo inesperado: fraude electoral y lucha política en Costa Rica (1901–1948)* (San José: EUCR, 1999), pp. 115–26. These figures do not include 1944 because the PVP joined the PRN in the Victory Bloc alliance. And, there are no provincial figures for Limón in 1946 because the Communist Party only ran a slate of candidates in San José in this year.

[11] While committee reports and Congressional debate do not shed light on the motives for the reform, U.S. State Department correspondence reveals that the success of the Communist Party led to "... a great deal of agitation ... in favor of making voting compulsory, providing for a system of fines to penalize delinquent citizens." "Communism," Despatch No. [not available] (28 February 1934), Leo R. Sack to Secretary of State, USNA 818.00/1447, p. 6. For analysis of the party's electoral performance, see Iván Molina, "El desempeño electoral del Partido Comunista de Costa Rica (1931–1948)," *Revista Parlamentaria*, Vol. 7, No. 1 (April 1999), pp. 491–521.

print on political behavior. With the establishment of the secret franchise, parties lost opportunities to commit the least controversial types of fraud. Paradoxically enough, institutional change encouraged parties to commit increasingly egregious acts of fraud.

The Nature and Spatial Basis of Fraud

Between 1925 and 1938, parties filed 412 accusations of fraud (see Table 5.1). The vast majority of these – 87 percent (or 357) of the charges – were channeled in forty-three petitions. Parties made the rest of the accusations during the tally of the vote that Provincial Electoral Councils conducted. On average, petitioners filed fifty-nine complaints per elections during this period.

The periphery continued to be responsible for most infractions of electoral law. Though less than a quarter of the electorate resided in outlying provinces, parties filed 61 percent of their complaints against election results in the periphery. In a pattern established since the turn of the century, parties and public officials stuffed the ballot box in regions with the largest share of wage laborers, with the largest proportion of illiterates, and where most of the population lived in scattered and isolated rural hamlets. Economically dependent on powerful landlords and dispersed over a larger area, voters in the periphery became the target of unscrupulous politicians.

Institutional differences, however, also contribute to explaining the concentration of fraud in outlying provinces. As in earlier periods, electoral laws encouraged politicians to field candidates in the periphery because most seats three quarters, to be precise – were apportioned to parties that out-polled their rivals. In the center, in contrast, seats went to parties that obtained one quotient worth of votes. That the threshold for winning a Congressional slot was higher in the center than in the periphery led to lower levels of political competitiveness in core provinces. Once we control for the size of the electorate, in general elections there were 28,845 eligible voters per party in the center and 8,333 in the preriphery. In contrast, in midterm elections there were 5,977 eligible voters per party in the center and 3,586 in the periphery. Again, these reduced numbers were the product of local party formation in midterm races: forty-six parties in the center and eighteen in the periphery. Proportionally, however, there were 1.4 local parties in the periphery for every one local party in the center. As a result of a more competitive political environment, there were 659 eligible voters for every accusation in the periphery and only 3,790 in the center.

Table 5.1. *Number of Accusations of Electoral Fraud, by Province and by General and Midterm Election, 1925–38*

Province	Midterm 1925	General 1928	Midterm 1930	General 1932	Midterm 1934	General 1936	Midterm 1938	Total
Center								
San José	14	1		37	4	14	4	74
Alajuela	13		6	10	1			30
Cartago	9	20	3	10	1		7	50
Heredia	4					2		6
Periphery								
Guanacaste	24		32	68			50	174
Puntarenas				24	29			53
Limón			16	9				25
TOTAL	64	21	57	158	35	16	61	412

Source: La Gaceta (1925–38).

164

Electoral reform also succeeded in reducing overall rates of fraud. Between 1925 and 1938, there were 1,890 eligible voters per accusation of fraud. Between 1913 and 1923, in contrast, there were 1,085 per eligible voter. And, by disaggregating for region, we discover that most of the fall in rates of electoral fraud occurred in the center. In the period before the establishment of the secret franchise, there were 1,813 eligible voters per accusation of fraud in the center. After 1925, this ratio nearly doubled by declining to 3,790 eligible voters for each charge of fraud. In the periphery, the fall was less pronounced: It went from 426 eligible voters per accusation between 1913 and 1923 to 656 charges of fraud between 1925 and 1938 – a 40 percent fall in rates of accusation.

By dramatically reducing the amount of information parties held about the preferences of voters, the elimination of the public franchise undercut the ability of parties to commit procedural violations of electoral law. It was pointless to claim that polling station officials had, for example, incorrectly recorded votes if citizens were voting in private. Paradoxically enough, the reforms of the mid-1920s encouraged parties to commit more and more flagrant acts of fraud even as they shrank overall rates of fraud because, simply put, they had no choice but to stuff the ballot box if they wished to triumph in increasingly competitive elections.

Information in Table 5.2 upholds this interpretation. Parties accused polling station officials of committing more serious kinds of fraud after the establishment of the secret franchise. These include accusations that officials excluded poll watchers from sitting in on polling station deliberations and had permitted parties to substitute voters. Parties also filed numerous complaints that these and other actions had led parties to inflate their vote totals illegally. Such charges increased from 33 percent of all accusations made against polling stations between 1913 and 1923 to 58 percent of all such complaints between 1925 and 1938. This pattern holds even when controlling for regional variations. Between 1913 and 1923, 18 percent of the charges filed against polling stations in the center were of the more serious sort. In the subsequent period, they increased to 46 percent of all such accusations. The trend was similar in the periphery, where the most egregious types of fraud went from 66 to 77 percent of the total.

A particularly blatant (and colorful) example of electoral fraud occurred at the Hospice of Incurables in the Canton of Goicoechea in the Province of San José. A PRN activist accused the hospice director of forcing patients to vote for the opposition candidate during the 1936 general elections. According to the petitioner, the hospice director organized the staff so that

Table 5.2. *Accusations of Electoral Fraud, by Province, 1925–38*

Accusation	Category of Fraud	Center				Periphery			Total
		San José	Alajuela	Cartago	Heredia	Guanacaste	Puntarenas	Limón	
Against polling stations[a]	1	43	16	44	6	126	10	19	264
Technical defects of provincial electoral council	2					2			2
Official favoritism toward a party	2	3				11	12	4	30
Liquor distributed on election day	2	2				7	1		10
Provincial electoral council favored a party	2					1			1
Purchase of votes	3	7	10			9	24	1	51
Official intimidation against voters	3					4		1	5
Nonofficial intimidation against voters	3	1							1
Grand electoral council acted illegally	3	5	1						6
District electoral council acted illegally	3	2							2
Official coercion against voters	4	6	1	1		12	5		25
Official coercion against polling stations	4	2		1					3
Nonofficial coercion against voters	4	1		1		1			3
Person elected not qualified for post[b]	4	2	1	1		1	1		6
Party incorrectly registered[a]				2					2
Others[a]			1						1
TOTAL		74	30	50	6	174	53	25	412

Notes:
[a] See Table 5.3.
[b] These cases did not apply in our classification.
Source: La Gaceta (1925–38).

"the patients were coerced into voting for don Octavio Beeche [of the PUN], and were threatened with being expelled [from the hospice unless they did so]." "Furthermore," the petitioner complained, "one of the infirm induced voters to cast ballots for Beeche . . ." so that "voting could not be done in conformity with the law . . ." and was therefore ". . . was not secret. . . ."[12]

Even though most denunciations of officially sponsored coercion occurred in the periphery, Table 5.2 indicates that the center went from housing 11 percent (or six of fifty-three) of these accusations between 1913 and 1923 to 39 percent (or eleven of twenty-eight) of them between 1925 and 1938. As in the preceding period, the petition reveals that only 11 percent (three of twenty-eight) of the charges of coercion were leveled against landlords, two of which took place in the center.

The reforms of the 1920s thus led to the development of new ways of fabricating votes and a corresponding discourse to portray new and brazen acts of fraud (see Table 5.3). Unable to monitor the behavior of voters, parties resorted to more flagrant acts of fraud to decrease the uncertainty of electoral competition. Pundits referred to any large-scale fabrication of votes as a "downpour (*chorreo*)" of votes. They also dubbed any effort that pressed a large number of men to vote for a particular party as a "chain (*cadena*)."

Filed after the 1932 general elections, a PRN petition furnishes a wonderful example of both types of fraud. PRN militants argued that "two trucks, transporting PUR voters, passed and repassed the same streets" to use ". . . more than three thousand identification cards" kept "in a dark place, a hideout of this illegality and crime. . . ." At first, the PRN supporters "thought it concerned trips to animate their supporters." But, as they

. . . observed the trucks, it struck us that [PUR supporters] left the PUR club, arrived at the voting place, and its passengers would enter and vote, return to the truck, and it would newly go to the club and, once again, the same passengers would repeat the trip and the vote, and all in a few minutes.

"Understanding what was at stake," the petitioner explained, "and seeing among the PUR followers a friend of ours, who testified how the PUR club contained a large deposit of identification cards that were given to

---

[12] "Demanda de nulidad (18 February 1936)," *La Gaceta*, No. 44 (22 February 1936), p. 325. Despite suffrage restrictions, the director was a woman actively involved in politics.

Table 5.3. *Accusations of Electoral Fraud against Polling Stations by Province, 1925–38*

Accusation	Category of Fraud	Center				Periphery			Total
		San José	Alajuela	Cartago	Heredia	Guanacaste	Puntarenas	Limón	
Technical or legal defects	1	23	13	20	3	32	1	3	95
Voting booth in inappropriate place	2			3		4		2	9
Election held off schedule	2			1		4	1		6
No voting held	2		1	1					2
Party representative expelled or threatened	3	1				24	2		27
Permitted substitution of voters	3	4				12	1	6	23
Number of votes was inflated	3	3	1		1	14	3	1	23
Voting was public	3	5	1	2		7	2		17
Voters cast multiple ballots	3	3		6		4		1	14
Number of ballots exceeds number of voters	3			1	1	3		4	9
Polling station refused to give voters their ID	3					8			8
Ballots were altered	3			8					8
ID retrieved by wrong person	3	4						1	5
Votes were annulled	3					4			4
Ballot box altered	3			1		3			4
Voters did not meet requirements	3			1		1			2
Number of ballots does not equal number of ID cards	3					2			2
Ballots stolen	3				1				1
Voters were intimidated	3					1			1
Identification not requested of voters	3					1			1
Votes not received	3					2			2
Ballots were substituted	3							1	1
TOTAL		43	16	44	6	126	10	19	264

Source: La Gaceta (1925–38).

168

the truck's passengers," the PRN militants concluded that its rivals were casting "criminally false votes."[13]

Political folklore suggests that a key source of illegal votes consisted of parties organizing their followers to cast ballots using the identification cards of the deceased or of nonexistent persons or of using cards purchased from citizens. Before the 1944 elections, for example, reports circulated that the government had manufactured as many as forty thousand electoral identification cards to ensure that its candidates were elected to executive and legislative offices. Confidential U.S. diplomatic correspondence indicates that the market rate of voter identification cards oscillated between 2 and 20 colones a piece during the early 1940s. At 1943 minimum wage rates for agricultural laborers on coffee estates, parties were paying the equivalent of two- to five-days' pay for each identification card.[14]

The petitions, however, do not contain very many accusations of the illegal use or purchase of votes. Only one petition denounced that "the authorities" were condoning "the open purchase and sale of votes" in exchange for promises from citizens that they would ". . . abstain from exercising their suffrage rights."[15] Nevertheless, petitioners did accuse their rivals of having their followers retrieve ID cards that belonged to others and using them on election day. Furthermore, that petitioners charged individuals with casting more than one ballot on election day or of not meeting suffrage requirements suggests that there was an illegal trade in ID cards. Between 1925 and 1938, 11 percent (44 of 412) of all accusations of fraud were of these types.

Electoral fraud also became worse over time. Classifying all accusations of fraud between 1925 and 1938, Table 5.4 indicates that parties made 30

---

[13] "Reclamaciones presentadas acerca de las elecciones verificadas el dia 14 de febrero de 1932 (n.d.)," Ibid, No. 84 (21 April 1932), p. 450.

[14] The price of voter identification cards stems from "Details of a Conversation Which Took Place on Saturday Afternoon February 27, 1943 [between Harry Fernández and Edward D. Cuffe]." USNA-DS, 818.00/1751, especially pp. 3–4. We calculated minimum wage rates for the coffee sector from "Labor: Its Unions, Institutions and Political Power in Costa Rica," Despatch No. 989 (January 10, 1944), Edward G. Trueblood to Secretary of State, USNA-DS 818.504/75, pp. 24 and 26. The number of cards allegedly controlled by the government is mentioned in "Presidential Campaign Enters Last Phase," Despatch No. 951 (7 January 1944), Edward G. Trueblood to Secretary of State, USNA-DS 818.00/1912, p. 4.

[15] "Demanda de nulidad (15 February 1934)," La Gaceta, No. 94 (27 April 1934), p. 747. Though we could not determine the partisan identification of the petitioners, the petition was filed against the PRN, the party in power.

Table 5.4. Accusations of Electoral Fraud, by General and Midterm Elections, 1925–38

Accusation	Category of Fraud	Midterm 1925	General 1928	Midterm 1930	General 1932	Midterm 1934	General 1936	Midterm 1938	Total
Against polling stations[a]	1	60	19	35	83	15	4	48	264
Technical defects of provincial electoral council		2							2
Official favoritism toward a party	2			11	2	12	3	2	30
Liquor distributed on election day	2			1	5	1	2	1	10
Provincial electoral council favored a party	2				1				1
Purchase of votes	3				43	2	5	1	51
Official intimidation against voters	3			1	2			2	5
Nonofficial intimidation against voters	3						1		1
Grand electoral council acted illegally	3			1	2			3	6
District electoral council acted illegally	3				2				2
Official coercion against voters	4	2	1	2	11	4	1	4	25
Official coercion against polling stations	4				3				3
Nonofficial coercion against voters	4				3				3
Person elected not qualified for post[b]			1	3	1	1			6
Party incorrectly registered[b]				2					2
Others[b]				1					1
TOTAL		64	21	57	158	35	16	61	412

Notes:
[a] See Table 5.5.
[b] These cases did not apply in our classification.
Source: La Gaceta (1925–38).

170

percent (45 of 148) of their complaints between 1934 and 1938. Only 18 percent (28 of 148) of the accusations made between 1925 and 1938 referred to elections of 1925, 1928, and 1930. We do not include charges parties filed against the 1932 general elections to prevent the results of a highly competitive election from distorting overall trends. After the 1932 general elections, parties filed 38 percent (158 of 412) of the charges they formulated during this period. Excluding the complaints made by parties against polling stations – 36 percent (148 of 412) of the total – between 1925 and 1938, these charges consisted of flagrant violations of electoral law. These included accusations of the purchase of votes, that officials favored progovernment candidates, and that the authorities used coercion against opposition voters.

As Table 5.5 shows, parties also complained that polling station officials committed more egregious types of fraud with time. Complaints about procedural flaws and legal defects went from 85 percent (fifty-one of sixty) of all accusations filed after the 1925 midterm elections to 10 percent (five of forty-eight) in the 1938 midterm elections. Petitioners increasingly accused polling station officials of condoning the substitution of voters, of allowing voting to take place in public, and of altering ballots.

Institutional reform also explains why parties accused their rivals of illegally inflating vote totals more often than of reducing the accusing party's vote totals. As we saw in Chapter 3, parties invested approximately the same amount of time to increasing their vote totals illegally as they spent trying to lower their opponents' vote totals between 1913 and 1923. The public ballot allowed them to keep a running tally of how many votes they were behind or ahead of their opponents. Once legal reform made it impossible for them to ascertain their respective positions, parties shifted to amassing as many votes as possible, whether by mobilizing more voters or by quite literally stuffing the ballot box. Table 5.6 reveals that 78 percent of the 232 accusations (56 percent of the total between 1925–38) that can be classified as either increasing or decreasing vote totals denounced acts that allowed parties to ratchet up their vote totals.

The Intensity and Magnitude of Fraud

Between 1925 and 1938, the worst two types of fraud accounted for 62 percent of all accusations. This figure represented a 20 percent increase in category three and four types of fraud from the prior period of study. After the establishment of the secret franchise, 54 percent of all charges made

Table 5.5. *Accusations of Electoral Fraud Against Polling Stations, by General and Midterm Election, 1925–38*

Accusation	Category of Fraud	Midterm 1925	General 1928	Midterm 1930	General 1932	Midterm 1934	General 1936	Midterm 1938	Total
Technical or legal defects	1	51	12	8	14	5		5	95
Voting booth in inappropriate place	2		1	1	5	1		1	9
Election held off schedule	2		1		1	1		3	6
No voting held	2		1	1					2
Party representative expelled or threatened	3	1		9	6	1	1	9	27
Permitted substitution of voters	3			5	10	1		7	23
Number of votes was inflated	3	2		6	8	4	1	2	23
Voting was public	3	3			7	2	1	4	17
Voters cast multiple ballots	3			1	13				14
Number of ballots exceeds number of voters	3	1	1	4	1			2	9
Polling station refused to give voters their ID	3				5			3	8
Ballots were altered	3		1					7	8
ID retrieved by wrong person	3				5				5
Votes were annulled	3				3			1	4
Ballot box altered	3	1	1					2	4
Voters did not meet requirements	3		1		1				2
Number of ballots does not equal number of ID cards	3				2				2
Ballots stolen	3						1		1
Voters were intimidated	3				1				1
Identification not requested of voters	3							1	1
Votes not received	3	1						1	2
Ballots were substituted	3				1				1
TOTAL		60	19	35	83	15	4	48	264

Source: La Gaceta (1925–38).

172

Table 5.6. *Accusations of Fraud, Classified by Whether the Act Increased or Decreased Vote Totals, 1925–38*

Province	+	−	Election	+	−	Impugned Votes	+	−
Center								
San José	28	14	1925	10	1	1–9	16	15
Alajuela	16	1	1928	3	4	10–49	15	5
Cartago	19	4	1930	23	3	50–99	5	4
Heredia	2	1	1932	94	31	100–499	7	2
			1934	12	2	500–999		
			1936	8	2	1000+		1
Periphery								
Guanacaste	69	26	1938	34	9			
Puntarenas	34	2						
Limón	16	4						
TOTAL	184	52	TOTAL	184	52	TOTAL[a]	43	27

Note:

[a] The totals are not equivalent because accusations did not always indicate the number of impugned votes.

Source: *La Gaceta* (1925–38).

in the center consisted of the worst types of fraud. And, in the periphery, the proportion was even worse: 67 percent of all accusations were of types three and four. In line with our more qualitative analysis of electoral fraud, the efforts of parties to stuff the ballot box were getting worse, a trend that is particularly notable in the center. While the share of fraud types three and four increased by 5 percent in the periphery, they went up by 35 percent in the center.

Like in previous periods, parties denounced acts of fraud in a rather small number of polling stations. In the 1928 presidential election, they filed petitions against 1.7 percent (or 12 of 689) of polling stations. In 1932, they questioned the results of 13.5 percent (or 92 of 681) of all polling stations. In 1936, they impugned the results of just 1 percent (or 7 out of 713) of all polling stations. The proportion of polling stations questioned was roughly similar in midterm elections. In 1925 and 1930, parties denounced acts of fraud in 9 percent (or 58 out of 678) and 4 percent (or 30 out of 670) polling stations, respectively. And, in 1934 and 1938, the share of impugned polling stations was 3 percent (22 out of 665) and 3 percent (24 out of 7343), respectively. Table 5.7 summarizes this information.

Table 5.7. *Questioned Polling Stations, 1925–38*

Election Year	Percent Questioned	Victor's Lead	Percentage Difference
1925	8.6	21.2	12.6
1928	1.7	18.3	16.6
1930	4.5	21.7	17.2
1932	13.5	17.5	4.0
1934	3.3	38.9	35.6
1936	1.0	25.2	24.2
1938	3.3	52.8	49.5

Source: *La Gaceta* (1925–38), and Iván Molina, "Estadísticas electorales de Costa Rica (1897–1948): Una contribución documental," *Revista Parlamentaria* (San José, Costa Rica), Vol. 9, No. 2 (August 2001), pp. 404–17.

Table 5.7 also displays the margin of votes obtained by the victor over his nearest rival during these elections. Even if we assume that every vote at impugned polling stations is fraudulent, fraud did not determine the outcome of general elections held between 1925 and 1938. In the 1928, 1932, and 1936 presidential elections, the margin of votes separating victorious parties from second runners-up was 18.3, 17.5, and 25.2 percent of the vote, respectively. Simply put, parties that won presidential elections did actually attract larger shares of the votes. Similarly, parties that triumphed in midterm elections obtained vote totals greater than the share of impugned polling stations. In the 1925, 1930, 1934, and 1938 midterm elections, victors garnered 21.2, 21.7, 38.9, and 52.8 percent of the popular vote.

As the nature of fraud was becoming worse, the most flagrant violations of electoral law were also becoming concentrated in fewer and fewer polling stations. Between 1901 and 1909, parties denounced electoral results in about 6 percent of all polling stations. In the subsequent period, this figure increased to 8 percent. And, after the reforms of the mid-1920s, petitioners argued that their rivals fabricated fraudulent votes at an average of 5 percent of all polling stations.

That the ability of parties to forecast election results declined precipitously after the establishment of the secret franchise explains the seemingly contradictory trend toward worse types of fraud occurring in a smaller share of polling stations. Unless public opinion clearly favored one candidate, all bets were off – a not unexpected outcome, and one that helps to explain why so many deputies opposed President Jiménez's reform bills in the mid-1920s. The dramatic jump in the uncertainty of election results, after all, led the PR to claim that the public franchise was, all things considered, not such a bad way of running an election. Surprise, disappointment, and anger with electoral results also led factions to organize revolts against the central government in every election year between 1928 and 1932.[16]

Institutional Controls

According to the electoral laws of the mid-1920s, the Grand Electoral Council (GCE) could annul votes. Responsible for the initial tally of the vote, the GCE could disregard ballots because they did not possess the appropriate signatures, because they were defaced, or for similar such reasons. The GCE and Provincial Electoral Councils annulled votes in 43 and 24 percent of the provincial elections in the center and periphery, respectively, between 1925 and 1938. Although electoral laws authorized these agencies to discard votes, Provincial Electoral Councils modified vote totals in fewer elections than in the preceding period. Between 1913 and 1923, they had annulled votes in 75 and 39 percent of provincial elections.

The president, however, reserved the right to approve the GCE's decisions. Congress remained the only branch of government constitutionally empowered to rule on the validity of petitions to nullify electoral results. Especially if the opposition held a Congressional majority, endowing the GCE with some of these responsibilities created the conditions for executive-legislative conflicts. The reforms of the mid-1920s also created the possibility that the GCE, if it took its mandate seriously, could come into conflict with the president.

Conflicts between the president and members of the GCE led to resignations and dismissals after the 1930 and 1938 midterm elections. After the 1930 midterm election, the GCE and the Provincial Electoral Council of Alajuela did not tally 312 votes that PUN President Cleto Gonzalez (1928–32) had, through an administrative order, requested be counted as legitimate.[17] In 1938, PRN President León Cortés (1936–40) had

---

[16] For a more detailed analysis of the relationship between fraud and rebellion, see Fabrice Lehoucq, "Institutional Foundations of Democratic Cooperation in Costa Rica," *Journal of Latin American Studies*, Vol. 26, No. 1 (February 1996), pp. 329–55.

[17] "Poder Ejecutivo (6 March 1930)," *La Gaceta*, No. 55 (7 March 1930), p. 363, and "Gobernación (12 March 1930)," Ibid, No. (23 March 1930), p. 448. This section draws upon Iván Molina, "La Comisión de Credenciales y Renuncias del Congreso: Un capítulo olvidado de la política costarricense (1902–1948)," in Ronny Viales, ed., *Memoria del IV Congreso Panamericano de Historia* (México, Instituto Panamericano de Geografía e Historia, 2001), pp. 113–31.

dismissed all three GCE members because they had not tallied ninety-one absentee ballots cast in the Province of Cartago in favor of his party's candidates in the Province of San José. This action resulted in the PRN filling yet another legislative seat and thereby depriving the Communist Party of a representative in Congress.[18]

Between 1925 and 1938, the Credentials Committee ruled in favor of only one petition unanimously. It rejected thirty-five of them outright and split its vote on the remaining seven petitions. The success of petitioners declines even further when we recognize that Congress approved only one of forty-three petitions filed during this period. Congress justified its behavior by claiming that petitioners had not furnished sufficient evidence to prove their accusations or because the nullification of impugned votes would not have changed electoral results.

Interestingly, Congress as a whole rejected the petition that received the undivided support of the Credentials Committee. Submitted by a Reformist National Union Party (PUNr) observer, this petition contested the election of PUN candidates Francisco Gutiérrez and Filadelfo Granados as deputy and his alternate, respectively, in the Province of Limón in 1930. This petition denounced a host of irregularities, including the inflation of votes, that some voters cast more than one ballot, and the like.[19] In its report, the Credentials Committee declared

even if it is said that the usual practice in electoral debates in Limón consists of simulating votes and filling out ballots and the registry in any way, the aim of Costa Ricans should be that these things not continue to occur. . . . As a result, [we do] not recommend that Congress approve of the most recent elections . . . and we ask Congress to identify a new date so that, appropriately controlled, new elections can be held. . . .[20]

Upon hearing of the Committee's decision, the PUNr petitioner published a pamphlet called *A Glorious Page of the Congress of Costa Rica*, praising the Committee's actions. According to the PUNr observer, the Committee's decision only needed Congressional approval for all of the citizenry to exclaim, "glorious Congress, how well you knew how to fulfil your mandate."[21] At first, Congress voted nineteen to nineteen to accept

[18] "Consejo Nacional Electoral (8 April 1938)," Ibid, No. (21 April 1938), p. 741.
[19] "Demanda de nulidad (19 February 1930)," *La Gaceta*, No. 96 (30 April 1930), p. 621.
[20] "Dictamen de la Comisión de Credenciales (25 April 1930)," Ibid, No. 96 (30 April 1930), p. 622.
[21] Eduardo Maroto Touret, *Una página gloriosa del Congreso de Costa Rica: la nulidad de las elecciones de Limón* (San José: Imprenta Alsina, 1930), p. 3.

the PUN*r* petition. In its second vote, deputies voted, by twenty-two to sixteen, against the petition. Unfortunately, surviving records of the Congressional response to this request do not shed light on why the Committee ultimately shied away from becoming bathed in glory.

The only petition that Congress endorsed did not meet with the undivided support of the Credentials Committee. In its minority report, the Credentials Committee rejected virtually all charges contained in a 1932 PRN petition. It made only one exception when it accepted the call to annul four votes in a district in the Canton of Puriscal in the Province of San José. In its majority report, the Committee disagreed, but ruled in favor of another request that questioned the GCE's decision not to tally 323 absentee ballots cast for the San José races. By ruling against the GCE, the Committee majority – consisting of one PUN and one Constitutional Republican Party (PRC) deputy – helped to elect another PUN candidate to Congress. By ignoring this issue, the minority report – written by an Esquivelista Provincial Union Party deputy sympathetic to the PRN – kept this seat in the hands of the PRN. Dominated by a PRN majority of twenty-four seats, Congress voted to endorse the minority report.[22]

One interpretation of the low rate of Congressional approval of petitions between 1925 and 1938 is that institutional mechanisms of arbitrating electoral conflicts were becoming increasingly ineffective. That rates of petitioning began to decline upholds the validity of this hypothesis. In the 1936, 1938, and 1940 elections, for example, parties filed an average of three petitions. Between 1925 and 1934, they submitted an average of 6.8 petitions per election. And, between 1913 and 1934, parties presented an average 6.3 petitions to Congress after each election. The difficulty of finding justice in electoral matters was expressed with clarity by PR*i* (Independent PR) Deputy Roberto Quirós in May of 1938:

> ... I want to leave, for the record, my negative vote of the report issued by the Credentials Committee, which recommends the approval of the minutes and the provisional declaration of deputies in the Province of Alajuela, since no petition to nullify electoral results was presented because it was judged as inconvenient to do so – because, all things considered, no practical results would have been achieved – sufficient moral reasons exist to declare that the elections that took place in this province [in February 1938] are affronts to President [León] Cortés, whom

[22] "Demanda de nulidad (7 April 1932)," *La Gaceta*, No. (30 April 1932), pp. 491–7. Deputies voted to accept the minority's report during o.s. no. 2 (2 May 1932), art. 3, Ibid, No. 97 (6 May 1932), p. 526. The final vote was twenty-nine to thirteen in favor of the petition.

I assume was unaware of the plots hatched by his fellow party members and supporters.[23]

Yet, the decrease in the number of petitions presented to Congress could also be sour grapes. By the mid-1930s, the PRN had come to dominate politics. Though it – like every other party – was no doubt stuffing the ballot box, the PRN was also highly successful in attracting the support of electoral majorities. Between 1934 and 1940, its margin of victory was an average of 46 percentage points greater than the proportion of impugned polling stations. So, opposition deputy Quirós's complaints appear to be true, but for reasons quite different from those he advanced. Opposition parties may have gradually stopped petitioning Congress about electoral results because they would be unable to prove that fraud was extensive enough to oveturn their defeat.

An Imperial Presidency, Polarization, and Electoral Fraud

By the 1940s, the dangers of the functional division of electoral governance again became apparent. With his party in control of 89 percent of legislative seats, Rafael Ángel Calderón Guardia (1940–4) was able to combine his discretionary authority of the executive with the Congressional power to certify election results to monopolize state power. As opposition to his government mounted, the president pursued a reformist agenda in alliance with the Communist Party that injected an ideological dimension into political conflict. Both the centralization of power and ideological warfare polarized political competition and upset the equilibrium upholding the political stability of the republic.

The Ruling Bloc Splits

Relationships between Calderón and his predecessor, Cortés, had never been ideal. Cortés had only reluctantly backed Calderón once he had extracted a commitment from Calderón to sponsor his bid to become president in 1944. Cortés attempted to maintain his political influence by leaving relatives and supporters in key state positions to ensure that the new president would not renege upon his promise.[24]

---

[23] O.s. no. 2 (2 May 1938), art. 2, Ibid, No. 100 (7 May 1938), p. 873.

[24] "Hard Political Bargain Driven by President Cortés with Dr. Calderón Guardia," Despatch No. 984 (27 November 1939), William Hornibrook to Secretary of State,

The PRN's unity was shattered on 1 May 1941 when the president and his legislative supporters refused to support the ex-president's son, Otto Cortés, in his bid to be reelected president of Congress. By a vote of thirty-two to thirteen, deputies elected Teodoro Picado of the PRN the new president of Congress, a post to which he was elected annually until 1944.[25] One by one, the president purged the remaining relatives and supporters of the former president from the government payroll.[26]

Having been shuffled out of positions of power, the *cortesista* faction retaliated. On 22 May 1941, Deputies Cortés and Francisco Urbina sponsored a Congressional motion requesting that the president explain whether it was true that he was participating in or condoning governmental corruption. They claimed that the president had sold captured German and Italian ships to his friends at a substantial discount. They argued that Calderón had personally profited from the illegal sale of Panamanian lottery tickets on national territory. And, they announced that the president ignored irregularities occurring in the ministry of public health.[27] *Cortesistas* also took aim on the secretary of the interior and public security, Francisco Calderón – the president's brother, chief advisor, and PRN party whip. They accused the regime of economic mismanagement that led to the rapid increase in the rate of inflation and the growing fiscal deficit.[28] As the breach between these factions widened,

USNA-DS 818.00/1591. Minister Hornibrook learned of this deal from "a close political friend of Dr. Calderón Guardia, in whom I have the utmost confidence." He does not disclose the name of his source.

[25] "Por 32 votos contra 13, triunfó la fórmula Picado Guardia y la reelección del resto del directorio del congreso, habiéndose producido un voto en blanco que se dio a la mayoría," *La Prensa Libre*, No. 12,329 (1 May 1941), pp. 1, 8.

[26] "Political," Despatch No. 3090 (19 April 1941), Dudley G. Dwyre to Secretary of State, USNA-DS 818.00/1636, pp. 3–4; "Political," Despatch No. 3112 (25 April 1941), Dudley G. Dwyre to Secretary of State, USNA-DS 818.00/1637, p. 2. The former president's relatives ultimately relieved of their government sinecures included Claudio Cortés (brother and manager of the Pacific Railway), Luís Fernández (brother-in-law and minister to Washington), Javier Cortés (son and consul general in New York), and Arturo Fernández (nephew and consul general in San Francisco).

[27] "Formulan sensacionales cargos al gobierno en el congreso los diputados Cortés Fernández y Urbina González," and the president's reply, "Mi protesta participa de justificada indignación," *Diario de Costa Rica*, No. 6,492 (23 May 1941), pp. 5, 8, 10, and pp. 1, 6. Representative Cortés Fernández and Urbina González's counterreply is "Olvidó el Señor Presidente de la República que vivíamos en un régimen donde los poderes supremos son libres," Ibid, No. 6,493 (24 May 1941), pp. 1, 5.

[28] The government was particularly sensitive to these attacks because the budget deficit was over 1 percent of GDP during most of the 1940s (and the government collected less than

stories began to circulate that Cortés was considering a run for the presidency in 1944.[29]

Social Reform and Coalitional Politics

As criticism mounted, the president counterattacked. To outshine his rival's electoral appeal, the president worked with the PRN majority in Congress to enact major social programs – projects that PRN leaders had been designing to meet the challenge posed by the steady growth of the Left since the mid-1930s.[30] In 1941, deputies approved the creation of the Social Security Institute, a pension and health care system for all salaried employees. Two years later, the PRN majority in Congress promulgated a Labor Code to regulate work practices and arbitrate disputes between and employers and workers. In the same year, it gave final approval to the incorporation of a set of social guarantees into the constitution.

Despite having condemned the government for fabricating votes in the 1942 midterm elections, the Communist Party endorsed the president's social reforms. Over the next year, the president and the Communist Party leader, Manuel Mora, began to make joint appearances at political rallies.[31] The gradual shift to the left was electorally attractive: according to

5 percent of GDP in the form of taxes). In 1942 and 1943, the deficit became 2.6 percent of GDP. Even in the worst years of the Great Depression, the budget deficit was 0.4 percent of GDP. The most thorough anti-calderonista attack on the economic problems of this period remains a special edition of the Center for the Study of National Problems (CEPN)'s journal, *Surco*, No. 47 (May–June 1944), dedicated to lambasting the behavior of Calderón's administration. Also, see *El ideario costarricense: resultado de una encuesta nacional* (San José: Editorial Surco, 1943), especially pp. 61–80. The best study of the Costa Rican economy during this period remains Rodrigo Facio, *La moneda y la banca central en Costa Rica* (San José: Editorial Costa Rica, 1973 [originally published by the Fondo de Cultura Económica in Mexico City in 1947]). Also, see Iván Molina, "Ciclo electoral y políticas públicas en Costa Rica (1890–1948)," *Revista Mexicana de Sociología*, Vol. 63, No. 3 (July–September 2001), pp. 67–98.

[29] "Political Conditions: Incidents Provoked between the Adherents of Cortés and Police Officials in Puntarenas," Despatch No. 1448 (1 March 1943), Robert M. Scotten to Secretary of State, USNA 818.00/1750, pp. 1–2; "Political Activity – Costa Rica (2 July 1943)," J. Edgar Hoover (Director, FBI) to Adolf A. Berle, Jr. (Assistant Secretary of State), USNA-DS 818.00/1779, pp. 1–2; "Recent Political Activity (30 August 1943)," J. Edgar Hoover to Adolf A. Berle, USNA-DS 818.00/1810, p. 3.

[30] Molina, "El desempeño electoral del Partido Comunista de Costa Rica (1931–1948)."

[31] *El otro Calderón Guardia*, interview with don Ivonne Clays Spoelder [Calderón's first wife] conducted by Guillermo Villegas Hoffmeister (San José: Casa Gráfica, 1985), pp. 45–7. Mora Valverde and Calderón's joint participation in political rallies is described in Gerardo Con-

U.S. diplomatic correspondence, the BOC could mobilize as many as 30,000 voters or 20 percent of the electorate.[32] In a Catholic country packed with small and medium-sized property holders and dominated by powerful export interests, Marxist platforms alienated many voters. Others, while not members of the BOC but sympathetic to its reformist goals, also became critical of the Communist Party for supporting a government they viewed as corrupt and dictatorial. A leading member of the CEPN estimated that the Left's alignment with the government lost it the support of approximately five thousand to six thousand votes.[33]

Some of the political disadvantages of an alliance with the Bloc were mitigated when delegates, attending the party's National Conference on 13 June 1943, voted in favor of dissolving the Bloc. In its place, they created a new, ostensibly non-Communist party dedicated to promoting progressive social legislation and unifying all anti-oligarchic and antifascist forces. The search for respectability received ecclesiastical blessing the next day when Archbishop Víctor Manuel Sanabria declared that members of the church could join the PVP without prejudicing their status as faithful Roman Catholics. Five months later, the PRN and the PVP formed the Victory Bloc, a coalition to support Congressional leader Picado's bid for the presidency.[34]

treras and José Manuel Cerdas, *Los años cuarenta: historia de una política de alianzas* (San José: Editorial Porvenir, 1988), pp. 82–99, and Eugene D. Miller, "Labour and the War-Time Alliance in Costa Rica, 1943–1948," *Journal of Latin American Studies*, Vol. 25, No. 3 (October 1993), pp. 515–41. Like much existing historiography on this relationship, Contreras and Cerdas suggest that Calderón went looking for the support of Left. For a different perspective, see Gustavo Adolfo Soto Valverde, *La Iglesia costarricense y la cuestión social: antecedentes, análisis y proyecciones de la reforma social costarricense de 1940–1943* (San José: EUNED, 1985), especially pp. 289–97. Lehoucq evaluate these claims and sides with Soto Valverde in his "Class Conflict, Political Crises and the Breakdown of Democratic Practices: Reassessing the Origins of the 1948 Civil War," *Journal of Latin American Studies*, Vol. 23, No. 1 (February 1991), pp. 37–60. For a discussion of the strategic benefits of this alliance for the PRN and the PVP, see Molina and Lehoucq, *Urnas de lo inesperado*, pp. 150–1, 156–62.

[32] "Political Pact Between Picado and Mora," USNA-DS 818.00/1886, p. 1. We believe this figure overestimates the true size of the Communist electorate by approximately ten thousand votes. See Molina, "El desempeño electoral del Partido Comunista."

[33] "Influence of Labor in Costa Rican Politics and the Social Legislation Resulting Therefrom," Despatch No. 1697 (21 April 1943), Leslie E. Reed to the Secretary of State, USNA-DS 818.00/1755, p. 4. The name of source is not revealed in this despatch.

[34] "Political Pact Between Picado and Mora," Despatch No. 653 (5 October 1943), Edward G. Trueblood to Secretary of State, USNA-DS 818.00/1886. Quotations from the pact in preceding sentences are taken from the Embassy's translation of the agreement, which is an appendix of this despatch. A copy of this agreement is reprinted in Fernando Soto Harrison, *Qué pasó en los años cuarenta* (San José: EUNED, 1991), pp. 67–9.

The political alignment begun two years earlier was complete. From being a bulwark of the PRN, Cortés had become the leader of the opposition grouped in the Democratic Party (PD). Deprived of his government connections, he ran a race against a candidate backed by an executive employing the resources at his disposal for partisan advantage. Calderón's espousal of social reform also put his rivals on the defensive. In response, the government's critics denounced his sponsorship of the Victory Bloc as a ploy typical of "caldero-comunismo," a label they employed to charge the government with having combined corruption, electoral fraud, and opportunism to install a bolshevik-tainted dictatorship in Costa Rica. By injecting an ideological dimension to a conflict between rival political factions as the Cold War was getting under way, the formation of a progressive alliance further polarized the struggle for state power.[35]

The Nature and Spatial Basis of Electoral Fraud

Between 1942 and 1946, parties submitted 291 accusations of fraud contained in fourteen petitions to Congress. Petitioners filed 86 percent (251 of 291) of these charges against government behavior in the 1946 midterm elections. Opposition parties did not file any petitions contesting Calderón's victory in 1940, when he obtained 84 percent of the popular vote.

Tables 5.8 and 5.9 indicate that the practice of fraud underwent a fundamental change by the mid-1940s. In previous decades, parties had disproportionately denounced their rivals for violating electoral laws in the periphery. By the mid-1940s, petitioners began to accuse their opponents of violating electoral laws in the central provinces, where over three-quarters of all voters lived. Of the thirty-eight accusations lodged in the aftermath of the 1944 elections, exactly two-thirds were distributed in the core Provinces of Alajuela, Heredia, and San José.

The 1946 midterm elections most starkly reveal this fundamental change in the geographic distribution of electoral fraud. Seventy percent of the 251 charges that opposition parties filed against the government concerned electoral results in the center. Furthermore, a whopping 16 percent consisted of accusations that the authorities had attempted to

---

[35] For more on the international context of these times, see Jacobo Schifter, *Las alianzas conflictivas: las relaciones entre Estados Unidos y Costa Rica desde la segunda guerra mundial a la guerra fría* (San José: Asociación Libro Libre, 1986).

Table 5.8. *Accusations of Electoral Fraud by Province, 1942–6*

Accusation	Category of Fraud	Center				Periphery			Total
		San José	Alajuela	Cartago	Heredia	Guanacaste	Puntarenas	Limón	
Against polling stations[a]	2	71	22	16	34	12	25	20	200
Official favoritism toward a party	2	6		1		1		1	9
Liquor distributed on election day	2	3		1		2	1		7
Nonofficial intimidation against voters	3		10						10
Official intimidation against voters	3	4			1	2	1		8
District electoral council acted illegally	3		1						1
Provincial electoral council acted illegally	3							1	1
Official coercion against voters	4	6			10	3	11	2	32
Official coercion against polling stations	4	4	9	1			1		15
Others[b]						2		1	3
Unspecified[b]		1				4			5
TOTAL		95	42	19	45	26	39	25	291

Notes:
[a] See Table 5.10.
[b] These cases did not apply in our classification.
Source: La Gaceta (1942–6).

183

Table 5.9. *Accusations of Electoral Fraud, by General and Midterm Elections, 1942–6*

Accusation	Category of Fraud	Midterm 1942	General 1944	Midterm 1946	Total
Against polling stations[a]	1		27	173	200
Official favoritism toward a party	2		1	8	9
Liquor distributed on election day	2		7		7
Nonofficial intimidation against voters	3		10		10
Official intimidation against voters	3		5	3	8
District electoral council acted illegally	3		1		1
Provincial electoral council acted illegally	3		1		1
Official coercion against voters	4		4	28	32
Official coercion against polling stations	4		1	14	15
Others[b]			3		3
Unspecified[b]		2		3	5
TOTAL		2	38	251	291

Notes:
[a] See Table 5.11.
[b] These cases did not apply in our classification.
Source: *La Gaceta* (1942–6).

coerce voters or polling stations. Such charges account for only 11 percent of all accusations between 1913 and 1923, and 7 percent between 1925 and 1938. And again, 64 percent (thirty of forty-seven) of these charges were leveled against authorities in the central provinces of the republic.

Not only did accusations of fraud become concentrated in the center, but parties began to denounce infractions of electoral laws at rates not seen since the first decades of the twentieth century. In the center, fraud became almost twice as common in the 1940s as it had been between 1925 and 1938. By the 1940s, there were 2,187 eligible voters in the center for every accusation of fraud – up from 3,790 eligible voters during the preceding period. In contrast, fraud became less commonplace in the periphery over time. From 659 eligible voters per accusation of electoral fraud between 1925 and 1938, rates increased to 1,655 eligible voters per accusation by the 1940s. So, even if parties committed and denounced acts of fraud more often in relative terms in outlying than in core provinces, long-term trends indicate that rates in the center were catching up with those of the periphery.

These figures also reveal that social structural and electoral laws still made the periphery into a place that encouraged parties to violate and to document acts of fraud at slightly higher levels than in the center. This was a product of the fact that citizens of the periphery lived in isolated, scattered hamlets and were more likely to be illiterate, ethnically discriminated against, and more economically dependent. Differences between center and periphery also stemmed from the fact that electoral laws led to more competitive races in the outlying provinces. While proportional representation distributed 90 percent of the seats in the center, 57 percent of the seats in the periphery went to parties that only had to out-poll their rivals. That annulling a small number of votes to pull out ahead of their opponents was easier in provinces that allocated seats principally through plurality rule meant that competition for votes would be stiffer in the periphery than the center. Once we control for the size of the electorate, in general elections there were 27,958 eligible voters per party in the center and 9,554 in the periphery. In midterm elections, there were 22,324 eligible voters per party in the center and 10,885 in the periphery. Though proportionally there were 1.5 local parties in the periphery for every one in the center, political polarization explains why local party formation diminished in midterm races (six parties in the center and three in the periphery), and also why fraud rates increased in the center.

Other characteristics of the petitions confirm that electoral fraud was becoming both worse and more widespread. Tables 5.10 and 5.11 reveal that 69 percent of the charges made in the 1944 and 1946 elections were lodged against polling stations. Unlike in previous years, charges of a procedural sort, such as the absence of relevant signatures, accounted for just 11 percent of all such accusations. This is a marked decline from the percentage of procedural violations contained in the petitions in preceding periods. Minor infractions of electoral law comprised 60 and 36 percent of all the accusations against polling stations between 1913 and 1923, and 1925 and 1938, respectively.

As the number of procedural violations of electoral law began to fall, petitions began to accuse polling station officials of increasingly serious offenses. A particularly colorful account of fraud reveals how the "caldero-communist" machine used the Pacific Railroad in the 1946 midterm

Table 5.10. *Accusations Against Polling Stations by Province, 1942–6*

Accusations	Category of Fraud	Center				Periphery			Total
		San José	Alajuela	Cartago	Heredia	Guanacaste	Puntarenas	Limón	
Technical or legal defects	1	13	2				3	3	21
Election held off schedule	2	6	2	2			9		19
Voting booth in inappropriate place	2	1				1			2
No voting held	2	1				1			2
Permitted substitution of voters	3	8	10	1	9	2	2	5	37
Party representative expelled or threatened	3	9	1	2	1	4	7	1	25
Number of votes was inflated	3	9		3	1		3	4	20
Number of ballots exceeds number of voters	3		1	2	11				14
Voting was public	3				9	3			12
Ballot box altered	3	5		2	2			1	10
Votes were annulled	3	7		1	1				9
ID retrieved by wrong person	3	4	2				1		7
Voters cast multiple ballots	3	1						5	6
Ballots were substituted	3	1	3						4
Nonauthorized persons tallied vote	3	4							4
Officials did not return pollbooks	3			3					3
Ballots stolen	3	1						1	2
Pollbooks released to nonauthorized persons	3		1						1
Inappropriate tally of absentee ballots	3	1							1
Pollbooks and ballots boxes opened ahead of schedule	3					1			1
TOTAL		71	22	16	34	12	25	20	200

Source: La Gaceta (1942–6).

Table 5.11. *Accusations against Polling Stations, by General and Midterm Election, 1942–6*

Accusations	Category of Fraud	Midterm 1942	General 1944	Midterm 1946	Total
Technical or legal defects	1		1	20	21
Election held off schedule	2		2	17	19
Voting booth in inappropriate place	2		1	1	2
No voting held	2		1	1	2
Permitted substitution of voters	3		5	32	37
Party representative expelled or threatened	3		10	15	25
Number of votes was inflated	3			20	20
Number of ballots exceeds number of voters	3			14	14
Voting was public	3			12	12
Ballot box altered	3		1	9	10
Votes were annulled	3			9	9
ID retrieved by wrong person	3		5	2	7
Voters cast multiple ballots	3			6	6
Ballots were substituted	3			4	4
Nonauthorized persons tallied vote	3			4	4
Officials did not return pollbooks	3			3	3
Ballots stolen	3			2	2
Pollbooks released to nonauthorized persons	3			1	1
Inappropriate tally of absentee ballots	3			1	1
Pollbooks and ballots boxes opened ahead of schedule	3		1		1
TOTAL			27	173	200

Source: *La Gaceta* (1942–6).

elections to stuff the ballot box. A large number of Railroad employees, "armed to the teeth and brandishing electoral identification cards that did not belong to them," disembarked from the train and demanded ballots with which to cast votes in the second polling station of San Rafael Este, a rural community near the City of Alajuela. Despite protests from opposition poll watchers, the president of the polling station furnished official ballots to these alleged voters who did not have photographic electoral identification cards or certificates proving that they were registered voters in other districts, since many of the identification cards they presented belonged to deceased or absent persons or voters from other districts.

In several polling stations in the central canton of the Province of Alajuela, opposition members protesting such behavior also were "confronted in a threatening manner by the visitors from the train, who identified themselves by the pressure they brought to bear on all those who opposed them and by the presence of their revolvers."[36]

Throughout the 1940s, parties continued spending their energy on amassing votes, not on reducing those of their rivals. On average, petitioners accused their rivals of illegally increasing their vote totals 74 percent more often than they accused rivals of undercutting the petitioners' vote totals. The only exception to this pattern is the 1944 election, where we can classify only a handful of the accusations on this basis. And, between 1913 and 1923, the share of accusations that impugned fifty or more votes was 32 percent, it decreased to 24 percent between 1925 and 1938, then increased to 41 percent in the 1944 and 1946 elections. Table 5.12 summarizes this information.

Most fraud occurred in rural areas. Even if there was a shift in fraudulent activity from the periphery to the center during the 1940s, the petitioners made nearly three-fourths of their accusations against acts that took place in the countryside. In the center, 73 percent of the charges concerned the behavior of officials and parties in rural areas. The remainder occurred in villages, and not one impugned acts committed in cities. Similarly, 78 percent of the acts occurring in the periphery took place in rural areas. Only 20 and 2 percent claimed that officials and parties perpetuated fraud in villages and cities, respectively.[37] Electoral fraud took place, simply put, where most voters lived.

Electoral Fraud and Institutional Controls

Whether fraud was any more decisive to election in the 1940s is a question that lurks in the background of all efforts to make sense of the most controversial period in Costa Rican politics. According to the opposition,

---

[36] "Demanda de nulidad de la Provincia de Alajuela: Cantones Central, de Orotina y de Atenas (21 February 1946)," Ibid, p. 383.

[37] Iván Molina, "Fraude local y política nacional. El caso de Costa Rica (1901–1948)," *Cuadernos de Historia* (Santiago, Chile), No. 17 (December 1997), pp. 235–7.

Table 5.12. *Accusations of Fraud, Classified by Whether They Increased or Decreased Vote Totals, 1942–6*

Province	+	−	Election	+	−	Impugned Votes	+	−
Center								
San José	39	17	1940			1–9		1
Alajuela	28	7	1942			10–49	19	7
Cartago	6	4	1944	7	9	50–99	7	3
Heredia	41	2	1946	156	33	100–499	6	3
			1948			500–999		
						1000+		
Periphery								
Guanacaste	11	3						
Puntarenas	20	4						
Limón	18	1						
TOTAL	163	42	TOTAL	163	42	TOTAL*a*	32	14

Note:
a The totals are not equivalent because accusations did not always indicate the number of impugned votes.
Source: *La Gaceta* (1942–6).

the practice of electoral fraud rose to unprecedented heights during these years. Indeed, their opponents claim that Calderón and Picado succeeded in retaining control of the state precisely because the "caldero-communists" fabricated votes on a scale never seen before in the republic.

Government critics are certainly correct to point out that fraud became qualitatively more severe in the 1940s. According to our four-point classification of acts of fraud, categories three and four account for 78 percent of the accusations account made between 1944 and 1946. These are acts that are manifestly aimed at changing election results illegally and involve the coercion of voters and opposition poll watchers. And, for the first time since the turn of the century, the worst types of fraud accounted for a greater share of the center's accusations (81 percent) than those of the periphery (73 percent). In the outlying provinces of the republic, 72 percent of all charges consist of the two worst types of fraud.

As in earlier periods, the opposition failed to persuade Congress that fraud had robbed it of electoral victories. The Credentials Committee unanimously rejected the fourteen petitions filed between 1942 and 1946. It justified its action by claiming that the petitions did not muster enough evidence to support their allegations or because accepting these charges would not have altered presidential election results or distribution of legislative seats. That the PRN and PVP dominated these committees naturally makes their recommendations suspect. Of the three committees in existence during this period, eight members belonged to the PRN and one to the PVP. None belonged to any of the opposition parties.[38]

A closer look at the petitions, however, reveals that fraud could not have been responsible for the opposition's defeat in the 1942 midterm and 1944 general elections. The petitions filed against the 1942 elections questioned the validity of votes at less than 1 percent of all polling stations. In aggregate terms, however, government forces amassed slightly more than 45 percent more votes than opposition candidates. After the 1944 elections, the opposition impugned the results at 9 percent (or 30 of 324) of all polling stations.[39] Even if we assume that all votes cast at these stations were fraudulent, the Victory Bloc's presidential candidate obtained more than twice as many votes (or 90,403 compared to 46,403 votes) as the opposition leader. Interestingly, in the months before the election, the PRN predicted that it would attract the support of 77,500 voters and that its opponents would receive 42,500 votes. Though the PRN underestimated turnout, it did correctly forecast that the government would receive 65 to the opposition's 35 percent share of the valid vote – which is, quite remarkably, within 1 percent of the actual shares of the vote obtained by each party![40]

The opposition allegations regarding results in the 1946 midterm elections are somewhat more credible, but still do not alter overall election results. The PD and other opposition parties impugned the results at 10 percent (or 85 of 857) of all polling stations. Though the share of questioned polling stations remains smaller than the government's 14-point margin of victory (56 to 42 percent), it does raise the possibility that the PRN and PVP succeeded in electing at least several more representa-

---

[38] Iván Molina, "La Comisión de Credenciales y Renuncias del Congreso.
[39] "Dictamen de la Comisión de Credenciales y Renuncias (1 March 1944)," *La Gaceta*, No. 53 (4 March 1944), pp. 365–6. The members of the committee were Julio Muñoz Fonseca (PRN), Pablo Mercedes Rodríguez Rodríguez (PRN), and Ramón Leiva Cubillo (PRN).
[40] Data cited in Fabrice Lehoucq, "The Origins of Democracy in Costa Rica in Comparative Perspective," p. 191.

tives than they would have legitimately elected.[41] Yet, the distribution of legislative seats remains basically unchanged by comparing the number of votes alleged to be fraudulent in each province – the level at which Congressional seats are distributed – with the PRN or the PVP's margin of victory. Opposition charges possess more validity only in Guanacaste, where it had succeeded in attracting 2,438 votes – just eleven votes short of having captured one of the four legislative seats available in this province. At most, the opposition could have elected ten instead of the nine representatives it actually did win in the 1946 midterm elections. [42]

Conclusion

The establishment of the secret franchise did change the behavior of parties. No longer able to monitor the behavior of "their" voters, parties began to resort to increasingly blatant acts of fraud to win highly competitive elections. Both in the center and the periphery, infractions of electoral laws got worse. After the mid-1920s, parties went from largely accusing their adversaries of procedural violations of the law to charging them with intimidating voters, preventing party representatives from observing polling station deliberations, and stealing ballots. By the 1930s, these and similar types of acts account for more than 50 percent of the charges found in the petitions and related legal material.

Institutional change explains why blatant acts of fraud increased as a share of all accusations of fraud. Without the running tally of the vote that the public franchise made possible, parties could no longer accuse polling station officials of committing minor infractions of electoral law. Furthermore, the secret franchise left parties with few alternatives but, quite literally, to stuff the ballot box. Indeed, parties went to great lengths to retain control of the distribution of paper ballots during the mid-1920s precisely because creating safeguards for voters would undermine their ability to manipulate events on election day for partisan advantage.

---

[41] These percentages are based upon the final tally of 100,502 votes reached by the GCE. The GCE annulled 2,637 votes during the tally of the vote it conducted with Provincial Electoral Councils. Over two-thirds of these votes belonged to the PRN and the PVP, and 26 percent were deposited in favor of the PD. Provincial-level parties lost the remaining 1 percent of votes. Molina and Lehoucq, *Urnas de lo inesperado*, p. 175.

[42] This summarizes a more extensive discussion found in Lehoucq, "The Origins of Democracy in Costa Rica in Comparative Perspective," pp. 252–5.

Paradoxically enough, though, reform did reduce overall rates of fraud. Even if fraud was becoming more blatant, it was becoming less common once we control for the fact that the size of the electorate was constantly expanding. Between 1928 and 1946, rates of fraud fell by one-half in relation to the period between 1901 and 1925. Decline in accusations of fraud was a product of the fact that, by the mid-1930s, the PRN was winning elections by margins sufficiently large enough to discourage its opponents from claiming that fraud was responsible for their defeat.

As in previous periods, the periphery accounted for close to one-half of the accusations of fraud, though it housed only about a quarter of the electorate. A more illiterate, economically dependent population living in isolated settlements created a society less able to defend itself from assaults on its liberties. Spatial differences in the distribution of the electorate (fewer voters in the periphery than in the center) also explains why institutional arrangements encouraged parties to behave differently in core and outlying provinces. Simply put, because plurality formulae apportioned over half the periphery's legislative seats, parties were encouraged to discredit the votes of their rivals. In the center, by contrast, the use of proportional representation to allocate Congressional seats discouraged parties from filing petitions because it required impugning enough votes to obtain the quotient necessary to elect another representative. That the probability that parties could censure enough votes to win an additional legislative seat in the periphery was typically greater than in core provinces generated a markedly more competitive environment precisely where voters were more rural, illiterate, and economically disadvantaged.

Perhaps our most important finding in this chapter is that, by the 1940s, the polarization of political competition redistributed fraud from the periphery to the center. Although formerly this region where less than one-half of all accusations of electoral fraud took place, the center began to account for more than two-thirds of all infractions of electoral law. Even if, in relation to the regions' respective numbers of voters, rates of fraud were still somewhat higher in the periphery than the center during the 1940s (1,655 compared to 2,187 eligible voters per accusation), the center witnessed a dramatic increase in the incidence of fraud from the previous ten-year period. In comparison with the period between 1927 and 1938, accusations of fraud became almost twice as common in the center during the 1940s. Over the same periods, fraud became nearly three times less frequent in the periphery.

Conclusion

National-level political dynamics began to fuel the increase in the frequency and intensity of fraudulent activity in the center during the 1940s. Once the regime's popularity began to wane, the PRN-PVP alliance employed the powers of the executive to prevent the opposition from increasing its Congressional representation and from electing its candidate to the presidency. Based upon our analysis of the petitions to nullify electoral results, however, it is unlikely that officially sanctioned fraud was responsible for the Bloc's continuation in power during the 1940s. That the Bloc's margin of victory was always greater than the share of impugned polling stations indicates that the opposition's charges of widespread fraud were probably exaggerated – though understandably so, as we suggest below.

Two factors help explain why this decade has become known as one of the most infamous and fraud-ridden in Costa Rican politics. First, the petitions increasingly began to denounce blatantly coercive acts of fraud. As we argue in this chapter, this trend was a product, paradoxically enough, of the institutional innovations of the mid-1920s as well as of national-level political polarization. Even if electoral misconduct, at the aggregate level, was becoming less common with time, it was becoming more flagrant and therefore apparent to all. Second, violations of electoral law could not but become the main topic of political discourse once the more literate and tightly linked communities of the center became targets of officially sponsored acts of fraud.

Despite well-documented and widely propagated opposition claims, we conclude that electoral fraud was not responsible for the PRN and PVP's success at winning elections during the 1940s. Though the size of progovernment majorities declined with time, they were sufficiently large to win election after election. The PRN-PVP's margin of victory always exceeded the share of votes said to be fraudulent. Despite its increasing popularity and its ever more detailed denunciations of fraud, the opposition was still unable wrest control of the state from the PRN and the PVP. Election results indicate that the Credentials Committee and Congress did not act unreasonably by rejecting petitions, even if the PRN and PVP found it in their partisan interests to do so.

No matter who really won these elections, a system of laws that facilitated the rigging of the ballot box worked to no one's advantage. The laws obviously helped to reduce the opposition's electoral performance. Most important, elections robbed the progovernment coalition of the legitimacy that victory at the polls conferred. For, despite the coalition's triumph, accusations of fraud tarnished its mandate. This was the ultimate cost of a fraud-ridden republican system: It could so muddle the verdict of the ballot box that not even winners could reap the rewards of what was a highly questioned victory.

6

Political Polarization, Electoral Reform,
and Civil War, 1946–9

Introduction

Amid charges of fraud, the Victory Bloc won the 1944 elections. To the opposition, Teodoro Picado's election to the presidency was an imposition orchestrated from the heights of power. To progovernment forces, Picado's victory was the product of a well-organized campaign that had successfully won the support of an electoral majority. The immediate consequence of an ambiguous election was to foment the development of both pro- and antigovernment hardliners. PRN and PVP sectors began to organize efforts to retain control, whatever the price, of state power. The opposition fragmented as parties excluded from the political arena began to plot the government's overthrow.[1]

As the mid-1920s, circumstances did not bode well for electoral reform. Indeed, the political crisis was much worse: Though opposition forces

---

[1] Since Picado's election to the presidency, rumors had been circulating that different individuals were organizing insurrections against the government. It was rumored that Manuel Quesada – the leader of a military revolt against the government after he lost the 1932 presidential election ("Bellavistazo") – was said to planning a coup. Fernando Castro – a wealthy coffee grower and lawyer for the United Fruit Company – was simultaneously involved in talks with the government as he met with other hardliners to discuss the possibility of sponsoring a revolt against Picado. And, it was no secret that José Figueres, an enemy of Rafael Ángel Calderón Guardia's, was organizing a clandestine effort to bring down the government. Figueres had been exiled by Calderón in 1942 after publicly denouncing governmental corruption on the radio. He doubted that the regime would ever willingly relinquish control of the state, especially since his election to Congress had been so flagrantly invalidated by electoral officials. Plots against the government were carefully monitored by the U.S. Embassy. See "Transmitting Report Prepared by Livingston D. Watrous, 'Review of Administration of President Picado,'" Despatch No. 298 (12 April 1945), Hallet Johnson to the Secretary of State, U.S. National Archives (hereafter cited as USNA) DS 818.00/4–1245.

questioned the legitimacy of the government in both periods, only the 1940s witnessed the development of an opposition faction dedicated to overthrowing the government through the use of force. Furthermore, unlike President Ricardo Jiménez, Picado could not count upon the PRN or the PVP's undivided support. Most PRN deputies remained loyal to *calderonista* faction of the party (henceforth cited as PRNc).

Despite these constraints, theory suggests that reformers held several advantages. First, opposition deputies would be favorably disposed toward reform. In line with office-seeking perspectives, they had an interest in change that promised to redistribute state power from pro- to antigovernment forces. Second, the constitutional prohibition against running for consecutive reelection encouraged the president to think about his long-term career prospects. Third, the possibilities for enacting long-term democratic reforms actually brightened because no party could single-handedly torpedo bills that threatened its domination of Congress. Like in the mid-1920s, a split legislature created the opportunity for a president to use the power of the veto to pivot between parties and to amplify the president's political influence. Unless deputies supported enough of the president's proposals, the executive could retaliate by vetoing bills Congressional rivals favored. Finally, the existence of a political crisis compelled Picado to exploit these opportunities for reform. Regardless of how he felt about institutional change, the inability to forge a consensus with opposition moderates only increased the probability that they would support a hardline insurrection against his regime. A combination of institutional incentives, public demand for reform, and a simmering political crisis therefore served to fuse the president's short-term interest in political survival with his long-term interests in returning to high office.

In this chapter, we also explore why far-reaching institutional changes, contrary to expectations, did not thwart the polarization of electoral competition. A series of contingent events succeeded in undermining the fragile consensus in favor of reform and turned the 1948 presidential race into the acrimonious, violence-tainted affair for which it is known. We therefore explain how opposition hardliners hijacked political competition and thereby outflanked the moderates who had the most to gain from the peace necessary to expand their already significant share of state power.

The first section of this chapter presents an overview of Picado's reform bill. The next section analyzes the impact of legislative alignments on the possibility for enacting far-reaching changes. The chapter then turns to evaluating the ability of three models of institutional change to explain support and opposition to 1946 reform bill. We then explore why passage of the Electoral Code, the principal achievement of pro- and antigovernment moderates, stabilized political competition for only a short period of time. The chapter explains why institutional arrangements encouraged government and opposition hardliners to polarize the race for the presidency. We suggest that there are good reasons to believe that the opposition may have cooked the Electoral Registry to ensure a victory for its candidate, Otilio Ulate, over the PRN leader, Rafael Ángel Calderón Guardia. The chapter concludes by reviewing the outcome of the 1948 civil war and the 1949 Constituent Assembly's decision to expand the reach of the 1946 Electoral Code.

Regime Survival and Electoral Reform

President Picado found himself in a rather unpleasant strategic dilemma. Doing nothing promised to promote the coalescence of opposition moderates and hardliners and further destabilize politics. Fashioning a deal with opposition centrists could prove that the benefits of cooperating were greater than confronting the government. Reaching out to his opponents, however, promised to alienate supporters. As office-seeking theories suggest, progovernment forces had no interest in reform because credible legal changes promised to reduce their share of state power.

Perhaps the president could, as institutionalist models suggest, pivot between government and opposition deputies to reform electoral laws. Negotiating with the opposition would demonstrate that he was not beholden to the progovernment alliance. Working with the PD would also defuse political tensions by depriving antigovernment hardliners of the support of opposition moderates. Given opposition distrust of the government, however, Picado had to commit himself to a far-reaching set of changes. How could he do this and take along enough progovernment deputies?

The Production and Scope of the Reform Bill

As part of a broader strategy to stabilize political competition, Interior Secretary Fernando Soto was quietly taking steps to produce a reform bill. In early 1945, he obtained the cooperation of a distinguished group of jurists to draft a law for a new electoral registry. Their bill called for a Civic Registry purged of the names of dead or nonexistent citizens and with distributing photographic identification cards to all registered voters.[2] In response to the interior secretary's recommendations, the president of Congress selected three deputies to form a Special Reform Committee. It consisted of Deputies Víctor Manuel Elizondo (PD), Francisco Fonseca (PRN), and Luis Carballo (PVP). For unknown reasons, Elizondo resigned from the committee in early January 1945. The legislative president selected Juan Rodríguez (a PRN independent) to fill Elizondo's place.[3]

With two exceptions, the Special Committee's draft project did not aim to alter the closed-list, largely proportional representational system of electoral laws.[4] Under prevailing electoral laws, only parties in the provinces sending three or more representatives to Congress that achieved what was called a quotient – a figure produced by dividing the total number of popular votes by contested legislative seats – could obtain leftover Congressional posts for which no party had a quotient. Existing laws excluded parties that failed to obtain a quotient from competing for left-over legislative seats (*el sistema de arrastre*), even if their vote totals were greater than the residual number of votes held by larger parties. Under the proposed Electoral Code, however, minority as well as majority parties in each province with the largest number of votes and at least 75 percent of a quotient could try to obtain unaccounted seats.[5]

The proposed law mainly aimed to eliminate the president's discretionary authority in electoral matters. It stripped him of the ability to

---

[2] See "Para garantizar la pureza del sufragio, la Secretaría de Gobernación envió ayer un proyecto al Congreso," *La Tribuna*, No. 7,330 (16 March 1945), pp. 1, 5, which contains a statement by the interior secretary and the Congress Special Reform Committee's introductory remarks on its draft project, p. 7. Known for their political neutrality, the jurists who prepared that bill were Supreme Court Magistrates Víctor Guardia, José María Vargas, and Alfredo Zúñiga. An incomplete version of the latter is contained in Soto's insightful political memoirs, *Qué pasó en los años cuarenta* (San José: EUNED, 1991), pp. 197–206. The complete text of what was called the Organic Law of the Civic Registry was published in Ibid, No. 7,332 (18 March 1945), pp. 12–3.

[3] E.s No. 66 (11 January 1945), art. 2, *La Gaceta*, No. 15 (21 January 1945), p. 190.

[4] "Proyecto (28 June 1945)," Ibid, No. 155 (12 July 1945), pp. 1160–75.

[5] This system is known as the largest remainders system of proportional representation. By mid-1947, PVP deputies succeeded in enacting a law lowering this threshold to 50 percent. See "Ley No. 1096 (27 August 1947)," *Colección de Leyes y Decretos* (San José: Imprenta Nacional 1947).

manipulate the executive's powers of appointment and of adjudication. It transferred both to the newly created National Electoral Tribunal (TNE), an institution modeled upon the weaker Grand Electoral Council (GCE). Unlike the GCE, the TNE would have its three members and alternates selected by each branch of government. Among its responsibilities, the TNE chose the members of Provincial Electoral Councils and was entrusted with arbitrating conflicts about the interpretation of electoral law. Most importantly, the TNE was responsible for issuing a provisional verdict of electoral results. Congress, however, retained the authority to certify election results in an extraordinary session convened for this purpose.

To ensure that incumbents did not possess an unfair advantage, the Electoral Code empowered registered parties to name poll watchers during every phase of the electoral process. Poll watchers could supervise the registration of voters, the printing of ballots, and, most importantly, the initial tally of the vote conducted at each polling station. To prevent any individual from voting more than once on election day, the Electoral Code also advocated the suppression of absentee ballots (*votos a computar*). Historically, these ballots accounted for, at most, 0.5 of all votes. In the 1942 and 1944 elections, however, they increased to 4.2 and 2.7 percent of all votes, respectively – fueling opposition claims that the PRN-dominated government was using every means available to maintain itself in power.[6] The reform bill even called for eliminating the ability of public servants to vote if they found themselves outside their home districts on election day. It also included an amended draft law for a new electoral registry that Supreme Court magistrates had presented to Congress on 15 March 1945.

Legislative Alignments and Strategic Possibilities

In the 1944–6 Congress, the PRN held 65 percent (or thirty of forty-six) of legislative seats. Most of these, or 41 percent of the total number of deputies, were loyal to former President Calderón. The remaining 11 percent of PRN deputies were either followers of the president or inde-pendents. Finally, one PRN deputy was a self-declared supporter of León

---

[6] Iván Molina and Fabrice Lehoucq, *Urnas de lo inesperado: fraude electoral y lucha política en Costa Rica (1901–1948)* (San José: EUCR, 1999), p. 180 (note 15).

Cortés, reflecting the fact that the former president once led the party Calderón now largely controlled.[7]

In line with office-seeking theories of institutional reform, most PRN legislators did not want to reform electoral laws. As the majority party, they opposed efforts that endangered their party's control of the executive and legislative branches of government. That midterm elections were to be held in February 1946 only reinforced their trepidation about tinkering with electoral legislation.

Office-seeking theories also predicted that the thirteen opposition deputies would support the reform bill. Like the PRN *cortesista* renegade, they too would likely endorse a bill that increased their ability to gain control of the executive and legislative branches of government. These theories also explain why the four PVP deputies, even as members of the governing coalition, did come out in support of the reform bill. Under an effective set of electoral safeguards, the PVP could expect to increase its share of legislative seats because it, like any other electoral minority, could henceforth compete for residual seats.

Yet office-seeking theories cannot explain why the president would float a bill of reforms that promised to increase the uncertainty of electoral outcomes. As titular leader of the PRN, he could not benefit from a set of reforms that threatened to redistribute Congressional power from pro- to antigovernment parties. If the opposition gained control of Congress, it would complicate the tasking of obtaining approval of his policies. Moreover, if the PRN lost its Congressional majority, the PD would hold the power of accepting the validity of the 1948 election results. Not surprisingly, the potential loss of executive and legislative power unsettled PRN leaders.

There are several reasons why Picado might reform electoral laws. First, he was not a machine politician. He had only served in Congress for one term before running for president. Indeed, Picado was known as a politically ambitious man of letters whose reputation the 1944 elections had sullied. As sociological theories suggest, Picado might make politically counterintuitive decisions because he was not a short-sighted party hack.

---

[7] "Composition of Costa Rican Congress," Despatch No. 583 (5 June 1945), Hallet Johnson to Secretary of State, USNA-DS 818.00/6–545, and "Political," Despatch No. 1737 (7 August 1944), Rufus H. Lane, Jr., to Secretary of State, USNA-DS 818.00/8–744, p. 2. Discipline in PRN*c* was maintained by the ex-president's brother, Francisco Calderón, who continued to serve as campaign manager, chief political advisor, and principal whip of the *calderonista* faction of the party.

Second, the constitutional prohibition against consecutive reelection did generate incentives for Picado at least to consider the long-term benefits of becoming identified as a political reformer. Whatever he did, he was out of the presidency in 1948. Perhaps, though, Picado could build a reputation as a reformer whom the electorate would remember in the future.

The absence of a stable Congressional majority also provided the president with an opportunity to advance institutional reform. That all legislation required the president's approval unless two-thirds of all deputies voted to override an executive veto turned Picado into a pivotal player in politics. None other than the politically ambitious Interior Secretary Soto was advising the president to allow his adversaries to win the 1946 midterm elections as part of a broader strategy to have the government break free of the PRNc. As he explained to the U.S. ambassador, "it would be better for the [president] and for the country should the opposition win the Congressional elections, since otherwise Picado would become the stooge of the Calderons and of [Manuel] Mora." If, on the other hand, "the opposition should control Congress, Picado could play one party off against the other."[8]

Fighting the PRN leadership over a key piece of legislation, however, was risky. The president could both fail to get a reform bill passed through Congress and become branded as a party traitor. His efforts would fail unless the president had the support of the PD (36 percent of the deputies), the PVP (12 percent), and, most crucially, at least some of the PRN independents (11 percent). Though electoral interests encouraged the PD and PVP to back institutional reform, the support of PRN independents was uncertain. As members of the majority, they held an interest in maintaining the PRN's political hegemony. Yet, as independents or followers of the president, Picado could persuade the PRN independents to back a series of reforms that promised to stabilize political competition.

Killer Amendments and Their Outcomes: The Pressure Mounts

Soon after the Special Committee presented its bill to Congress, PRNc deputies presented 76 percent of the 134 amendments that representatives

---

[8] "Proferred Resignation of Secretary of Government Not Accepted; Question of Free Elections to the Forefront in Increasingly Disturbed Political Situation," Despatch No. 1243 (19 November 1945), Hallett Johnson to Secretary of State, USNA-DS 818.002/ 11–1945 CS/VJ, p. 3. Soto threaten to resign unless certain guarantees were in place for the 1946 midterm elections. This will be discussed in greater detail later in this chapter.

submitted to the Special Committee regarding the bill.[9] Two amendments were particularly threatening to the reform bill: One consisted of the reinstatement of public voting, and the other called for extending voting rights to women. If approved, these amendments promised to sink the bill, either by triggering a presidential veto or the formation of a coalition to oppose them.

PRN*c* Representative Pablo Rodríguez called for the reinstatement of the public franchise. Joined by PRN independent Deputy José María Pinaud, Pablo Rodríguez defended the superiority of the public over the secret franchise. Both pointed out that public balloting did not prevent parties from mobilizing majorities against unpopular presidents in the past. Like other proponents of the public franchise, Pinaud contended that the secret ballot had robbed citizens of "their morality and civic virility." In short, argued Pinaud,

The secret ballot is the result of the most shameful farce, the worst farce against democracy. It is a lie that the secret ballot is secret; it has been established that it is violated by removing a plank, creating a crevice, or by looking at the voter through a window to indicate, during the hour when he is to deposit his vote, for whom he should vote.[10]

Deputy Juan Rodríguez, one of the authors of the reform bill, responded by pointing out that fraud did not stem from the secret franchise. Instead, it was a product of the loopholes in electoral law that the reform bill promised to close. PD Deputy Jorge Ortiz echoed his arguments. He disagreed that "... a man arrives at the ballot box happier, feeling more free, and appears to be more valiant with the public vote." "This may be very pretty to say," Ortiz claimed, but

What is real is that our peasants are subject to many circumstances of an economic character that all men of government should understand. When these peasants are free of debts and other economic obligations with their employers, then it would be a good idea to have the public ballot.[11]

---

[9] They were published in *La Gaceta*, Nos. 174–6 (4, 5, and 6 August 1945), pp. 1351–2, 1357–8, and 1365.

[10] E.s. no. 7 (26 September 1945), art. 4, Ibid, No. 225 (7 October 1945), p. 1765. The previous quotation appears in e.s. no. 8 (27 September 1945), art. 4, Ibid, No. 227 (10 October 1945), p. 1777.

[11] E.s. no. 10 (1 October 1945), art. 4, Ibid, No. 228 (11 October 1945), p. 1786. Deputy Juan Rodríguez's arguments appear in e.s. no. 7, pp. 1765–6.

Table 6.1. *Roll-Call Votes on Reestablishing the Public Franchise, 1945*

First Ballot					
Vote on the Amendment[a]	Party Affiliation				Total
	PD	PRN*c*	PRN*i*	PVP	
In favor	4	14	3		21
Against	5	6	2	4	17
TOTAL	9	20	5	4	38
Second Ballot					
Vote on the Amendment[a]	Party Affiliation				Total
	PD	PRN*c*	PRN*i*	PVP	
In favor	5	13	3		21
Against	8	8	2	5	23
TOTAL	13	21	5	5	44

Note:
[a] With three Degrees of Freedom, the chi-square result for the first vote is 7.169 (Asymp. Sig [2-sided] = .067). Six cells have expected counts of less than 5 (the minimum expected count is 1.79). For the second vote, the chi-square result is 7.006 (Asymp. Sig. [2-sided] = .072). Four cells have an expected count of less than 5. The minimum expected count is 2.39.

Sources: For party affiliations, see "Composition of Costa Rican Congress," Despatch No. 583 (5 June 1945), Hallet Johnson to Secretary of State, USNA-DS 818.00/6-545. For the votes, see e.s. nos. 10 and 11 (1 and 2 October 1945), arts. 4 and 3, *La Gaceta*, Nos. 228–9 (11–2 October 1945), pp. 1786, 1794.

On 1 October, deputies voted twenty-one to seventeen to repeal the secret franchise. In line with office-seeking perspectives, 70 percent of PRN deputies voted in favor of the killer amendment. Electoral interests also persuaded the PVP to override its interests as a member of the governing coalition. By rejecting a bill that promised to increase its share of legislative seats, the PVP demonstrated its independence as well as its distrust of the PRN*c*. These results, which are significant at the .07 level, indicate the partisanship was an important force behind the behavior of representatives on this issue (see Table 6.1).

Yet, these results do indicate that some parties did not behave in accordance with office-seeking perspectives on institutional change. Both PRN independents and opposition representatives could not speak with one voice on the reform bill. Though three of the five PRN independents voted for the bill, two found the ties of party loyalty too binding to ignore. Curiously, five of the nine PD deputies actually voted in favor of reinstating the public franchise – an action that came dangerously close to prompting a presidential veto. Perhaps they, like PRN independent Pinaud, believed that the secret franchise had succeeded only in concealing – and not eradicating – ballot-rigging. Though the incidence of fraud declined after parties effectively dismantled the secret franchise in the mid-1920s, our analysis does reveal that parties resorted to increasingly blatant acts of fraud with time. So, while Pinaud's assessment is not entirely accurate, it does possess more than a grain of truth to it. According to Manual Mora, the PVP leader, PD hardliners wanted the president to veto the reform bill to prevent the reapproachment among pro- and antigovernment moderates. By sabotaging the president's effort to reform electoral laws, Mora suggested, PD deputies could demonstrate the government's inability to resolve its dispute with the opposition.[12]

Hoping to reverse the decision to reinstate the public franchise, PRN independent Deputy Juan Rodríguez called for a revote. In twenty-four hours, both sides on the issue of reform mobilized their legislative supports. By a twenty-three to twenty-two majority, reformers barely defeated the effort to load the reform bill with a killer amendment. The forces in favor of the reform bill eked out a victory by out-mobilizing their rivals. None of the deputies who voted on the prior day switched their vote. Of the four deputies who did not appear for the second vote, three were members of the PRN backing the reinstatement of the public ballot. Of the ten new deputies who came on 2 October, seven supported the secret franchise and three did not.[13] Table 6.1 presents these results.

Chi-square results indicate that partisanship shaped representative's decisions. Again, all PVP deputies voted against reestablishing the public franchise. Sixty-two percent of the PRN*c* deputies voted in favor of repealing the secret franchise. About the same proportion of PRN independents supported the killer amendment, indicating that they were no more willing to listen to the president's call for compromise than the *calderonistas*. On

---

[12] E.s. no. 11 (2 October 1945), art. 3, Ibid, No. 229 (12 October 1945), p. 794.
[13] In a series of conversations Lehoucq held with Fernando Soto, the secretary of the interior during this time period and a principal backer of reform, Mr. Soto made this point. These interviews took place in San José during February 1996 in Mr. Soto's home.

this occasion, however, most PD deputies voted to maintain the secret franchise. As predicted by office-seeking theories of reform, opposition deputies voted against loading the president's bill with an amendment that would only set back the cause of reform. Twenty-four hours apparently was enough time for most PD representatives to discover that fair elections would permit them to expand their numbers in Congress and possibly to win the 1948 presidential elections.

After barely defeating the effort to repeal the secret franchise, reformist deputies faced another PRN*c* killer amendment. Again, PRN*c* Deputy Pablo Rodríguez was the author of an amendment recommending that women be granted suffrage rights. Some representatives claimed that enfranchising women required only a change in law, as the constitution did not explicitly grant citizenship rights only to men. Other deputies argued that this reform required a constitutional amendment. As *La Prensa Libre* noted, a group of deputies was pushing to grant women voting rights as a way to force the president to veto the bill on constitutional grounds. Finally, deputies agreed to postpone debate on the matter by soliciting the expert opinion of the College of Lawyers.[14]

The board of directors of the College of Lawyers issued an opinion that helped the cause of reform even as it argued that suffrage rights for women could be effected only through constitutional reform – a change that required approval of two-thirds of all deputies in two different sessions of the legislature. While the board expressed sympathy for such a change, it contended that a "historical" interpretation of citizenship rights suggested that the authors of the 1871 constitution believed only men were entitled to choose public officials. Fully aware of the politically charged atmosphere surrounding the issue, the board also pointed out that

Relying upon a constitutional interpretation to extend the vote to women and basing it upon ordinary law would be to establish, for the future, a situation of complete insecurity. . . . It could be abrogated at any moment by the simple procedures that exist for abrogating laws or by annulling elections, given political alignments prevailing in Congress in particular circumstances.[15]

---

[14] "Maniobra política para que la nueva Ley Electoral sea vetada por el Ejecutivo," *La Prensa Libre*, No. 13,524 (21 September 1945), pp. 1, 3. The decision to approach the College of Lawyers was made during e.s. no. 6 (25 September 1945), art. 6, *La Gaceta*, No. 222 (4 October 1945), p. 1743.

[15] "Informe dado por la Junta Directiva del Colegio de Abogados sobre la consulta que el Congreso Constitucional le hicera en relación con el voto femenino (8 October 1945)," Ibid, No. 229 (12 October 1945), p. 1797.

The effect of this opinion was to put those in favor of reform in the paradoxical position of opposing suffrage rights for women if they did not want to scuttle approval of the Electoral Code. According to *La Prensa Libre* reporters, most deputies in favor of the progressive-sounding amendment were members of the PRN majority. For, unlike in the mid-1920s, no feminist movement was clamoring for extending voting rights to women, even if prominent legal experts, like Marco Tulio Zeledón, disagreed with the board of directors' "historical" opinion. Like other proponents of female franchise rights, he reminded everyone that the constitution did not refer to men, but only to citizens.[16]

Dissent with the board of directors did not reenergize antireform forces. The conservative, if controversial, legal opinion silenced amendment supporters. Congress kept postponing debate of the amendment until it simply disappeared from the congressional agenda. According to an informal poll taken among representatives in mid-October, *La Prensa Libre* reported that little support existed for extending voting rights to women.[17]

Debate, Delay, and Compromise

Having been beaten on several key votes, the PRN*c* turned to weakening the reform bill. By insisting upon discussion of all of the amendments, the PRN*c* also sought to delay enactment of the Electoral Code. The party's actions provoked another series of skirmishes threatening to sink the reform bill.

---

[16] Professor Zeledón, of the Liceo de Costa Rica, offered his views in "Ninguno de los artículos de nuestra Carta Magna excluye a la mujer de concurrir con el hombre a las urnas electorales," *La Prensa Libre*, No. 13,532 (1 October 1945), p. 1. Also, see "No hay absurdo antidemocrático más grande ni injusticia más palpable, que negar el voto a la mujer costarricense [dijo Lic. Don Héctor Beeche]," Ibid, No. 13,528 (26 September 1945), pp. 1, 9. The absence of a feminist movement struggling for female voting rights is discussed in "Los movimientos feministas de otras epocas en pro del derecho del sufragio han desaparecido," Ibid, No. 13,531 (29 September 1945), p. 5. The claim that most deputies in favor of female voting rights belonged to the majority stems from "Maniobra política para que la nueva Ley Electoral sea vetada por el Ejecutivo," Ibid, No. 13,524 (21 September 1945), p. 1.

[17] "No tiene ambiente el voto femenino en el Congreso," *La Prensa Libre*, No. 13,645 (18 October 1945), pp. 1, 13. In e.s. no. 15 ([8 October 1945], art. 4, *La Gaceta*, No. 233 [18 October 1945], p. 1825), discussion of the amendment is postponed until 15 October. And, in this session (e.s. no. 19 [15 October 1945], art. 6, Ibid, No. 235 [20 October 1945], p. 1841), the amendment again was raised and dropped during e.s. no. 25 (23 October 1945), art. 5, Ibid, No. 242 (28 October 1945), p. 1884.

PRN*c* Deputy Pablo Rodríguez submitted a motion to modify the reform bill's call to abolish absentee ballots. He requested that the law make exceptions for police officers, poll watchers, and other officials serving outside their home districts on election day. Though no one denied that such voting was easily corrupted, PRN independents José Albertazzi and Aristides Baltodano argued that prohibiting these citizens from casting ballots deprived them of their suffrage rights. Though Congress did not take a roll-call vote on this measure, the legislative transcript reveals that both factions of the PRN united to weaken the reform bill.[18]

With debate on crucial matters dragging on, proreform forces made repeated requests that deputies shorten their speeches and withdraw the large number of amendments that Congress had not yet discussed. "With the exception of 25 percent of the amendments," claimed PD Deputy Víctor Manuel Elizondo, "all other motions lacked importance." For, as a *La Prensa Libre* journalist noted on 18 October, unless Congress approved the Electoral Code in the following ten days, it would not be in effect for the midterm elections.[19]

It was within this context that PD Deputies Fernando Lara and Eladio Trejos obtained Congressional approval to petition Picado to issue executive decrees to ensure that the midterm elections would be "held with a minimum number of electoral guarantees." Their motion called upon the president to require citizens to present photographic identification before voting, to reorganize all Electoral Councils to include members of all political parties, and to restrict the use of absentee ballots. Finally, the opposition also requested that the president request that Congress enact laws empowering each branch of government to appoint its magistrate to the TNE. It also requested that the president gain Congressional approval so that the TNE could use the proposed system for allocating legislative seats in the 1946 midterm elections.[20]

---

[18] Juan Rodríguez's motion was approved during e.s. no. 23 (19 October 1945), art. 2, Ibid, No. 242 (28 October 1945), pp. 1882–3. The amendment submitted by Pablo Rodríguez was approved in e.s. no. 21 (17 October 1945), art. 9, Ibid, p. 1882. The quotation appears in e.s. No. 20 (16 October 1945), art. 7, Ibid, No. 241 (27 October 1945), p. 1874.

[19] "Con el Código Electoral no se harán las elecciones de Febrero," *La Prensa Libre*, No. 13,645 (18 October 1945), p. 1. Deputy Elizondo made the claim during e.s. no. 20 (16 October 1945), art. 7, p. 1874.

[20] E.s. no. 33 (5 November 1945), art. 4, *La Gaceta*, No. 255 (13 November 1945), pp. 1989–1990.

Pressured by PRN*c* leaders, the president declined the opposition request. He claimed that making the use of photographic identification compulsory would deprive thirty-thousand citizens – or 19 percent of the electorate – of their suffrage rights because they had never retrieved their identification cards from the Registry. He pointed out that reorganizing Provincial Electoral Councils, whose members were appointed to four-year terms in 1943, was not possible. Finally, all other reforms Deputies Lara and Trejos requested could not be implemented because they were based upon the Electoral Code, a project still under debate.[21]

Reformist forces counterattacked by themselves exerting pressure on the president. Amid opposition attacks on the government, Interior Secretary Soto turned in his resignation to Picado.[22] By abandoning the government, Soto threatened to rob it of what little credibility it had with opposition moderates. His action signaled the end of reform and increased the possibility that opposition moderates would join opposition hard-liners to topple the government. On 21 November, the president capitu-lated and issued a decree convening Congress to consider amendments to existing electoral laws.[23]

Opposition deputies requested that deputies suspend parliamentary procedure to expedite approval of these measures. After provoking a heated debate, Congress defeated their motion by a vote of thirty-one to fourteen. Again, analysis of the roll-call results shows that the majority was overwhelmingly opposed to preferential treatment for electoral safeguards: 84 percent of the PRN and 100 percent of the PVP representatives voted against these measures. Only members of the opposition voted to dispense with normal parliamentary procedures.[24] Table 6.2 summarizes these results.

---

[21] Picado's letter is not part of the transcript of Congressional debates published in Ibid. Its contents, however, were summarized by "No hay cambio de Juntas Electorales," *La Prensa Libre*, No. 13,665 (15 November 1945), p. 1. The estimate of voters who would be deprived of their franchise rights stemmed from the Civil Registry and the Office of Direct Taxation.

[22] On Soto's resignation, see "La renuncia de Soto Harrison," Ibid, No. 13,667 (17 Novem-ber 1945), p. 1, and "Proferred Resignation of Minister of Government Not Accepted," USNA-DS 818.002/11–1945, pp. 1–3. Several interviews Lehoucq held with Soto in San José during February 1946 also contributed to making sense of this period.

[23] "Proyecto (23 November 1945)," *La Gaceta*, No. 268 (28 November 1945), p. 2101. The president's convocation, dated 21 November, was printed as part of e.s. no. 45 (22 Novem-ber 1945), art. 2, Ibid, No. 11 (15 January 1946), p. 145.

[24] E.s. no. 46 (23 November 1945), art. 3, Ibid, No. 11 (15 January 1946), pp. 97–8.

Table 6.2. *Roll-Call Votes on Suspending Parliamentary Procedures and the Amendments to Existing Electoral Laws, 1945*

First Ballot					
Vote on the Amendment[a]	Party Affiliation				Total
	PD	PRN*c*	PRN*i*	PVP	
In favor	10	2	2		14
Against		25	2	4	31
TOTAL	10	27	4	4	45
Second Ballot					
Vote on the Amendment[a]	Party Affiliation				Total
	PD	PRN*c*	PRN*i*	PVP	
In favor	13	13	3	2	31
Against		10	1	1	23
TOTAL	13	23	4	3	43

Note:

[a] With three Degrees of Freedom, the chi-square result for the first vote is 31.694 (Asymp. Sig [2-sided] = .000). Five cells have expected counts of less than 5 (the minimum expected count is 1.24). For the second vote, the chi-square result is 7.865 (Asymp. Sig. [2-sided] = .049). Five cells have an expected count of less than 5. The minimum expected count is .84.

Sources: For party affiliations, see Table 6.1. For the vote, e.s. no. 46 (23 November 1945), art. 3, *La Gaceta*, No. 11 (15 January 1946), pp. 97–8.

Consisting of representatives of pro- and antigovernment parties, the Committee on Legislation issued its report on the proposed measures. Seeking to strike a common ground, it endorsed most of the opposition's proposals except the mandatory use of photographic identification. It called for the formation of the TNE within five days of the promulgation of this law. All parties also agreed that they would cooperate to ensure that the Electoral Code would be in effect for the 1948 elections.[25] On this

[25] "Dictamen de la Comisión de Legislación (28 November 1945)," Ibid, No. 270 (30 November 1945), p. 2116. The members of this committee were Bernardo Benavides (PRN), Mora (PVP), and Luis Carlos Suárez (PD). The Committee also incorporated suggestions made by Froilán Bolaños of the PRN. The consensus in favor of approving the Electoral Code in time for the 1948 elections was not mentioned in the Committee report, but was reported by "Dispensa de trámites para el dictamen en el asunto electoral," *La Prensa Libre*, No. 13,677 (28 November 1945), p. 1.

occasion, 60 percent of the PRN deputies sided in favor of suspending parliamentary procedure. Ten deputies changed their votes to support this reform, largely because the transitory articles had become less radical. Along with two-thirds of the PVP and all twelve of the opposition deputies, Congress endorsed a measure that advanced the cause of reform. Table 6.2 also contains these results.

PRN deputies, however, did not stop attacking the bill. They floated an amendment to loosen the restrictions on absentee balloting, claiming that they would unfairly deprive agricultural workers outside their home districts on election day of their voting rights. After negotiating with the opposition, the deputies endorsed, in first debate, a bill that allowed citizens outside their home districts to cast absentee ballots if they had filed a request to do so with their local polling station. After several more delays, Congress approved the compromise bill in third and final debate in early December.[26]

As Congress approved the transitory measures, deputies completed discussion of remaining amendments. On 20 December, legislators passed the bill in third debate and supported a motion to dispense with its detailed discussion. After reviewing the entire bill, a legislative committee sent it to the executive. On 18 January 1946, the president and his interior secretary signed the bill into law.[27] The arduous struggle to reshape the electoral landscape of the republic was complete.

The Political Center Stabilizes

With the passage of these reformist measures, government moderates had something to show for their efforts. If PRN independents broke party ranks to make common cause with the communists and the opposition, the PRN*c* could be defeated. Like the president, PRN independents recognized that reform would promote stability by discouraging opposition

---

[26] Deputies endorse this bill in third and final debate during e.s. no. 57 (5 December 1945), art. 4, *La Gaceta*, No. 18 (23 January 1946), p. 145. The controversial motion is presented during e.s. no. 52 (3 December 1945), art. 5, Ibid, pp. 139–40. Also, see "En el Congreso no existe el deseo de otorgar la libertad electoral [declaraciones del Diputado Fernando Lara Bustamante]," *La Prensa Libre*, No. 13,684 (6 December 1945), pp. 1, 6.

[27] República de Costa Rica, *Código Electoral* (San José: Imprenta Nacional, 1946). The third debate occurred during e.s. No. 65 (20 December 1945), art. 4, *La Gaceta*, No. 19 (24 January 1946), p. 183. The first debate was during e.s. no. 60 (13 December 1945), art. 5, Ibid, p. 182.

moderates from supporting hardline revolts against the government. With the support of PRN moderates, the PVP and the PD could reform laws so that each would have an easier time increasing its share of elected offices.

Institutionalist theories therefore accurately explain why politicians enacted the 1946 Electoral Code. As long as the president stood above the partisan fray, he could pivot between pro- and antigovernment forces to enact far-reaching reforms. The ban on the consecutive reelection of presidents allowed Picado to act upon the public demand for clean government. The structure of executive-legislative relations and the Congressional balance of power empowered him to assemble a coalition just large enough to reform electoral laws.

This strategy worked because it only required a handful of politicians to think about the long-term interests of the republic. Pivoting was successful precisely because it harnessed the self-interest of pro- and antigovernment parties that would otherwise not support Picado's policies. Out of electoral self-interest, opposition deputies supported reforms to facilitate expanding their parties' share of state power. By altering the formula to allocate "leftover" seats in multimember districts, he gained the support of a small, but disciplined number of communist deputies. The president had only to convince a handful of PRN deputies to take a leap into the unknown.

As Interior Secretary Soto predicted, playing the middle was working to stabilize political competition. In its lead article, *La Prensa Libre* noted that irregularities did occur in the 1946 midterm elections, but not on a scale to render the results completely invalid. The opposition obtained 39 percent (nine of twenty-three) of the seats. In contrast to previous elections, most of the votes that the GCE annulled belonged to progovernment parties.[28] Roberto Campabadal, the opposition's representative in the Presidential House on election day, complimented Picado for his efforts to resolve all complaints brought to his attention. A day later, Otilio Ulate, National Union Party (PUN) leader, and Dr. Antonio Peña, a member of the Social Democratic Party (PSD), led a delegation to the Presidential House, where they expressed to the president their satisfaction with election results.[29] Perhaps no better portrayal of their effects exists than that

---

[28] Molina and Lehoucq, *Urnas de lo inesperado*, p. 175.
[29] "Las elecciones verificadas ayer," *La Prensa Libre*, No. 13,734 (11 February 1946), pp. 1, 9.

of the Third Secretary at the U.S. Embassy. With these elections, the president had

> ... enormously increased his personal prestige. Prior to the elections the opinion was almost universal that Picado was no more than a "prisoner" of the "caldero-communists," and that as such he would be a ready tool for their presumed electoral machinations. However, the president's reiterated insistence upon the freedom of elections, his obviously impartial decisions in the many complaints presented to him, and his calm and collected way of organizing the government machinery to avoid violence have won him praise from all sides.[30]

Electoral Competition, Polarization, and Civil War

The Electoral Code was the greatest achievement of government and opposition moderates. Yet, it did not thwart the polarization of political competition and the outbreak of a civil war – a set of issues almost as tantalizing as the puzzle of the enactment of the Code itself. In this section, we explore how a series of contingent events empowered hardliners as they undermined the position of moderates. Despite the polarization of political competition, parties nevertheless continued to invest time and energy in revamping electoral institutions. The reform of electoral institutions was so successful, in fact, that it allowed the opposition to defeat the government in the 1948 elections – a victory that, we suggest, makes sense only through serious consideration of PRN allegations that it, and not the opposition, was the victim of electoral fraud.

Rival Strategic Calculations: The Opposition Splits

Opposition hardliners began to denounce the validity of the 1946 midterm elections soon after the authorities tallied the popular vote. Impugning election results in every province of the republic, hardliners demanded that opposition deputies honor of the agreement reached by opposition parties to boycott Congress if fraud had been responsible for their defeat. Dominated by representatives of the Social Democratic Party (PSD) and National Union Party (PUN) – which were sending only two of the nine

---

[30] "Results of Midterm Congressional Elections," Despatch No. 1600 (14 February 1946), Livingston Watrous to Secretary of State, USNA-DS 818.00/2–1446, p. 5. The previous citation appeared on page 3 of this despatch.

opposition deputies elected in 1946 to Congress – the Tribunal of Honor ruled that opposition deputies should not attend Congressional sessions.[31]

The leading opposition moderate, however, disagreed with this assessment of election results. Cortés concluded that all antigovernment deputies should attend Congress since they had been legitimately elected in 1944 or 1946. While conceding that the midterm elections were "neither entirely or approximately legal," he claimed that large-scale repression did not characterize them. The presence of opposition poll watchers, he suggested, was responsible for relatively fair elections in the central parts of the republic. Based upon these results, Cortés publicly rejected the use of violence to topple Picado's government. Instead, he announced his intention to speak with the president to select a presidential candidate acceptable to the government and its critics. Unofficial reports said that he was willing to endorse Fernando Castro or Fernando Esquivel, influential members of the PD, as compromise candidates.[32]

Doubts about winning a civil war may not be the only reason opposition moderates favored compromise with the government. Our analysis of the petitions to nullify the 1946 electoral results suggests another: that the opposition may not have been as popular as it expected to be. By subtracting the number of votes alleged to be fraudulent from the total number of votes received by progovernment parties, the share of legislative seats captured by the opposition does not change. At most, opposition charges for the Province of Guanacaste, if true, might have boosted the opposition's total number of deputies from nine to ten of the twenty-three up for grabs in the midterm elections.[33] Faced with the

---

[31] "Dividida la opinión en el seno del Tribunal de Honor Electoral de la Oposición," "Apelación ante el Partido Demócrata del Fallo del Tribunal de Honor que recomienda la inasistencia de los diputados," *La Prensa Libre*, Nos. 13,781, and 13,791 (6 and 23 April 1946), pp. 1 and 1, 8. This PUN, led by Otilio Ulate, should not be confused with the PUN of Cleto González of the 1900s and 1920s.

[32] "El último reportaje político de don León Cortés," *La Prensa Libre*, No. 13,752 (6 March 1946), pp. 1, 2, 3. Sergio Carballo R., the editor of *La Prensa Libre* who had conducted this interview with Cortés three days before the latter died, later told Ralph Hilton, a member of the U.S. Embassy in Costa Rica, that the former president was willing to endorse either of these individuals as a compromise presidential candidate. This information was not published as part of this famous interview, claimed Carballo R., because he did not have another opportunity to confer with Cortés before the former president died unexpectedly. See "Memorandum from Ralph Hilton to the Ambassador," Enclosure No. 2 to Despatch No. 1794 (6 April 1946), Hallet Johnson to Secretary of State, USNA-DS 818.00/4–646.

[33] Lehoucq, "The Origins of Democracy in Costa Rica in Comparative Perspective," pp. 249–55.

fundamental uncertainty of the ballot box, opposition moderates may have had good reason to forge an alliance with the president instead of provoking a confrontation with the government, either on the battlefield or in the electoral arena.

This analysis also explains why opposition hardliners remained intransigent. If the coalescence of moderates became the basis of a stable political arrangement, the political marginalization of hardliners would deepen. Their ability both to claim credit for political reforms and to inflame the passions of the electorate would evaporate. With the fewest representatives in Congress, the PSD, PUN, and extreme *cortesistas* had the least to gain from a settlement brokered by the dominant forces of the polity.

The Collapse of the Centrist Compromise

The gradual but steady shift to the political center was dealt a serious blow soon after the midterm elections. In early March, Cortés died of a massive stroke. His death left the opposition bereft of a leader with the popularity and therefore the credibility to negotiate with the government.

Attempting to build upon foundations Cortés laid, opposition factions tried to seal a mutually beneficial agreement with the government on several occasions. The PD Executive Committee held several long conversations with the president, PRN*c* whip Francisco Calderón, and PVP chief Mora.[34] Claiming to speak for the opposition Tribunal of Honor, Otilio Ulate, the PUN leader, also spoke with the president about the provision of additional electoral guarantees. These conversations soon produced results: In exchange for replacing governmental officials unpopular with the opposition, the president's adversaries ended their boycott of Congress.[35] These talks reached fruition by 5 August, when the PD and the president agreed to select consensus candidates to fill TNE posts. Picado also committed himself to reorganizing the newly created Electoral Registry to ensure that all citizens would possess photographic identification cards by the 1948 general elections. Finally, the president assured the

---

[34] The other members of the Executive Committee were Otto Cortés Fernández (first vice-president), Fernando Lara Bustamante (second vice-president), Ricardo Castro Beeche (treasurer), and Eladio Trejos Flores and Fernando Volio Sancho (secretaries). See "Se instaló el Comité Ejecutivo del Partido Demócrata," *La Prensa Libre*, No. 13,832 (11 June 1946), p. 1.

[35] Lehoucq, "The Origins of Democracy in Costa Rica in Comparative Perspective," pp. 261–2.

opposition that he would "veto all reforms of the Electoral Code contrary to liberty or the efficacy of the franchise."[36]

As opposition moderates were scurrying to effect a series of compromises with the president, opposition hardliners intensified their efforts to discredit political moderates. A faction headed by the former president's son, Otto Cortés, broke away from the PD. It began forming a new group, the Independent Cortesista Party, with hardline leader José Figueres.[37] In control of the leading and arguably most widely read newspaper, the *Diario de Costa Rica*, PUN leader Ulate condemned that the PD had negotiated with Calderón and Mora instead of with the president.[38] Though in favor of agreeing with the government, Ulate denounced negotiations with those who had perpetuated fraud in the elections of 1944 and 1946. Unlike PD leaders, the PUN leader had only spoken with the president of his own efforts to effect a political settlement. The distinction, he claimed was important: "one can deal with those who, by means of a sin committed in his interest, attain power and declare that they wish to erase the stain of left by the sin." "One cannot interact," Ulate added, "with the perpetrators of the sin itself."[39]

Under these and many other attacks, the agreement crafted by pro- and antigovernment forces disintegrated by early September. In a letter to the president, the PD Executive Committee explained that, despite the removal of public officials the opposition distrusted, many other officials of questionable character remained in their posts. PD leaders also pointed out that, under existing laws and constitutional statutes, the (PRNc-dominated) Congress retained its constitutional authority to certify the validity of election results. It demanded that the president turn over

---

[36] Quotations are from "El Partido Demócrata presentó un memorándum de garantías mínimas," *La Prensa Libre*, No. 13,875 (5 August 1946), pp. 1, 3. The text of the agreement was not published until a month later in "Al juicio sereno de los costarricenses somete el comité del Partido Demócrata sus últimas actuaciones políticas," Ibid, No. 13,909 (12 September 1946), pp. 1, 2.

[37] "Abandonará la vía del sufragio el Partido Social Demócrata," *Diario de Costa Rica*, No. 8,100 (22 March 1946), p. 1. The PSD's weekly newspaper, *Acción Demócrata*, after March 1946 consistently followed a hard line against the government.

[38] Comité Ejecutivo del Partido Unión Nacional, "Ante el Pacto," *Diario de Costa Rica* (8 August 1946), p. 4.

[39] "Ulate le habló anoche al país: fijo su posición y la del Partido Unión Nacional en el proceso sobre garantías electorales [texto del discurso pronunciado por el señor Ulate, desde las estaciones radiodifusoras 'Alma Tica,' 'Radio Monumental,' 'Titania,' y 'La Voz del Hogar,' por el sistema de cadena]," Ibid, No. 8,217 (15 August 1946), pp. 1, 4.

control of the security forces to the TNE on election day. After its letter went unanswered for over a week, PD leaders informed the public that it was no longer cooperating with the government.[40]

In the wake of León Cortés's death, the latent conflicts of interest among opposition leaders had become manifest. While all held an interest in seeing the government fall, each jockeyed to become the opposition chief. Indeed, the absence of a leader with an undisputed national stature encouraged a frenzied competition among rival politicians, each of whom claimed to be the only person capable of standing up to the caldero-communist regime. In their search for electoral support, each succeeded in polarizing public opinion by discrediting rivals who used the language of cooperation and compromise.

The other reason responsible for the collapse of the talks between the government and opposition moderates was Calderón's return to the country in late August. According to Professor Luis Dobles, an influential member of the PD, Calderón's reappearance had "completely changed the political panorama" by raising the possibility that the government would use fraud to ensure the former president's reelection to the presidency. The possibility of another presidential candidacy by the ex-president, argued Dobles, was a frightening specter because

Dr. Calderón has control over the totality of force required to steal a free election. The military barracks and police are all and completely his partisans, the governors and mayors loyal to him, and the Congress is controlled by his supporters. No corner of the country exists where his political machine does not extend its reach.

Under such conditions, "the political struggle would be unequal and unfair." It is for these reasons, Dobles concluded, that "the people do not believe that they will have the right to choose" their leaders.[41]

Along with contributing to the polarization of political competition, hardline opposition attacks on the government and especially on the PD

---

[40] This letter, along with other relevant documents, is published in "Al juicio sereno de los costarricenses somete el comité del Partido Demócrata sus últimas actuaciones políticas," *La Prensa Libre*, No. 13,909 (12 September 1946), p. 3. A more thorough discussion of the collapse of the moderates' accord is Lehoucq, "The Origins of Democracy in Costa Rica in Comparative Perspective," pp. 256–70.

[41] "El regreso del Dr. Calderón Guardia ha cambiado totalmente el panorama político y ha hecho que empiece a avivarse una agitación mucho más honda y mucho más seria [palabras del Profesor Luis Dobles Segreda, en sus brillante discurso del sábado]," Ibid, No. 13,906 (9 September 1946), p. 4.

seem to have persuaded, paradoxically enough, Calderón to contemplate entering the race for the presidency. By generating divisions among the government's critics, Ulate and other opposition hardliners undermined the political standing of the opposition as a whole. Intentionally or not, opposition hardliners created an opportunity for a popular, though divisive, candidate such as Calderón to defeat several not very well-known rivals.

Political Polarization and Electoral Reform

Led by opposition presidential candidate Ulate, opposition forces publicly issued threats – occasionally veiled, other times quite explicit – to engage in civil disobedience or even to start a war unless elections were fair. The most hardline sectors of the opposition escalated their attacks on the property of progovernment supporters. Acts of subversion increased from five in 1946 to seventy-two in 1947.[42] With hardliners in control of the opposition, progovernment factions stopped floating proposals to reach a wide-ranging accord with their opponents. Yet, neither the government nor the opposition ever called for the cancellation of elections.

Uncertainty about the results of violence in part explains why parties committed time and financial resources to revamp electoral institutions. Unless a party was convinced it could triumph in a civil war, it was rational to hedge its bets by ensuring that elections were as fair and as transparent as possible. By far the most daunting task consisted of the production of an accurate list of voters. Each of the approximately 163,000 names on the electoral rolls had to be checked against the lists possessed by the Civil Registry, the executive agency in charge of tabulating the names of all born in the republic. Reports suggested that, after 1942, governments had stopped adding the names of new citizens to or deleting those of the deceased from the General Index of the Electorate.[43]

---

[42] Mercedes Muñoz, "Mitos y realidades de una democracia desarmada: Costa Rica," *Polémica*, 2nd Series, No. 10 (January–April 1990), p. 45. This tabulation is based upon a reading of the *Diario de Costa Rica* and *La Tribuna*. An observer of the times reports that hardliners committed thirty-eight acts of violence, five of which failed. See Eunice Odio, "Exposición sobre política actual de Costa Rica," in her *Obras completas*, Vol. 2 (San José: EUCR, 1996), pp. 26–8 (the Guatemalan newspaper *El Imparcial* originally published this article between 4 and 12 December 1947).

[43] This and the subsequent paragraphs draw upon Benjamín Odio's long defense of his activities, "El Ex-director del Registro Electoral expone al país su actuación," *Diario de Costa*

Under the terms negotiated between government and opposition, the Electoral Registry also had to produce photographic identification cards for each voter. Though many voters had some form of identification, it was not of a type "backed by relevant documents or by authenticated personal records," in the words of Benjamín Odio, the first director of the new Registry. Since 1934, the authorities had permitted voters to use a personal identification card devised by the Department of Direct Taxation to expedite payment of a quasi-income tax (*el impuesto cedular de ingresos*) enacted the previous year. As a result, Odio estimated that approximately 80 percent of all adult males possessed defective forms of identification. And verifying their accuracy required reviewing "no less than 700,000 documents, including photographic negatives, photographs and tax accounts" – the approximate number of documents, according to Odio, that the taxation office sent the Electoral Registry.[44]

Election Results and the Charges of Fraud

Official results suggest that the PUN candidate had received 54,931 votes to 44,438 votes for the PRN leader. As they recovered from the shock of apparent defeat, the PRN and the PVP began to argue that only fraud had prevented Calderón from winning the presidency. It was inconceivable, they suggested, that the opposition could have defeated a politician whose administration had enacted popular social reforms. In a statement aimed at promoting political reconciliation, the PUN leader promised to respect the rights of his rivals and thanked the president for having held fair elections.[45]

With one member abstaining and two voting in favor, the TNE declared the PUN candidate to be the provisional president-elect on 28 February.

Rica, No. 8,656 (19 February 1948), pp. 1, 7, 8. The estimate of registered voters contained in this paragraph is from "163,000 ciudadanos podrán votar en las próximas elecciones," *La Prensa Libre*, No. 14,077 (1 April 1947), pp. 1, 10. A similar report appeared as "Expurgación de 160,000 ciudadanos inscritos en el padrón electoral," *La Tribuna*, No. 7,870 (14 January 1947), p. 1. Table 1.3 indicates that Registry officials had extensively revised the General Index in 1946.

[44] This figure stems from "El Ex-director del Registro Electoral expone al país su actuación." The estimate of all voters possessing identification cards by late 1946 was made by Víctor Manuel Castro, director of the Office of Identification, in "El 80% de los ciudadanos aptos para votar tienen ya su cédula de identidad con fotografía," *La Prensa Libre*, No. 13,966 (19 November 1946), p. 4.

[45] "Nuestro triunfo no será nunca expresión de poder; aquí mandará la razón y gobernará la justicia," Ibid, No. 14,332 (9 February 1948), p. 1.

The majority based its judgment upon the certificates of results signed by party observers and members of polling stations (and which the PUN supplied), once some fire – those responsible for the fire remain unknown to this day – during the evening of 9 February destroyed some ballots and related documents. The majority avoided confronting the issue of fraud by maintaining that, according to article 186 of the Electoral Code, "our mission is limited to the examination of the arithmetic and legal computation of the votes received. . . . Consequently," Magistrates Gerardo Guzmán and José María Vargas pointed out, "we do not possess the faculties to begin to know and resolve the general issue of the nullification of the elections." Magistrate Max Koberg abstained from voting in favor or against the decision reached by his colleagues because he believed that the tally of the vote was only "half-completed" and was based upon a computation made in part without party supervision. Instead, he recommended that the Tribunal ask Congress whether it should complete its work.[46]

In the petition he submitted to Congress, Calderón alleged that the electoral rolls were defective, incomplete, and biased against the PRN. According to Calderón, the Registry included 32,500 names that it had failed to publish in *La Gaceta*. By violating procedure, the Registry had prevented citizens from contesting the registration of deceased or non-existent persons. Second, the PRN claimed that 3,035 of its members, who had submitted by stated deadlines either requests to be registered or changes in residence, had not received the documentation necessary to vote on election day. Third, the PRN leader argued that 37,035 of his party's supporters never obtained photographic identification cards, although they had made these requests on a timely basis.[47]

Interestingly, neither the PRN nor the PUN impugned the behavior of government officials and poll watchers. Calderón's petition to nullify electoral results, in fact, was unlike any other in the history of the republic. Because the PRN controlled the state, it could not claim that parti-

---

[46] All quotations are from the decision reached by Magistrates Guzmán Quirós and Vargas Pacheco, published in *La Gaceta*, No. 50 (29 February 1948), pp. 368–9. Koberg's verdict was published on pp. 369–70. Clotilde Obregón, *El proceso electoral y el Poder Ejecutive en Costa Rica* (San José: EUCR, 2000), p. 332.

[47] The petition submitted by the PRN was published in *La Gaceta*, Nos. 50 and 56 (29 February and 7 March 1948), pp. 366–8 and 409–20. Aguilar Bulgarelli, *Costa Rica y sus hechos políticos de 1948*, pp. 277–8 (ftn. 23), errs when he claims that the documentary appendices of this petition cannot be found, thus preventing analysis of the Calderón's charges of fraud. While it may be true that the originals are not in the archives of either the Legislative Assembly of the Supreme Tribunal of Elections, they were published in the aforementioned edition of *La Gaceta*.

sanship had led the authorities to harass its supporters, steal ballot boxes, or otherwise throw elections results. Instead, the PRN concentrated upon undermining the legitimacy of the Registry – the linchpin of the electoral system that pro- and antigovernment moderates had designed. That turnout had fallen from 136,806 (or 91 percent) of the eligible voters in 1944 to 103,451 (or 63 percent) of the eligible voters in 1948 lends an air of plausibility to Calderón's argument that the Registry deprived thousands of PRN supporters of their suffrage rights.

In a spirited defense of his activities, the Registry director, Odio, argued that the fall in voter turnout rates proved that his agency had successfully purged the electoral rolls of the names of thousands of deceased, nonexistent, or ineligible men. Before election day, in fact, an undisclosed source from this agency claimed that its personnel had removed nearly 46,658 invalid names from electoral rolls.[48] After making deductions for false registrations and the twenty to 25 percent voter abstention rate, Odio added, only about one hundred thousand men should have voted in 1948. Using similar sorts of reasoning, the vice consul of the U.S. Embassy argued that turnout was "strikingly similar" to an adjusted number of the ballots cast in 1944. If 20 percent of the total represented fraudulent ballots, approximately 109,444 citizens participated in the 1944 elections and, based upon provisional results, 98,201 citizens went to the polls in 1948.[49] For both the Registry director and the U.S. vice consul, progovernment claims that the reorganization of the Registry had deprived PRN and PVP voters of suffrage rights were specious because, simply put, these voters did not exist.

What is troubling about both analyses is that they seriously underestimate the actual size of the electorate. According to official estimates, there were 163,100 and 176,979 eligible males in 1944 and 1948, respectively. Our own estimates suggest that there were 149,583 and 164,465 potential voters in 1944 and 1948, respectively.[50] So, even if official figures are inflated by an average of 7.7 percent, the difference between government

---

[48] Odio's calculations are from "El Ex-director expone al país su actuación," p. 7. The estimate of purged registrations stems from "TEMAS DEL MOMENTO: Alarmante Informe," *La Prensa Libre*, No. 14,216 (22 September 1947), p. 2. The source appears to have been someone in the Electoral Registry if not Odio himself.

[49] "Presidential Elections," Despatch No. 79 (13 February 1948), Alex A. Cohen to Secretary of State, USNA-DS 818.00/1348, pp. 1–2.

[50] This and followings paragraphs draw heavily from Iván Molina, "El resultado de las elecciones de 1948 en Costa Rica: Una revisión a la luz de nuevos datos," *Revista de Historia de América* (México, D. F.), No. 130 (January–June 2001).

numbers and our own estimates is much smaller than the breach separating the Registrar and the U.S. vice consul's numbers from these figures. Furthermore, Odio's own postelection estimates contradict the preelection numbers he must have known about (and approved) as director of the Electoral Registry.[51]

It was also no secret that voter turnout rates were going to fall drastically in 1948. Indeed, in the weeks before election day, no one less than the president of the TNE called on disenfranchised citizens "to manifest the greatness of their spirit and to resign themselves to electoral passivity." Like other knowledgeable observers of politics, he knew that administrative logjams were going to dampen turnout on election day.[52] And the PRN's charges gain in plausibility when, in the weeks after election day, Odio went into hiding and joined the antigovernment insurrection.

A closer look at election results also suggests that partisanship was at work in the Electoral Registry. In the 1948 presidential elections, an average of 70 percent of the electorate turned out to vote in the core. Only 42 percent of the eligible voters cast ballots in the periphery in what everyone considers to be the elections of the century. Not coincidentally, these lopsided results mirror regional patterns of partisan strength. In 1946 and 1948, the PRN and the PVP won the periphery by overwhelming majorities. In these elections, the opposition obtained, with one partial exception, more votes than its rivals in the four provinces of the center.[53] Differences in turnout between pro- and antigovernment strongholds suggest that the Registry did deprive thousands of PRN and PVP voters of their suffrage rights, a conclusion the British ambassador F. G. Coultas believed was plausible.[54]

That the opposition failed to win the legislative elections also suggests that something went awry in 1948. According to the majority and minority verdicts, the TNE gave the PRN and PVP 55.4 and 51.6 percent of the popular vote in the Congressional race, respectively. While split-ticket voting was possible, it had never occurred on this scale before. In the

---

[51] "Registro Electoral," *Alcance a La Gaceta*, No. 29 (5 February 1948), pp. 1–9.

[52] "LOS MIEMBROS DEL TRIBUNAL SE DIRIGEN AL PAÍS: Declaraciones de Max Koberg Bolandi," *La Prensa Libre*, No. 14,330 (6 February 1948), pp. 1, 8.

[53] Although the opposition did attract slightly more votes than either the PRN or PVP in every election held in the center during these years, it had fewer votes than the total number of votes the PRN *and* PVP won in the Province of San José in the 1946 midterm elections.

[54] "Costa Rican Presidential Elections," Public Records Office, London, AN 0922, 21 February 1948, pp. 1–2.

highly charged atmosphere surrounding the 1948 election, it also is difficult to conceive of this many voters crossing the partisan divide. Proponents of the conventional wisdom can argue that this divergence stems from the fact that a different set of magistrates supervised the tally of the legislative vote. Upon issuing their verdict of the presidential election, the TNE magistrates resigned. Each branch of government (two of which the PRN and PVP dominated) then selected new magistrates to complete the tally of the vote. This criticism, of course, cuts both ways; one can argue that the first set of magistrates became as partial as the second are alleged to be. Furthermore, the TNE minority or majority differ only regarding the scale of the progovernment victory.

What is clear is that the first and second TNEs counted ballots in slightly different ways. While the first set of magistrates claimed there were 103,451 valid votes, the majority and minority reports of the second TNE tabulated 96,281 and 86,236, respectively. Different magistrates appear to have instructed officials to nullify votes on different grounds and to include or to ignore other ballots – a not unlikely outcome of an election like no other in the history of the republic. With 43 percent of the ballots counted (and two days after election day), the original TNE noted that the PRN and PVP were ahead by 51 to 49 percent of the legislative ballots.[55] Using different decision rules, a small number of split votes may very well have become magnified into the 4 to 5 percent difference in votes between government and opposition in the final vote tallies.

From the foregoing evidence, we can conclude that it is not improbable that the PRN won the 1948 presidential election. Even with thousands of PRN and PVP voters deprived of their suffrage rights, the opposition lost the congressional elections. Its candidate wins the presidential election only if we accept a verdict whose proponents went into hiding, resigned, or used inaccurate figures about the size of the electorate to defend their behavior. In perhaps one of the few cases in the annals of electoral history, an incumbent determined to prove his impartiality before his countrymen may very well have lost an election that his party may very well have won.

---

[55] "Escrutinio de votos hasta 3:30 p.m. Datos tomados en el Tribunal Electoral," *La Prensa Libre*, No. 14332 (9 February 1948), p. 1.

Negotiation, Civil War, and a New Constitution

Difficulties in interpreting the will of the electorate only heightened the uncertainty surrounding the results of the ballot box. Behind the scenes, progovernment factions squabbled about whether to accept the provisional verdict; antigovernment factions struggled to maintain their alliances as moderates and hardliners vehemently disagreed about how to react to Congress's decision to annul presidential election results. It was widely rumored, for example, that hardline leader Figueres and his followers had gone underground and were planning to attack the government. For their part, PRN leaders began to assemble goon squads and the PVP began to organize workers' militias.

Dominated by PRN and PVP representatives, the Credentials Committee accepted Calderón's demand to annul presidential electoral results. When the old Congress assembled on 1 March to issue a final declaration of results, a majority of 59 percent endorsed the Committee's recommendation. All but four PRN progovernment deputies voted to reject the TNE's provisional verdict. All fifteen opposition deputies, along with the four PRN renegades, opposed the Credentials Committee's decision.[56]

The decision to annul presidential election results triggered preparations for war even as it accelerated efforts to mediate the increasingly bitter conflict between pro- and antigovernment forces. Since election day, in fact, the archbishop of the country, Victor Sanabria, and TNE magistrates had been working to broker a peaceful settlement over the crisis of political succession. After Congress rejected Ulate's provisional election, the Association of Bankers joined forces with the archbishop to avert the outbreak of violence. For weeks, both worked around the clock to find a compromise candidate acceptable to pro- and antigoverment forces.[57] While PRN and PUN leaders negotiated to resolve the political impasse, word

---

[56] E.s. no. 1 (1 March 1948), art. 1, *La Gaceta*, No. 97 (30 April 1948), pp. 617–8. The four renegade PRN deputes were Bernardo Benavides, Francisco Fonseca (president of Congress), Tomás Guardia, and Arturo Volio. Two additional Republicans, José Miguel Jiménez and Manuel de Jesús Quirós, never reached Congress because they were kidnapped. It was rumored that they were abducted because they were planning to vote against the motion to invalidate the presidential elections. The majority and minority reports were published as "Dictamen de Mayoría (28 February 1948)," written by José Albertazzi (PRN) and Jaime Cerdas (PVP), and "Dictamen de Minoría (28 February 1948)," written by Otto Cortés (PD), in Ibid, No. 51 (2 March 1948), p. 373.

[57] Lehoucq, "The Origins of Democracy in Costa Rica in Comparative Perspective," pp. 320–33.

reached San José on 12 March that hardliners led by Figueres had attacked government troops sent to discover whether rumors were true that he was assembling an army on his *finca* (farm).

After a month of fighting, PRN and PUN leaders agreed to end the civil war. They decided that the new Congress, in its first ordinary session of the new year, should select Dr. Julio César Ovares as first designate to the presidency. Under this agreement, Dr. Ovares would rule as interim president for two years and the TNE would hold new elections. When this plan was presented to Figueres for approval, he rejected its terms and instead continued to lead the army that would eventually prove triumphant in the civil war.[58]

As the Army of National Liberation reached San José, it negotiated a set of pacts with its adversaries and other opposition sectors. Much to the chagrin of PUN leaders, Figueres and other hardliners forced the rest of the opposition to accept the creation of a de facto junta that would assume executive and legislative powers for eighteen months. Consisting of former opposition hardliners, the junta agreed to hold elections to elect delegates to attend a Constituent Assembly to write a new constitution for the republic. At the end of its period in office, the junta promised to relinquish state power to Ulate, who would govern with a newly elected Congress under the new constitution.

Dominated by the representatives from the PUN, the National Constituent Assembly rejected the junta's draft constitution calling for a dramatic expansion of the role of the state in domestic affairs. Marginalized within the Constituent Assembly (only four of forty-five delegates belonged to the pro-junta Social Democrats), hardline forces failed to prevent most convention participants from reducing the decree-making powers of the junta. Contrary to the wishes of the junta, the Constituent Assembly settled for simply restructuring the relations among the branches of government contained in the 1871 charter.

Among the Assembly's most far-reaching reforms was the decision to extend suffrage rights to all men and women above the age of twenty.[59]

---

[58] This and the previous paragraph condense Lehoucq, "The Origins of Democracy in Costa Rica in Comparative Perspective," pp. 320–33.

[59] For a discussion of the extension of suffrage rights to women consistent with our arguments, see Eugenia Rodríguez, "¿Por qué se aprobó el sufragio femenino en Costa Rica hasta 1949?" in Sara Poggio and Monserrat Sagot, eds., *Irrumpiendo en lo público: seis facetas de las mujeras en América Latina* (San José: LASA-Maestría Regional en Estudios de la Mujer, 2000), pp. 175–206.

The Assembly also voted to build upon the Electoral Code by making the newly named Supreme Tribunal of Elections completely responsible for electoral governance. With this decision, constitutional delegates stripped Congress of its longstanding authority to certify the results of presidential and legislative elections. They also empowered the Supreme Court of Justice to select, through a two-thirds vote of its members, the Tribunal's three magistrates and their alternates, each of whom would serve staggered, six-year terms in office. Despite the PUN's domination of the Constituent Assembly, the PUN agreed to strengthen electoral safeguards to reassure the junta that it was not going to consolidate a monopoly on elected offices. With the defeat and subsequent collapse of the army, the junta and its followers held the only arms left in the country. Cornered in different ways, both the junta and its PUN rivals found it in their interests to maintain the consensus in favor of electoral fairness – a consensus that intense partisan competition put to the test in the subsequent decade when close elections almost ignited another civil war between these rivals.[60]

Conclusion

After fifty years of trial and error, parties succeeded in writing a Code that remains the cornerstone of fair elections in Costa Rica. With the promulgation of the 1946 Code, opposition parties could send their representatives to observe voter registration and the tally of the vote. The Code also eliminated the president's role in election administration by making a tribunal solely responsible for electoral governance. The Code also called for revamping the Electoral Registry in time for the 1948 general elections.

Despite these safeguards, allegations of fraud surround the 1948 election results. In an event rare in the annals of political history, the

---

[60] For an analysis of the 1950s, see Kirk Bowman, "¿Fue el compromiso y consenso de las elites lo que llevó a la consolidación democrática en Costa Rica? Evidencia de los cincuenta," *Revista de Historia* (Heredia/San José), No. 41, (January–June 2000), pp. 91–127. Also, see his *Militarization, Democracy, and Development in Latin America* (University Park, PA: Penn State University Press, 2002). Bowman has unearthed a mountain of data to show that democracy was not consolidated in Costa Rica until well into the 1960s. For the initial formulation that the 1948 civil war led to a political stalemate necessary to sustain democracy, see Jacobo Schifter, "La democracia en Costa Rica como producto de la neutralización de clases," in Chester Zelaya, et al., *¿Democracia en Costa Rica?: Cinco opiniones polémicas* (San José: EUNED, 1983), pp. 345–435.

incumbent party became the victim and not the perpetrator of electoral fraud. Indeed, in all of the controversy that has engulfed election results, no one has ever suggested that the government used its powers to win these elections unfairly. Under continual attack by opposition hardliners, Picado's government kept its commitment to hold fair elections and unwittingly allowed opposition hardliners to hijack the Electoral Registry. In control of the reorganization of the Electoral Registry, opposition elements succeeded in depriving thousands of progovernment supporters of their suffrage rights.

Short-term electoral incentives cannot explain why President Picado sponsored a reform bill that would increase the uncertainty of election outcomes. By promising to strengthen electoral safeguards for opposition parties, he undertook a counterintuitive series of decisions that most members of the PRN opposed. The president backed institutional reform, we argue, as a way to underpin the survival of his government. Unless he reached out to opposition moderates – those who had a stake in prevailing political arrangements – the president faced the very real possibility that they would support the efforts of opposition hardliners to overthrow his government.

As sociological accounts suggest, Picado endorsed reform because he had values consistent with institutional change. He was not the typical sort of machine politician; he made his career as a politically ambitious man of letters, not by operating successfully larger political machines. Yet, as institutionalist approaches suggest, Picado endorsed reform of the system because the rules governing access to state power encouraged him to do so. The ban on the consecutive reelection of presidents liberated Picado from a narrow focus on reelection. Regardless of the impact of reform on the PRN, Picado had to step down at the end of his four-year term in office. And, by advancing the cause of democratic reform, Picado would improve his lagging political reputation and demonstrate his commitment to promoting changes of benefit to the entire body politic.

That no single faction dominated Congress, oddly enough, created an opportunity for a reform-oriented president. Relying upon the moderate opposition's interest in increasing its share of state power, Picado floated a reform bill that succeeded in attracting the support of opposition moderates. Furthermore, Picado obtained the support of the PVP by supporting a bill that promised to make it easier for small parties such as the PVP to elect their members to Congress. And, by reminding independent members of the PRN that the uncertainty of fair elections was preferable

Conclusion

to civil war, Picado succeeded in assembling a coalition just large enough
to prevail in Congressional votes. Indeed, without the support of a rump
faction within the PRN, the president would have failed to reform electoral laws and therefore to stabilize political competition. Fully in line with
reelection theories of political change, the PRN*c* ultimately failed to derail
a reform bill that led to its loss of state power and its subsequent defeat in
a two-month civil war.

Conclusion: Ballot-Rigging and Electoral Reform in Comparative Perspective

Introduction

This book began with the puzzle of why incumbents relinquish their power to stuff the ballot box. Making elections fairer and more transparent raises the possibility that elected officials may lose control of the state. And, for both incumbents and opposition movements, increasing safeguards for citizens only augments the uncertainty of electoral outcomes. Understanding why parties reform electoral laws from which they benefit is one of the core objectives of this book.

We also set out to meet the challenge of studying electoral fraud – a set of illicit activities that remain poorly understood. Though the past and present of democratization are replete with references to how incumbents steal elections, only a few studies analyze how parties stuff the ballot box. No research exists explaining how institutional reform shapes the nature, extent, and magnitude of electoral fraud. In this book, we examine the petitions to nullify electoral results – the formal complaints that parties filed with Congress in the aftermath of elections – to develop a quantitative and qualitative portrait of ballot-rigging during the first half of the twentieth century.

Stuffing the Ballot Box focuses on Costa Rica, a country where parties began to compete in regularly scheduled elections in the nineteenth century. We begin our analysis in 1901, when competitive party politics took off, and end it in 1948, when institutional reforms completely removed the executive and legislature from electoral governance. Like in Chile, England, and Uruguay, parties in Costa Rica gradually reformed institutions to permit increasing numbers of adults to vote. Like these (and other countries), however, parties did not willingly relinquish their ability

228

to manipulate the electoral arena for partisan advantage. Until well into the twentieth century, in fact, parties were not above using violence and fraud to gain control of the state. The use of multiple "currencies" of power is what makes Costa Rica an ideal case to analyze the sources of institutional change and the impact of legal reform on the nature of ballot-rigging.

Our research design allows us to control for a variety of social and institutional factors that affect the course of electoral reform. Throughout the first half of the twentieth century, over two-thirds of the population lived in rural areas. Major social or ethnic conflicts did not exist. During this period, the republic had a unitary and presidential system with a unicameral legislature. That social and constitutional structure remained basically unchanged permits identifying how institutional arrangements generate the strategic incentives that encourage some presidents and legislators to reform electoral laws.

In the first part of this conclusion, we present our central findings about the nature, extent, and magnitude of electoral fraud. One half of all accusations of ballot-rigging took place in the three provinces of the periphery even though they only contained between a fifth and a quarter of the electorate. This pattern, we show, is consistent with sociological portraits that point out that the population of the periphery was more illiterate, ethnically heterogeneous, and economically dependent than its counterparts in the four provinces of the center. With only one exception, rates of fraud – defined as the number of eligible voters per accusation of electoral misconduct – were typically two to three times higher in the periphery than in the center.

We nevertheless argue that an institutionalist account – one that highlights how electoral laws shape political behavior – can better make sense of the dynamics of ballot-rigging. We show how differences in the way electoral laws converted votes into seats had profound implications for party development and the production and denunciation of electoral fraud. In the periphery, parties that obtained pluralities of the vote sent their candidates to Congress because nearly three-quarters of the races involved competing for only one or two legislative seats per election. In the center, proportional representation typically determined the distribution of Congressional seats because biennially held elections allowed parties to compete for three or more legislative seats at a time. That only a quarter or less of the electorate lived in outlying provinces explains why those votes sent a minority of deputies to Congress and why their races typically involved small numbers of deputies. The use of first-past-the-post electoral systems explains why political competition was more intense where civil society was weakest. Because the margin of votes separating winners from losers was smaller in the periphery than in the center, parties had more incentives to denounce – and to commit – acts of fraud.

At the end of this section, we also suggest that fraud did not determine election results on most occasions. Ballot-rigging shaped the results only of two or, at most, three presidential elections during our period of study. Yet, even if ballot-rigging was not as pervasive as its critics claimed, it served to undermine the legitimacy of the political system. If parties faced a 17 or 25 percent chance of having fraud deprive them of presidential victory, they faced the very real possibility that they could lose the presidency even if they won the popular vote. As a result, parties faced few incentives to relinquish their ability to stuff the ballot box. The possibility that fraud could be decisive in hotly contested races reveals why the use of fraud could snowball into armed confrontations between pro- and antigovernment forces.

In the second part of the conclusion, we present our findings about the effectiveness of the classical theory of electoral governance. According to prevailing constitutional doctrine, the executive should organize the election. To keep him honest, constitutional designers entrusted the legislature with the certification of election results. By carefully examining the behavior of the Credentials Committee – the Congressional body that initially reviewed the petitions – and Congress as a whole, we generate an empirical basis to assess the performance of the classical approach to electoral governance. We conclude that splitting the "administrative" from the "political" functions did not succeed in eliminating charges of unfairness during ordinary elections. In close elections, the classical approach actually fomented conflict because it relied upon partisanship to adjudicate disputes about the allocation of state offices. As we shall see, nineteenth-century theories of constitutional design in a world of partisan competition became a politically explosive mix.

In the third part of this conclusion, we summarize our findings about the usefulness of three theories of institutional change. The most common explanation about why parties do not change the laws that permit them to stuff the ballot box is that incumbents do whatever is necessary to augment their share of state power. The second theory contends that class backgrounds, socialization, and international demonstration effects encourage politicians to make choices that run counter to their short-term electoral interests. Finally, an institutionalist perspective explains seemingly irrational choices because it delineates the incentives that politicians face in different arenas. What might be irrational in the legislative arena may be perfectly rational given the incentives politicians face in other institutional environments.

We then test implications of these approaches during four periods when parties debated far-reaching changes to electoral law. The first was the early 1910s, when reformers proposed a host of changes, including the establishment of the secret franchise. Slightly more than a decade later, reformers succeeded in enacting the secret franchise during a second period of reform. But, only two years later, during the third period, parties took the necessary steps to uphold the secrecy of the franchise. Until 1927, parties continued to supply voters with paper ballots that effectively allowed parties to monitor the behavior of voters. With the 1927 reforms, politicians agreed to centralize the production of ballots in the secretariat of the interior (*de Gobernación*). And, during the last reform period studied here, politicians enacted the 1946 Electoral Code that cleaned up the Electoral Registry and made election administration a responsibility of a semi-autonomous court system. Negotiated in an atmosphere of political polarization, this Code remains the foundation of existing electoral legislation in Costa Rica.

In the final part of this conclusion, we identify the implications of our findings for comparative politics and institutional analysis. We first discuss how our account of electoral fraud and reform undermines the conventional wisdom that, given a favorable social structure, the democratization of the Costa Rican polity was inevitable. We then suggest guidelines for future research on electoral fraud and how its study changes ways of understanding the rise and fall of democracy in the nineteenth and twentieth centuries. Finally, based upon our analysis of electoral reform, we suggest how political ambition, institutional arrangements, and electoral constituencies interact to propel or to thwart far-reaching political reforms.

Electoral Fraud: Principal Findings

Why do parties rig the results of the ballot box? What impact does fraud have on politics? For a phenomenon as ubiquitous as electoral fraud, most analysts rely upon little more than anecdotes to describe the ways in which parties tried to deprive their rivals of electoral victories. In this section, we identify two approaches to explain the patterns we detected in the more than thirteen hundred accusations of fraud we culled from 123 petitions to nullify electoral results and related legal material.[1]

Social Structural and Institutional Accounts: A Balance Sheet

We assess the usefulness of social structural and institutional approaches to explain the rhythm of electoral fraud. Social structural accounts argue that fraud will vary in proportion to social stratification. As social relations between dominant and subordinate classes become more unequal, elites will more likely use violence to maintain their control of the political system. Institutional perspectives, in contrast, suggest that electoral laws and other rules of the political game generate incentives for parties to fabricate votes. If ballot-rigging leads to victory, then fraud should vary with the competitiveness of political arrangements.

Except for the 1940s, parties concentrated their denunciations of fraud in the poorest and least populated parts of the country. Despite housing between a fifth and a quarter of the electorate, the periphery was the site where parties lodged approximately one-half of all accusations of electoral fraud between 1901 and 1938. Even when we control for their regions' respective number of potential voters, infractions of electoral law were more common in outlying than in core provinces. Between 1901 and 1946, there were 686 eligible voters per accusation of fraud in the periphery. In contrast, there were 2,466 eligible voters for each accusation made in the center.

The distribution of fraud between center and periphery therefore upholds the validity of sociological approaches. Social differentiation was much more pronounced in the periphery, where laborers were often completely landless and worked on large cattle or banana estates. Economically dependent upon plantation owners, citizens in the periphery faced parties and public officials more willing to use of fraud against largely illiterate voters living in scattered, isolated hamlets. The periphery also remains more ethnically complex than the center; it contained large numbers of people of African and indigenous descent. In contrast, the center held important numbers of coffee growers with small and medium-sized landholdings. These growers considered themselves to be white and superior to the peoples of the periphery. Citizens of the center lived in

---

[1] This section draws upon Iván Molina and Fabrice Lehoucq, "Political Competition and Electoral Fraud: A Latin American Case Study," *Journal of Interdisciplinary History*, Vol. 30, No. 2 (Autumn 1999), pp. 199–234.

tightly knit, literate communities capable of organizing themselves to protect their civil liberties.

Yet, our findings demonstrate that political institutions are equally – if not more – responsible for these regional distributions of accusations of ballot-rigging. Both in absolute and in relative terms, electoral laws made it easier for parties to win legislative seats in outlying provinces. Unlike most races in the center, most elections in the periphery allowed voters to choose one or two deputies at a time. In such races, majority rule determined the distribution of seats between parties. In the center, by contrast, only parties that obtained a quotient – the sum produced by dividing the number of valid votes by the number of seats – could send their candidates to Congress because most races involved parties competing for three or more legislative seats. Unless the quotient was small and/or the number of impugned votes was large, smaller parties stood little chance of ever electing one of their members to Congress. In outlying provinces, however, any party stood a better chance of winning a legislative seat because it only needed to out-poll each of its rivals. Parties, in other words, faced incentives to commit and, most important, to denounce acts of fraud precisely where voters were disproportionately poorer, were less literate, and faced more ethnic discrimination.

While both of our approaches are consistent with spatial differences in the distribution of fraud, only an institutionalist can explain why political competition was more intense in the periphery than in the center. In general elections between 1901 and 1948, there were 20,772 eligible voters per party in the center and 7,586 in the periphery. In midterm elections, there were 7,142 eligible voters per party in the center and 4,515 in the periphery. These reduced numbers were the product of local party formation in midterm races between 1915 and 1946: seventy-seven parties in the center and thirty in the periphery. Proportionally, however, there were 1.3 local parties in the periphery for every one local party in the center. By making it easier for parties to elect deputies in the periphery, electoral laws encouraged politicians to form local parties precisely where sociological approaches predict less political activity to have taken place. Figure 1 charts long-term trends in eligible voters per party at the national and regional levels.

Indeed, only an institutionalist approach can explain why levels of fraud declined over the long term. At the national level, rates of fraud fell by 50 percent after the promulgation of the secret franchise. They went from 1,288 to 1,939 eligible voters per accusation of fraud between 1901 and

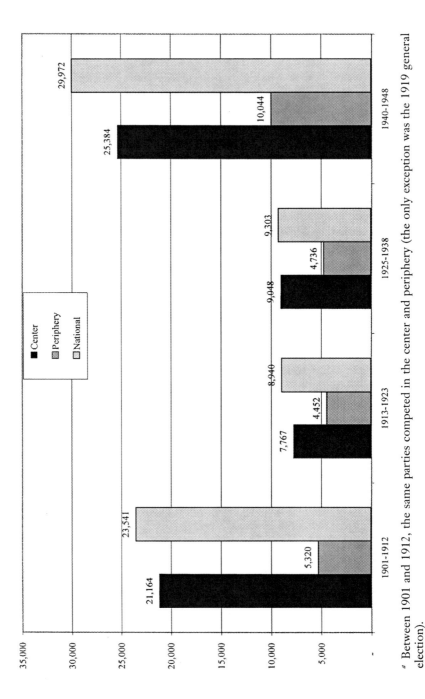

a Between 1901 and 1912, the same parties competed in the center and periphery (the only exception was the 1919 general election).

Figure 1. Eligible Voters per Political Party, 1901–48. *Source:* Iván Molina, "Estadísticas electorales de Costa Rica (1897–1948): Una contibución documental," *Revista Parlamentaria* (San José, Costa Rica), Vol. 9, No. 2 (August 2001), pp. 345–435.

1923 and between 1925 and 1946, respectively. Though levels of fraud were typically higher in the periphery than in the core, electoral reform succeeded in pushing them down everywhere in the republic. In outlying provinces, rates of fraud went from 517 to 943 per eligible voter during these periods – a fall of nearly 100 percent. In the center, rates of fraud went from 2,071 to 2,891 accusations per eligible voter – a drop of about 40 percent. Figure 2 lists rates of accusation by region and at the national level between 1901 and 1946.

Paradoxically enough, electoral reform encouraged parties to commit and to denounce increasingly blatant acts of fraud. Even if we control for geographic location, more openly coercive acts of fraud increased with time. Approximately a fifth of all accusations parties lodged in the center between 1901 and 1923 were category three and four types of accusations – acts of fraud, according to our classification, that involved coercion or could not but be interpreted as fraudulent in inspiration. The shares of the two most severe types of fraud increased to 54 percent between 1925 and 1938 and accounted for 81 percent of all such complaints made in the center during the 1940s. The rhythm of fraud is similar in the periphery, where fraud types three and four amount to 26 percent of all the accusations parties made between 1901 and 1912. The share of the two most egregious types of fraud increased to 62 percent of all charges between 1913 and 1923. After 1925, fraud types three and four account for approximately 67 percent of all accusations of fraud. Figure 3 displays trends of in types of accusation between 1901 and 1946.

Our fourfold classification also reveals that the thrust of fraud changed with the approval of the secret franchise. Before the mid-1920s, parties strove as often to increase their votes as well as to reduce the votes their rivals obtained. After the establishment of the secret franchise, however, parties spent significantly more time fabricating votes than reducing their adversaries' vote totals. Changing institutional incentives, we argue, were responsible for this shift in behavior. With the dismantling of the public ballot, parties no longer could keep a running tally of the vote. After the mid-1920s, however, it no longer made sense to disqualify, for example, voters casting votes for rivals, because parties, simply put, did not know how citizens were voting behind closed doors. Once laws protected the privacy rights of citizens, parties switched to inflating their own votes by, for example, buying identification cards or votes. This finding suggests that an increase in uncertainty is the principal outcome of the establishment of the secret franchise. Parties lose a great deal of information when

235

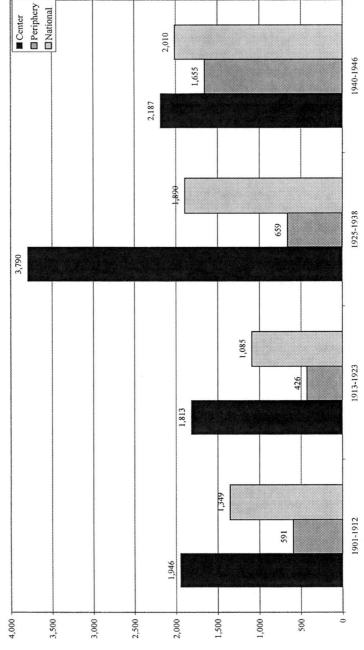

Figure 2. Eligible Voters per Accusation of Fraud, 1901–1946. *Source: La Gaceta* (1901–1946), and Iván Molina, "Estadísticas electorales de Costa Rica (1897–1948)."

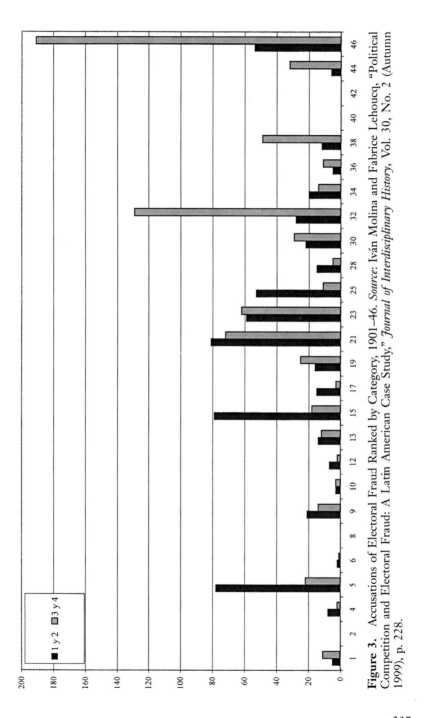

Figure 3. Accusations of Electoral Fraud Ranked by Category, 1901–46. *Source:* Iván Molina and Fabrice Lehoucq, "Political Competition and Electoral Fraud: A Latin American Case Study," *Journal of Interdisciplinary History,* Vol. 30, No. 2 (Autumn 1999), p. 228.

237

voters cast ballots in secrecy. They also forfeit their ability to monitor the behavior of voters. Both effects, oddly enough, encourage parties to fabricate votes to hedge their bets in increasingly competitive elections. One of the few other quantitative studies of electoral fraud indicates that the establishment of the secret franchise in 1890 in New York led parties to shift from buying votes to paying voters to stay at home in rural constituencies.[2] Ironically, the electoral corruption for which England was famous and that was the backdrop for the creation of the secret franchise in 1872 led to one of the most fraudulent elections, that of 1880. Three years later, Parliament enacted the Corrupt and Illegal Practices Act to curb the rampant vote-buying occurring during English elections.[3]

Finally, only an institutionalist approach can explain why fraud went from being an activity disproportionately occurring in the periphery to one principally taking place in the center. By the mid-1940s, the core provinces of the republic went from being the target of less than half to over two-thirds of the accusations of fraud. Containing three-fourths of all eligible voters, the center became a region that was, for the first time, experiencing its proportional share of electoral fraud.

Institutional arrangements also explain why, by the 1940s, most accusations of fraud occurred in the provinces where most voters lived. Though the 1927 electoral law strengthened the rights of voters and government opponents, it still vested the president with disciplinary authority over all electoral officials. Despite this law's requirement that citizens use photographic identification on election day, executives and legislators kept postponing the enactment of this legal provision. The classical approach to electoral governance also continued to encourage presidents to fill the legislature with their supporters so that Congress could certify their manipulation of the electoral arena. When the National Republican Party (PRN) found itself in control of the executive and legislative branches of government in the 1940s, President Rafael Ángel Calderón (1940–4) deployed the powers of the state to monopolize state power. Even if our analysis suggests that fraud was not responsible for the PRN's continuation in power, the scale of fraudulent activity scandalized many and fomented the

---

[2] Gary W. Cox and J. Morgan Kousser, "Turnout and Rural Corruption: New York as a Test Case," *American Journal of Political Science*, Vol. 25, No. 4 (November 1981), pp. 646–63.

[3] Gary W. Cox, *The Efficient Secret: The Cabinet and the Development of Political Parties in Victorian England* (New York: Cambridge University Press, 1987), pp. 10–1.

development of hardline sectors dedicated to overthrowing the PRN government.[4]

Indeed, the redistribution of fraud from the periphery to the center also helps to explain why political competition became further polarized during the 1940s. It was one thing for impoverished blacks, mulattos, and indigenous peoples of the periphery to be the victims of electoral fraud. It was quite another for parties to violate electoral liberties where a mostly literate and "white" electorate lived in a series of tightly linked communities. That violations of electoral law were becoming blatantly coercive also scandalized major sectors of the electorate and created support for hardline insurrections against President Teodoro Picado's government (1944–8).

The Magnitude of Electoral Fraud

For all of the ink spilled on ballot-rigging, fraud did not determine the outcome of most elections in prereform Costa Rica. The discourse of fraud was always larger than its reality. To see why, let us assume that all the votes cast at polling stations where parties alleged fraud had taken place were indeed fabrications. This, we should note, is a very generous way of compensating for any underreporting of ballot-rigging: between 1913 and 1946, parties only impugned, on average, about fifty votes at polling stations where they claimed their rivals were stealing votes (during these years, polling stations received an average of slightly less than one hundred votes).

On most occasions, the margin of votes separating winners from losers was greater than this very liberal estimate of electoral fraud. The difference separating winners from losers was greater than 10 percent in eighteen of twenty elections held between 1901 and 1946.[5] In all but two of these elections did the opposition impugn a percentage of votes greater than the margin of victory. So, with only two exceptions, the magnitude of electoral fraud is never greater than the margin of votes separating

---

[4] See Fabrice Lehoucq, "The Origins of Democracy in Costa Rica in Comparative Perspective," unpub. Ph.D. dissertation, Duke University, 1992, especially pp. 162–336, and his "Class Conflict, Political Crisis and Democratic Practices: Reassessing the Origins of the 1948 Civil War," *Journal of Latin American Studies*, Vol. 21, No. 1 (February 1991), pp. 37–60.

[5] In another election, a party filed a petition, but did not impugn polling station results. In yet a third, petitioners censured results at less than 1 percent of all polling stations. We exclude the 1940 election from this calculation because no party filed a petition against the PRN's 1940 victory.

winners from losers. And, 46 percent of all the complaints parties made between 1901 and 1946 belong in the two least severe categories of fraud – acts that are not obviously fraudulent in design or that refer only to procedural violations of electoral law.

The two occasions when fraud did determine the outcome of presidential elections help to make the point that, even for incumbents, stealing elections was not easy. This conclusion even holds for the first decade of the twentieth century, when legal safeguards for opposition parties were at their weakest. Though the share of impugned polling stations – 13 percent (or 75 of 568) – is greater than the PUN's 9 percent margin of victory in the 1905 general elections, we can only assume that the PUN stole the popular election by claiming that every ballot cast at these polling stations was fraudulent. Despite the suspension of the constitutional order and officially inspired machinations on election day, the PUN candidate obtained the support of only 41 percent of the electorate. The PUN jailing of close to half of all electors is what made the 1905–6 election scandalous.[6] Indeed, the PUN opted to manipulate the vote in Provincial Electoral Assembles precisely because the party was unable to fabricate a majority in favor of its presidential candidate, Cleto González, in popular elections.

Similarly, the PR managed to send Jiménez to the presidency in 1924 because it exploited institutional opportunities for winning high office, not because it amassed more votes than its rivals. When no party attracted the absolute majority of popular votes needed to be declared winner, the race was thrown into Congress, where the new legislature – half of whose members had just stood for election – selected the president from the two front runners. In a series of deft political maneuvers, the PR and Reformist Party (PfR) formed a majority on the Provincial Electoral Council of Heredia. In control of this Council, they annulled approximately 9 percent of the votes cast in the province on procedural grounds and therefore cleared the way for the PfR to win another Congressional seat. Both the PR and the PfR also succeeded in reordering the tally of the vote so that a PR candidate was selected as first alternate in the Province of Alajuela. And, because one deputy had resigned his seat from this province, the PR alternate became one of the members of the provincial delegation in Congress. Without such a maneuver, the Agricultural Party (PA) – whose candidate, Alberto Echandi, trailed Jiménez in the popular vote – would have

---

[6] Orlando Salazar Mora, *El apogeo de la república liberal en Costa Rica, 1870–1914* (San José: EUCR, 1989), pp. 219–20.

obtained two deputies. By depriving the PA of two seats, the PR and PfR were able to muster the bare number of legislative votes to make the PR candidate, Ricardo Jiménez, the president of the republic.[7]

Fraud had its greatest impact when voting was indirect. Until 1913, presidents took advantage of second-stage elections to jail opposition electors. After the establishment of direct elections, it became virtually impossible to steal a presidential election. As a rule, parties found it easiest to manipulate midterm elections in the periphery because turnout was at its lowest. Winning a few extra deputies here and there, as the 1923 legislative elections demonstrate, could tip the Congressional balance of power and shape presidential election results. Though fraud-induced changes in the legislative alignment of forces could complicate the president's ability to govern the country, the efficacy of this strategy ended in 1926 when Congress amended the constitution to create a popular run-off for the presidency.

Why, then, all of the fuss about electoral fraud? One reason is that, even as it became more difficult to shape election outcomes, well-organized parties could try and perhaps even succeed in winning a few extra votes here and there. This was certainly the case for local politics, where fraud could be deployed to alter municipal and legislative results. The possibility of gaining advantage through underhanded maneuvers was enough to unsettle most parties and to augment political uncertainty. That parties could blame their defeat on the illegal behavior of their rivals furnishes the second reason why charges of ballot-rigging persisted. Regardless of what parties knew or believed, it was rational to charge opponents with stuffing the ballot box. Blaming adversaries was preferable to identifying failures of party strategy.

Even if fraud did not determine the results of most elections, the threat and practice of electoral fraud corroded the body politic. Indeed, detailed, legal narratives of the violation of fundamental citizenship rights suggested that democracy was not consolidated. To the extent that fraud could be committed or denounced, it was rational for parties to take actions that only further undermined democratic institutions. In the end, a legal and constitutional framework permissive of fraudulent activities was itself a key obstacle to democratic consolidation.

---

[7] For the petition, see *La Gaceta*, No. 83 (16 April 1924), pp. 371–4. Accounts that place these events in perspective include Victoria Ramírez, *Jorge Volio y la revolución viviente* (San José: Editorial Guayacán, 1989), pp. 112–50, and Mario Samper, "Fuerzas sociopolíticas y procesos electorales en Costa Rica, 1920–1936," *Revista de Historia* (Heredia/San José), No. especial (1989), pp. 157–222.

Assessing the Classical Theory of Electoral Governance

One of the key issues that constitution-makers face is how to regulate the struggle for public office. Monarchies and other forms of nondemocratic governments never had to solve this problem. Indeed, they used blood-lines and/or violence to hand power from one faction to another. Republics, however, could not because they were predicated on the notion that the citizenry should choose its government. How exactly to organize the delicate task of adjudicating between conflicting claims about electoral results is an idea that continues to bedevil political scientists, legal theo-rists, and constitution-makers.[8]

Like other eighteenth- and nineteenth-century institutional designers, Costa Ricans chose to split authority over electoral governance between the executive and legislative branches of government. Constitutional the-orists made the organization of elections, like any other administrative matter, the executive's responsibility. To keep executives honest, they empowered the legislature to certify election results. Institutional rivalry, nineteenth-century thinkers believed, would encourage elected officials to produce fair and widely acceptable election results.

How did this system perform? In the most general terms, Congress did not do a very good job of holding the executive responsible for electoral misconduct. The Credentials Committee – the legislative body entrusted with initial scrutiny of election complaints – ruled in favor only of 4 percent (5 of 118) petitions that parties submitted between 1901 and 1948. The Committee divided its opinion approximately 14 percent of the time. As a whole, Congress did not do significantly better: It endorsed only 5 percent or seven of the petitions during this period. Parties, in other words, barely had one chance in twenty of getting the Credentials Com-mittee and Congress as a whole to rule in favor of their complaints.[9]

Defenders of the classical approach, can argue that the high rejection rate simply reflects the fact that most petitions failed to prove that fraud occurred or that it was decisive. Over a fifty-year period, in fact, the Cre-dentials Committee used one or a combination of three arguments to

---

[8] For a more extended discussion of the classical theory, see Fabrice Lehoucq, "Can Parties Police Themselves? Electoral Governance and Democratization," *International Political Science Review*, Vol. 23, No. 1 (January 2002), pp. 29–46.

[9] Data in this and the following paragraphs stem from Iván Molina, "La Comisión de Cre-denciales y Renuncias del Congreso: Un capítulo olvidado de la política costarricense (1902–1948)," in Ronny Viales, ed., *Memoria del IV Simposio Panamericano de Historia* (Mexico: Instituto Panamericano de Geografía e Historia, 2001), pp. 113–31.

dismiss most accusations of fraud. First, it claimed that petitioners had failed to offer evidence to support their allegations. Alternatively, the Committee concluded that the evidence was tainted. Second, the Committee argued that the charge in question was irregular, but not illegal. For example, a polling station opening a few minutes late was an incorrect action, but not an indictable offense. Third, the Committee employed counterfactual reasoning to assess the impact of the charges. Even if Congress would have accepted the accusations, the Committee often stated, it would not have affected election results.

As we have seen, these arguments are not entirely implausible. Nearly 50 percent of all accusations consist of the first and second types of fraud. Procedural violations of electoral law, in fact, represent more than half of the accusations of fraud that parties made before they established the secret franchise and centralized ballot production in the mid-1920s. We also echo the Committee's counterfactual validity tests. On most occasions, fraud – even under our very liberal interpretations of its magnitude – did not determine the outcome of hotly contested elections.

Nevertheless, we believe that the evidence in this book demonstrates that a nineteenth-century theory of electoral governance failed to produce fair and widely acceptable election results for three reasons. First, partisanship did rear its head, even if not always in a straightforward manner. Whether the party against which most accusations are made dominates or does not dominate, the Credentials Committee has little effect on its rulings. The Committee approved only approximately 4 percent (three of seventy-two and two of forty-two, respectively) of the petitions in both situations. Holding a Congressional majority, however, does have an impact on the success of petition writing. Congress approved only 4 percent (three of seventy-two) of the petitions when most accusations were lodged against the party that held a legislative majority. When, however, the majority was not the target of the complaints, Congress approved 10 percent (four of forty-two) of them. No wonder, then, that allegations of fraud and partiality accompanied every election before the establishment of an autonomous electoral tribunal.

Second, the classical approach failed to adjudicate between conflicts over election outcomes when they were most needed. Congress rejected opposition petitions when incumbents jailed hundreds of opposition electors to steal the 1906 presidential election. That the PUN controlled both the executive and legislative branches of government disabled the checks and balances necessary for Congress to have fulfilled its constitutional mandate.

Similarly, the classical approach could not arbitrate between competing interpretations regarding the 1923 popular election results. Because two parties colluded to form majorities on Provincial Electoral Councils tallying the vote, they managed to change the Congressional balance of power in their favor. Since no candidate had obtained a majority of the popular vote, the PR and PfR gained control of Congress to select their candidate as president amid allegations of fraud and unfairness.

Third, the checks and balances approach to electoral governance hinges upon an institutional boundary easier to conceptualize in theory than to delimit in practice. At the core of the dispute surrounding the 1923 elections was whether Electoral Councils, as creatures of the executive, could annul votes. According to Congress, they could not assume an attribute that came under the scope of certification – at least according to the legislative rulings about election outcomes since the early 1910s. When the PR and PfR majority came to power, however, it reversed precedent. Its decision to permit executive bodies to reject votes because annulling ballots is part of "verifying the initial tally of the vote," to quote from the 1923 Credentials Committee's opinion, shattered the distinction upon which the classical theory rested. That a partisan (and thus temporary) majority made this decision out of self-interest reveals only how obscure the boundary between the purely "administrative" and "political" functions of electoral governance was.

What this book demonstrates is that the classical approach generates reasonably acceptable election results under divided government. When two different parties control these branches, the nonpartisan world that nineteenth-century constitution-makers assumed to exist is roughly approximated. In a world without parties, there are good reasons to believe that representatives would be motivated to maximize the interests of their respective branch of government. Once politicians form parties, however, their loyalties fundamentally change. Indeed, in a world of partisan competition, the classical approach encourages executives to pack the legislature with members of their parties. When unified government exists, parties will collude to prevent the rivalry between the branches of government necessary for mutual monitoring to occur.

Stuffing the Ballot Box also shows that compliance with democratic institutions increased as parties gradually, and in fits and starts, removed the executive and legislature from electoral governance. In 1905, parties empowered the Supreme Court to review charges of fraud during popular elections. Five years later, Congress reasserted its authority to be the sole judge of electoral contests. In 1925, politicians established the Grand Electoral Council (GCE) to oversee the tally of the vote. Slightly more than two decades later, parties converted the Council into a tribunal. They made it completely responsible for the governance of elections, the supervision of the Electoral Registry, and the preliminary tally of the vote.

In 1949, constitution-makers stripped the legislature of the power to certify election results. By removing the last vestige of the classical theory from election governance, the Constituent Assembly made the Supreme Tribunal of Elections completely responsible for electoral affairs in this country. And, it was this independent court system, we contend, that helped maintain the peace between government and opposition during the 1950s. Both winners and losers of the 1948 civil war spent the following decade struggling for supremacy – a conflict that involved charges of fraud, a foreign invasion, and repeated confrontations between executive and legislative authority.[10] After this stormy decade, parties have competed in regularly scheduled elections that have become among the most competitive and honest in the world.

Electoral Reform: Theories and Evidence

If institutional arrangements help to generate what microeconomists call equilibria – that is, a set of mutually beneficial agreements from which no one has an incentive to defect unilaterally – a change in conditions must be responsible for their transformation. Economic development or demographic change, for example, can alter the distribution of resources between groups and thus their interest in reform. Politicians can also become aware of opportunities within institutional arrangements to advance their own careers. We now turn to understanding why parties did or did not exploit the possibilities for reform that institutions generated.[11]

---

[10] Kirk Bowman, "¿Fue el compromiso y consenso de las elites lo que llevó a la consolidación democrática en Costa Rica? Evidencia de los cincuenta," *Revista de Historia* (Heredia/San José), No. 41 (January–June 2000), pp. 91–127. Also, see his *Militarization, Democracy, and Development in Latin America*, unpub. ms., Atlanta, Sam Nunn School of International Affairs, Georgia Institute of Technology, 2000.

[11] This section draws upon Fabrice Lehoucq, "Institutionalizing Democracy: Constraint and Ambition in the Politics of Electoral Reform," *Comparative Politics*, Vol. 32, No. 4 (July 2000), pp. 459–77.

Office-Seeking Theories

Office-seeking theories suggest that reelection interests drive party behavior. In the words of Anthony Downs, the first exponent of this approach, "parties formulate policies to win elections, rather than win elections to formulate policies."[12] If this approach is valid, parties will support "efficient" reforms – those that benefit all parties – if they expect their political standing to improve with tendered reforms. But, parties are unlikely to back "redistributive" reforms if these changes promise to benefit other parties at their expense.[13] They will also oppose bills whose consequences are uncertain because they fear the redistributive consequences of such changes.

Office-seeking theories do reasonably well in explaining decisions to scuttle reform attempts. Of the fourteen presidential administrations between 1890 and 1948, only four proposed electoral reforms. The ability of office-seeking approaches to make sense of the behavior of presidents and deputies during four periods of reform, however, is more problematic.

It is certainly the case that the PR faction loyal to the perennial presidential candidate and Congressional leader, Máximo Fernández, did vote in accordance with the predictions of office-seeking theories. His deputies voted overwhelming against the secret franchise in 1912, despite the fact that they aspired to represent the interests of urban artisans and agricultural workers. By voting to retain the public ballot, the *fernandistas* (hereafter referred to as the PR*f*) cemented the role that parties played as mobilizers of voters and monitors of their behavior. They were also responsible for killing the president's electoral reform bill in committee in 1913 because, by the last year of Jiménez's term in office, they had gained the support of other PR deputies to wrest control of the Congressional presidency and of key committees from the faction loyal to the president, known as the *jimenistas* (and hereafter referred to as the PR*j*). The possibility of standing for reelection, in fact, had driven some PR*j* deputies to abandon the incumbent ineligible for consecutive reelection and to vote in favor of an electoral law that maintained the status quo with regard to the secret franchise.

Voting to eliminate two-stage elections in 1913 was, however, an important reform in the electoral interests of the PR*f*. Like every other party, it

---

[12] This remark is from Anthony Downs, *An Economic Theory of Democracy* (New York: Harper & Row, 1957), p. 28. Also, see Michael Laver and Norman Schofield, *Multiparty Democracy: The Politics of Coalition in Europe* (New York: Oxford University Press, 1994).

[13] George Tsebelis, *Nested Games: Rational Choice and Comparative Politics* (Berkeley, CA: University of California Press, 1990), ch. 4.

wanted to eliminate the period between popular and second-stage elections that had allowed incumbents to jail or otherwise harass opposition electors. And, parties had an interest in preventing their agents – electors chosen every four years – from voting against their wishes. In both general and especially in midterm elections, electors increased uncertainty because they could vote for candidates other than those the party leadership endorsed.

A look at the roll-call votes, however, suggests that not everyone in the PR voted in a narrowly self-interested manner. Though comprising the largest faction of the legislature, the PR*j* voted in favor of the secret franchise and, curiously enough, split its vote on direct elections for public office. The behavior of PR*j* representatives on these measures suggests that they did not vote in their narrow self-interest. By voting to establish the secret franchise, they supported a reform that promised to increase political uncertainty and therefore to undermine their ability to retain control of the state. And, by splitting their support on the direct elections amendment, the PR*j* again showed that it was not simply concerned with retaining control of public offices. President Jiménez's strong support for electoral reform also does not make sense from an office-seeking perspective because, as the leader of the PR, he should have opposed any measure that might lead to its electoral defeat. These results make the point that some politicians override their interest in reelection to make counterintuitive choices.

Much the same story can be told about subsequent periods, including those of the mid-1920s, when Jiménez returned to the presidency amid widespread allegations of fraud. As office-seeking theories would predict, the PA proposed a reform bill. Having just lost a bid to gain control of the presidency, the PA possessed an interest in institutional change. Exactly as a narrow focus on reelection suggests, the party only recommended measures extensive enough to prevent another of its candidates from being cheated of an electoral victory. Contrary to office-seeking perspectives, however, the president endorsed the PA's bill. Despite having been the beneficiary of fraud, he called for a major overhaul of electoral laws, including the establishment of the secret franchise and the extension of suffrage rights to women.

In line with office-seeking theories, however, Congress opposed expanding suffrage rights to females. Doubling the size of the electorate simply injected more uncertainty into political calculations than a majority wished to contemplate. Curiously, most deputies quickly approved the secret franchise in 1925. Unlike in the early 1910s, the measure did not become embroiled in a partisan debate. Indeed, both the legislative record and newspapers do little more than reveal that the measure passed in a voice vote. That parties retained the right to distribute paper ballots to voters suggests, however, that parties were still going to be able to monitor the behavior of "their" voters. Precisely because they appointed members to supervise polling center operations, parties requested that voters display their ballots before casting them.

A year before his second presidential term came to an end, Jiménez again confounds office-seeking perspectives. Among other things, he proposed that the state distribute paper ballots on election day – a measure that struck at parties' ability to control "their" voters. In response, deputies argued that the single ballot would disenfranchise illiterate men because these voters would be unable to decipher and mark their ballots. According to the 1927 population census, approximately a third of all men ten years or older were illiterate.[14] Yet, what motivated parties to oppose this change was not exactly their concern for uneducated voters. Stripping parties of their ability to distribute paper ballots threatened their capacity to monitor and to control the behavior of voters. In election races that were already quite competitive, a genuinely secret franchise promised to increase the uncertainty over the results of the ballot box.

What is fascinating about the politics of the 1927 law is that deputies voted for a law they did not want. Curiously enough, they did not attack the president or his proposals, even when Jiménez threatened to veto the bill being considered in Congress. Along with the president's decision to continue reforming electoral laws, the behavior of the legislative majority clashes with the interests that both the president and Congress have in maximizing their control over state offices. Why did they do it?

It obviously had little to do with their interest in reelection. Parties delayed, ignored, and otherwise tried to scuttle the 1927 reform bill because they did not want to lose control over voters. In line with office-seeking approaches of institutional reform, deputies did succeed in getting Jiménez to postpone the requirement that voters use photographic identification cards on election day. Arguing that the Electoral Registry would not have the time to produce these documents in time for the 1928 general election, deputies negotiated with the president to sign a law to delay implementation of this measure. That subsequent governments also sus-

---

[14] Republic of Costa Rica, *Censo de población de Costa Rica, 11 de mayo de 1927* (San José: Dirección General de Estadística y Censos, 1960), pp. 54–7.

pended this requirement suggests that no party wanted to take a step that would augment the uncertainty of electoral competition.

An office-seeking perspective explains why most deputies from the PRN, the majority party in Congress, fought Picado's 1946 reform bill. Proposed by the newly elected president, the Electoral Code promised to make the use of photographic identification cards mandatory on election day. The bill required purging electoral rolls of the names of dead or nonexistent individuals. And, it placed election administration in the hands of a semi-autonomous court system.

Reelection-based theories also explain why the opposition, congregated around the Democratic Party (PD), supported this bill. Although the Popular Vanguard Party (PVP) – the Costa Rican Communist Party – was part of the progovernment alliance that dominated Congress, it also endorsed the reform bill. That the provision for lowering the threshold that parties needed to compete for leftover seats in provinces where proportional representation distributed seats from an entire quotient to 75 percent of a quotient increased the probability that smaller parties could elect their Congressional candidates.[15] So, while the PVP had an interest in remaining in power, it also had an interest in a reform that promised to boost its share of legislative seats. But, office-seeking theories do not explain why a president endorsed a bill that threatened his party's control of both branches of government.

This overview suggests that office-seeking theories do reasonably well in accounting for most opposition to far-reaching institutional reforms. Most politicians fought measures that were likely to augment the uncertainty of electoral competition by reducing the ability of parties to manufacture fraud or control the electorate. Most presidents and deputies, in fact, never had to confront these issues because they simply did not raise them. But, the very fact that most politicians opposed reform makes the question of why some did back it that much more intriguing.

Sociological Approaches

Understanding the dilemmas that incumbents face is the way to begin resolving the puzzle of why any office-holding politician would agree to hold fairer and more transparent elections. One set of responses about why

---

[15] By mid-1947, PVP deputies succeeded in enacting a law lowering this threshold to 50 percent of a quotient. See "Ley No. 1096 (27 August 1947)," *Colección de Leyes y Decretos* (San José: Imprenta Nacional, 1948).

politicians run these risks focuses upon their social backgrounds and cognitive frameworks.[16] That parties choose noninstrumentally rational courses of action, sociologists contend, is prime facie evidence against the usefulness of office-seeking perspectives of political reform. Others focus on the behavior of workers and other social movements to understand the rhythm of electoral reform.[17]

Only a few parties combined demands for electoral reform with class-based appeals. As we have seen, the PRf did have a rhetorical commitment to social reform, but it failed to endorse the secret franchise or other reforms that promised to augment political uncertainty in the early 1910s. The PfR and the PVP were the only two leftist (and minority) parties that voted in favor of electoral reforms during the 1920s and 1940s, respectively. Yet, even the PfR chief could not push for safeguarding citizen's privacy rights. Like most other representatives of the mid-1920s, he could endorse the secret franchise, but not support the centralization of ballot distribution. With these partial exceptions, parties supportive of and those opposed to electoral reform could not be distinguished by their respective positions on social reform and property rights.

Upon closer inspection, it becomes much easier to understand why parties had an interest in attracting the support of as many (male) citizens as possible. The most conservative parties on social policy never called for restricting the franchise because alienating voters in what were highly competitive races would be highly counterproductive. This finding is in line with recent research on politics in prereform systems, which reveals that conservatives often backed broad suffrage rights as a way to wrest control of governments from their opponents. As a result, franchise rights were relatively extensive in many Latin American countries, especially by nineteenth- and early twentieth-century standards.[18] Strategic interests,

---

[16] The work of Seymour Martin Lipset is perhaps the most representative of this approach. See, for example, his "The Centrality of Political Culture," *Journal of Democracy*, Vol. 1, No. 1 (Fall 1990), pp. 80–3, as well as his *Three Lectures on Democracy* (Norman, OK: University of Oklahoma Press, forthcoming).

[17] See Dietrich Rueschemeyer, Evelyne Huber Stephens, and John D. Stephens, *Capitalist Development and Democracy* (Chicago: University of Chicago Press, 1992). Also, see Ruth Berins Collier and David Collier, *Shaping the Political Arena: Critical Junctures, the Labor Movement and Regime Dynamics in Latin America* (Princeton, NJ: Princeton University Press, 1991), and, more recently, Ruth Berins Collier, *Paths Toward Democracy: The Working Class and Elites in Western Europe and South America* (Cambridge, UK: Cambridge University Press, 1999).

[18] In nineteenth-century Brazil, a society with large sectors of its agricultural economy based upon slave labor and with an emperor until 1889, struggles to obtain control of local, state,

not ideological positioning, explains the democratic commitments of most parties.

While the international diffusion of ideas about the practice of republican politics did influence debates about electoral reform, it did not blunt the opposition of antireform forces that ignored or openly rejected such arguments. Many PR and P/R deputies in favor of suffrage reform during the mid-1920s, for example, argued that denying literate women the right to vote while illiterate males were voting was not fair, especially not in a world where advanced nations were destroying such barriers. The office-seeking interests of parties, however, overrode any desire some of their members may have had to create the secret franchise in the early 1910s or to extend franchise rights to women. As we saw, legislators could establish the secret franchise without actually guaranteeing that voting would be held in private by permitting parties to continue supplying voters with ballots on election day.

Similarly, sexist attitudes – rooted in a predominately rural, patriarchical society – certainly made many men unreceptive to empowering women. Yet, strategic considerations also played a fundamental role in shaping the outcome of the struggle to enfranchise women. Partisan politics also became a decisive force once President Jiménez, a well-respected leader of the PR, endorsed female suffrage rights in 1925. Despite the fact that its leader was the chief sponsor of this proposal, the PR split its vote on the measure even as the P/R supported it. That more than 70 percent of the PA opposed this bill suggests that the struggle for female suffrage

and national offices were typically competitive, often violent, and included an electorate estimated to be ". . . 50.6 percent of all free males, 21 years of age or older, regardless of race or literacy." Richard Graham *Patronage and Politics in Nineteenth-Century Brazil* (Stanford, CA: Stanford University Press, 1990), p. 108. It is also the case that universal manhood suffrage existed in Argentina since the 1820s, when the country became independent from Spain. See Hilda Sabato and Elías Palti, "¿Quién votaba en Buenos Aires? Práctica y teoría del sufragio, 1850–1880," *Desarrollo Económico* (Buenos Aires, Argentina), Vol. 30, No. 119 (October–December 1990), pp. 395–424. Despite the use of literacy and income requirements, the franchise was also broadly distributed in Colombia by the early twentieth century. Eduardo Posada-Carbó points out that hotly contested elections of the 1920s and 1930s included slightly less than half of all adult males. See his, "Limits of Power: Elections under the Conservative Hegemony in Colombia, 1886–1930," *Hispanic American Historical Review*, Vol. 77, No. 2 (May 1997), pp. 245–79. In these and other countries, it was urban-based liberals, not landed oligarchies, who opposed suffrage expansion or the establishment of the secret franchise because most voters lived in rural areas and could be mobilized to support conservative candidates. The best statement of this position is J. Samuel Valenzuela, *Democratización vía reforma: la expansión del sufragio en Chile* (Buenos Aires: IDES, 1985).

rights was doomed once it became identified as benefiting one side in what was ultimately a partisan struggle about the distribution of state power. The absence of a broad-based woman's movement also allowed politicians to torpedo this measure without angering any of their constituents. Political calculations, not social interests, determined when women would get the right to vote.[19]

What sociological approaches help explain is why individuals like Jiménez persisted in their efforts to reform electoral laws. For Jiménez was clearly a politician different from most of his contemporaries. When he was first elected to the presidency, he had distinguished himself as a jurist and an intellectual; his forays into politics did not begin until 1906, when he became a deputy for the first and only time. Picado also was not a traditional party hack. He held intellectual credentials: He had served as secretary of public education, a post typically held by a man of letters. Conversations with his former secretary of the interior, Fernando Soto, reveal that Picado was committed to reform, despite the enormous pressure the PRN*c* leadership brought to bear on the president to drop it.[20] By treating Picado as nothing more than a PRN stooge, the post–civil war historiography has unfortunately obscured his role in completing the decades-old struggle to reform electoral laws.

While a handful of parties combined social with electoral reform, most parties did not. While extraordinary individuals such as Jiménez played key roles in electoral reform, they had to struggle among politicians concerned with reelection and the distribution of pork. Both powerful ideas and remarkable individuals helped the cause of reform. Nevertheless, they did not determine when, why, and how presidents and legislators agreed to transform the rules governing access to state power.

Institutionalist Approaches

Explaining why some presidents enact far-reaching reforms requires outlining the choices they face, not just postulating the interests they have, political or otherwise. Barbara Geddes, for example, predicts that a necessary condition of redistributive reforms is the existence of a balance of

---

[19] See Eugenia Rodríguez, "¿Por qué se aprobó el sufragio femenino en Costa Rica hasta 1949?" in Sara Poggio and Monserrat Sagot, eds., *Irrumpiendo en lo público: seis facetas de las mujeres en América Latina* (San José: LASA-Maestría Regional en Estudios de la Mujer, 2000), pp. 175–206.

[20] Lehoucq's interviews with Fernando Soto Harrison in San José on 15 and 19 February 1996. Also, see Soto's *Qué pasó en los años cuarenta* (San José: EUNED, 1991).

power in the legislature. If the larger parties all have equal access to patronage and power, they will be less likely to oppose institutional changes because they expect tendered reforms to affect them equally.[21] While such access may have helped to encourage deputies to support reform, it was the impact of Congressional stalemates on the structure of executive-legislative relations that better explains the behavior of reformist presidents. The power to veto legislation allowed presidents to pivot between pro- and antigovernment forces to get recalcitrant legislators to support fundamental institutional changes.

Because no party possessed an outright majority during three of the four periods of reform, none proposed reforms that only promised to benefit their interests. Pro- and antigovernment forces were balanced in the legislature that established the secret franchise. In 1925, the PR and the P*f*R, in a coalition known as the Fusion, held 37 and 14 percent of legislative seats, respectively. The opposition PA held 49 percent of all seats. Two years later, when the centralization of ballot production and other measures made the secret franchise effective, the distribution of power was split among four factions. In the aftermath of the 1925 midterm elections, the PR split into two wings: One controlled 26 percent of all seats, and the other held 33 percent of all deputies. The PA's strength had dropped to 26 percent of the legislature, while the P*f*R held the loyalty of 16 percent of all Congressional representatives.

The legislature that passed the 1946 Electoral Code was split among three parties, one of which was divided into two factions. The *calderonistas* faction (hereafter cited as PRN*c*) held 41 percent of Congressional seats. Those more interested in reforming included the PD, holding 26 percent of all seats, and 22 percent of PRN deputies who were independent or loyal to the president. The PVP held the remaining 9 percent of seats.

A legislative standoff was barely absent (or barely present) in 1912, when Congress failed to establish the secret franchise. The PR*j* faction held 58 percent of the legislative seats. Its chief rival, the PR*f*, held 40 percent of the seats; a member of the Civil Party held the last seat in Congress. The two-thirds majority needed to amend the constitution could agree to eliminate two-stage elections, an "efficient" reform all parties favored. What doomed the redistributive reform was the two-thirds

---

[21] Barbara Geddes, *Politician's Dilemma: Building State Capacity in Latin America* (Berkeley, CA: University of California Press, 1994), pp. 94–5.

majority needed to enact it. Even with the splits in the progovernment PR faction, a majority of deputies could have established the secret franchise in 1912 if its passage required only an absolute majority of the deputies present.

Geddes also suggests that "additional pressure" is also indispensable for the enactment of redistributive reforms. In the early 1910s, newspapers do not reveal that public opinion was clamoring for fundamental electoral reforms. Interestingly, Jiménez did not organize a campaign to persuade citizens to pressure their deputies to support institutional change. By the mid-1920s, however, the president had become widely quoted in the press about the necessity of reform. When Congress's initial reactions were unfavorable, Jiménez came very close to attacking them. In one interview, for example, he was particularly blunt when he claimed that only "the eternal struggle of the past against the present and, second, the interests of parties" can explain opposition to the secret franchise.[22]

The president's use of the press was, we argue, part of a broader strategy to exploit the standoff in Congress to his advantage. Equally important was the use of the executive veto to force deputies to choose between approving bills that contained measures that he and they liked or no reform at all. Both going public and threatening a veto were, in fact, responsible for encouraging deputies to close the loopholes that allowed parties to pad the electoral rolls and to violate the secrecy of the franchise. Only after Jiménez vetoed Congress's draft of a new law did legislators compromise and enact most of president's requests. Then, and only then, did he sign the bill that became the 1925 Law of Elections.[23] Two years later, the president threatened to veto a new reform bill unless legislators maintained his provisions to safeguard the secrecy of the franchise. Still, no politician confronted the president, even though the committee that produced the bill that the president disliked expressed its opposition to his veto threat by tendering its collective resignation. After a stormy session in which deputies persuaded committee members to withdraw their resignations,

---

[22] "Ante la negativa del Partido Unión Nacional para aceptar el voto secreto en las próximas elecciones el Señor Presidente de la República declara que la discusión es inútil porque ese partido tiene mayoría en el Congreso," *La Tribuna*, No. 2036 (10 March 1927), p. 1.

[23] The president's defense of his veto is in "El veto del Señor Presidente a la Ley de Elecciones (3 July 1925)," *Diario de Costa Rica*, No. 1794 (4 July 1925), p. 3. The president's veto was also published in *La Gaceta*, No. 151 (4 July 1925), p. 1089. The final version of the bill containing the president's changes are to be found in articles 25 and 102. See "Decreto No. 75 (23 July 1925)," *Colección de Leyes y Decretos, Año 1925* (San José: Imprenta Nacional, 1926), pp. 131–68.

deputies agreed to incorporate most of the president's suggestions.[24] In a pre-election year, no party wanted to take responsibility for having torpedoed democratic reform or depriving citizens of their suffrage rights.

Much the same story can be told about the 1946 Electoral Code. Along with the pressure of public opinion, however, it was the threat of a civil war that hardened Picado's nerve in the face of PRN*c* opposition to the Code. Since his highly disputed election to the presidency, certain opposition sectors had begun to plot the overthrow of his government. Opposition moderates, led by former president León Cortés (1936–40), preferred to negotiate an agreement with the government. Urged on by his secretary of the interior, Picado sponsored a bill aiming to regain his adversary's confidence in electoral institutions. For, unless the government placated opposition moderates, they could very well support opposition hardliner efforts to topple the government.[25]

That the "additional incentives" consisted of the threat of civil war goes a long way toward explaining why the 1946 reform – but not those of the mid-1920s – succeeded in eliminating executive-sponsored fraud from electoral competition. Ironically enough, the enactment of the 1925 electoral law eliminated the sense of urgency necessary for persuading members of the ruling bloc that the uncertainty of reform was preferable to civil war and the possible loss of state power. Jiménez could go only so far before a veto threat failed to persuade enough deputies to broaden their preferences over institutional reform. Indeed, threats could backfire if a president demanded too much, because his legislative adversaries could then gain the support of two-thirds of all deputies to override the president's veto. The possibility of defeat, in fact, led Jiménez to drop key provisions – such as the enfranchisement of women and the mandatory use of photographic identification cards on election day – to salvage enough of his reform program.

[24] The president's denunciations were published on 21 July in *La Tribuna*. Unfortunately, this issue is missing from the Newspaper Room of the National Library. Efforts to find other copies have failed. Other newspapers refer to the president's remarks, but none report them. This reconstruction is based upon reports of Congressional reactions to his declarations summarized in minutes of Congressional sessions and newspaper reports where León Cortés reacts to the president's denunciations. See e.s. no. 4 (21 July 1927), art. 4, *La Gaceta*, No. 186 (13 August 1927), p. 1263 and especially "Incidente alrededor de un reportaje del señor presidente: renuncia colectiva de la Comisión Especial," *Diario de Costa Rica*, No. 2412 (21 July 1927), p. 5.

[25] Fabrice Lehoucq, "Institutional Change and Political Conflict: Evaluating Alternative Explanations of Electoral Reform in Costa Rica," *Electoral Studies*, Vol. 14, No. 2 (March 1995), pp. 23–45.

Implications and Comparative Perspectives

In this final section of our conclusion, we reflect on the implications our findings raise for three areas of scholarship. We begin by discussing the implications of our research for the study of the democratization of Costa Rican and Latin American politics, more generally. We then identify how to generalize the study of electoral fraud to assess the usefulness of social structural and institutional explanations of ballot-rigging. Finally, we end by showing how institutional constraints, electoral constituencies, political crises, and strategic choices interact to encourage politicians to do the unimaginable: to reform the institutions from which they benefit.

Rethinking Costa Rican Democratization

By analyzing a long history of presidential impositions, opposition insurrections, and the often violent intimidation of voters, this book contradicts the conventional wisdom that a high degree of social consensus explains why Costa Rica has become one of the world's most stable democracies. This book instead redirects attention to understanding how the interaction of institutional constraints and strategic behavior produced the trajectory that, in the long run, set Costa Rica apart from its Central American neighbors. Our book thus builds upon a handful of works that are beginning to question the prevailing consensus that social structure is responsible for Costa Rican exceptionalism.[26]

Most analysts typically suggest that the democratization of the Costa Rican political system was inevitable. Traditionalists, for example, argue that their political system is the natural outgrowth of an ethnically homogeneous and an egalitarian society dating to the colonial period. The

---

[26] See John A. Peeler, *Latin American Democracies: Colombia, Costa Rica, and Venezuela* (Chapel Hill, NC: University of North Carolina Press, 1985), and, more recently, his "Democracia inicial en América Latina: Costa Rica en el contexto de Chile y Uruguay," *Anuario de Estudios Centroamericanos*, Vol. 22, No. 2 (1996), pp. 65–90. Also, see Deborah J. Yashar, *Demanding Democracy: Reform and Reaction in Costa Rica and Guatemala, 1870s–1950s* (Stanford, CA: Stanford University Press, 1997). Though we disagree with her claim that Costa Rica and Guatemala were remarkably similar until the 1940s, we applaud Yashar's effort to revitalize social structural accounts by emphasizing the importance of elite choices during the critical conjuncture of the 1940s. Finally, see James Mahoney's *Path Dependence and Political Change: Liberal Origins of National Regimes in Central America* (Baltimore, MD: Johns Hopkins University Press, 2001), which argues that the liberal reforms in the late nineteenth century explain the divergent paths that Central American followed in the twentieth century.

absence of mineral wealth deterred many Spaniards from settling in what is now Costa Rica. Europeans and Indians quickly mixed to develop a society populated by independent, relatively poor farmers who allegedly became the ideal foundation for democratic government.[27]

Another more materialist explanation emphasizes the political consequences of the development of agrarian capitalism by the mid-nineteenth century. In arguments that echo those made by Barrington Moore in *The Social Origins of Dictatorship and Democracy*, historians and sociologists trace the origins of democracy in Costa Rica to the fact that landlords did not succeed in compelling the state to force peasants to labor on their estates.[28] According to Héctor Pérez-Brignoli, labor scarcity and an abundance of

---

[27] Perhaps the most influential version of this thesis remains Carlos Monge Alfaro, *Historia de Costa Rica* (San José: Trejos Hnos, 1966). Other notable examples include José Albertazzi Avendaño, "Unos apuntes simples sobre la democracia costarricense," *Don José Albertazzi y la democracia costarricense* (San José: UACA, 1988 [originally published in 1940]), pp. 43–63; Eugenio Rodríguez Vega, *Apuntes para una sociología costarricense* (San José: EUNED, 1979 [originally published in 1953]); and José Francisco Trejos, *Origen y desarrollo de la democracia en Costa Rica* (San José: Trejos, 1939). Useful surveys include Chester J. Zelaya, "Democracia con justicia social y libertad," in Chester J. Zelaya, ed., *¿Democracia en Costa Rica? Cinco opiniones polémicas* (San José: EUNED, 1983), pp. 11–34, as well as Marc Edelman and Joanne Kenen, "La culture politique du Costa Rica," *Les Temps Modernes*, Nos. 517–8 (August/September 1989). The principal English-language proponents of this explanation are James L. Busey, *Notes on Costa Rican Democracy* (Boulder, CO: University of Colorado Press, 1962); Charles D. Ameringer, *Democracy in Costa Rica* (New York; Praeger, 1982); John A. Booth, "Costa Rica: The Roots of Democratic Stability," in Larry Diamond, Jonathan Hartlyn, and Juan J. Linz, eds., *Democracy in Developing Countries: Latin America*, 2nd edition (Boulder, CO: Lynne Rienner, 1999), pp. 387–422. Samuel Z. Stone, *The Heritage of the Conquistadors* (Lincoln, NE: University of Nebraska Press, 1991).

[28] The classic statement of this position, of course, is Barrington Moore, *The Social Origins of Dictatorship and Democracy: Lord and Peasant in the Making of the Modern World* (Boston: Beacon Press, 1966). For a similar sort of study with a larger sample of cases, see Dietrich Rueschemeyer, Evelyne Huber Stephens, and John D. Stephens, *Capitalist Development and Democracy*. For Moorean interpretations of Central America, see Enrique Baloyra-Herp, "Reactionary Despotism in Central America," *Journal of Latin American Studies*, Vol. 15, No. 2 (1983), pp. 295–313; David Kauck, "Agricultural Commercialization and State Development in Central America: The Political Economy of the Coffee Industry from 1838 to 1940," unpub. Ph.D. diss., University of Washington, 1988; Mitchell A. Seligson, *The Peasants of Costa Rica and the Development of Agrarian Capitalism* (Madison, WI: University of Wisconsin Press, 1980); John Weeks, "An Interpretation of the Central American Past," *Latin American Research Review*, Vol. 21, No. 3 (1986), pp. 31–53; and, of course, Robert Williams, *States and Social Evolution: Coffee and the Rise of National Governments in Central America* (Chapel Hill, NC: University of North Carolina Press, 1994). Also, for the work that first raised many of these issues, see Edelberto Torres-Rivas, *History and Society in Central America* (Austin, TX: University of Texas Press, 1993), which is the translation of his *Interpretación del desarrollo social centroamericano*, which was first published in Santiago, Chile, in 1969.

land suitable for coffee cultivation facilitated democratization. Forced to negotiate with subaltern classes over wages and other labor conditions, the agrarian oligarchy failed to consolidate its hold on the economy and therefore on the political system.[29] Along with Pérez-Brignoli, Lowell Gudmundson, Jeffrey Paige, and Robert G. Williams are perhaps the most prominent Central Americanists to claim that it was the absence of a hegemonic landowning class that allowed democracy to flourish in Costa Rica.[30] And, in a number of pioneering articles, Víctor Hugo Acuña contends that it was the rural petty bourgeoisie that, in its own struggles with coffee exporters over the price paid for coffee during harvest time, championed the struggle for democracy.[31]

Whether traditional or modern, these arguments are simply too broad to make sense of the fact that electoral competition for state offices did not become consolidated until well into the twentieth century. Until the 1960s, politicians did not stop using violence to retain or to obtain state power.[32] And, as this book shows, parties went to extraordinary lengths to

[29] Héctor Pérez Brignoli, "Crecimiento agroexportador y regímenes políticos en Centroamérica: un ensayo de historia comparada," in Héctor Pérez Brignoli and Mario Samper, eds., *Tierra, café y sociedad: ensayos sobre la historia agraria centroamericana* (San José: FLACSO, 1994), pp. 25–54. For more discussion of the development of a coffee exporting society, see Lowell Gudmundson, *Costa Rica Before Coffee* (Baton Rouge, LA: LSU Press, 1987), and his "Peasant, Farmer, Proletarian: Class Formation in a Smallholder Coffee Economy, 1850–1950," *Hispanic American Historical Review*, Vol. 69, No. (May 1989), pp. 221–57; Carolyn Hall, *El café y el desarrollo histórico-geográfico de Costa Rica* (San José: Editorial Costa Rica, 1978); Iván Molina, *Costa Rica (1800–1850): el legado colonial y la génesis del capitalismo* (San José: EUCR, 1991); and Mario Samper K., *Generations of Settlers: Rural Households and Markets on the Costa Rican Frontier, 1850–1935* (Boulder, CO: Westview Press, 1990).
[30] Lowell Gudmundson, "Lord and Peasant in the Making of Modern Central America," in Evelyne Huber Stephens and Frank Safford, eds., *Agrarian Structure and Political Power in the Period of Export Expansion* (Pittsburgh, PA: University of Pittsburgh Press, 1995), pp. 151–76; Jeffrey Paige, *Coffee and Power: Revolution and the Rise of Democracy in Central America* (Cambridge, MA: Harvard University Press, 1997); and, Robert G. Williams, *States and Social Evolution*.
[31] Víctor Hugo Acuña, "La ideología de los pequeños y medianos productores cafetaleros costarricenses (1900–1961)," *Revista de Historia* (Heredia/San José), No. 16 (July–December 1987), pp. 137–59. Also, see his chapters from the collection of articles he produced with Iván Molina, *Historia social y económica de Costa Rica, 1750–1950* (San José: Editorial Porvenir, 1991).
[32] See Fabrice Lehoucq, "The Institutional Basis of Democratic Cooperation in Costa Rica," *Journal of Latin American Studies*, Vol. 28, No. 1 (May 1996), pp. 329–55. For a thorough account of how, well after the end of the 1948 civil war, Costa Rican politicians still used violence to settle their disputes about political succession, see Bowman, "¿Fue el compromiso y consenso de las élites lo que llevó a la consolidación democrática en Costa Rica?" Also, see his *Militarization, Democracy, and Development in Latin America*.

scuttle the enactment of reforms that would eliminate their ability to manipulate the electoral arena for partisan advantage. In the end, only the threat of civil war enabled reformist executives to assemble legislative coalitions of antigovernment and independent deputies to strip legislation of the loopholes allowing parties to stuff the ballot box. Social structural approaches are simply too general to explain why parties frequently ignored the results of the ballot box and typically opposed democratic reforms – the very facts that any theory of democratization must explain.

Our analysis suggests that it is misleading to argue that oligarchs, industrialists, middle classes, peasants, and workers pioneer the development of democratic (and authoritarian) regimes.[33] While struggles between landlords and peasants can generate political cleavages, only parties that represent these groups can build (or destroy) democracy. And the rules governing access to state power shape the decision to comply (or to ignore) the results of the ballot box. Parties – and not classes or interest groups – remain the key players in politics. Our analysis of electoral fraud and reform suggests that explaining the development of democratic institutions requires taking account of how state interests, institutional arrangements, party systems, and partisan identities interact to encourage politicians to build democratic institutions.[34]

This book also shows that the absence of severe ethnic and class conflicts hardly deprives political life of serious conflict. The very struggle to control executive and legislative offices generated insurrections, uncertainty, and ongoing political rivalries because public authority was the key

---

[33] On the role of industrialists and oligarchs, see Jeffrey Paige, *Coffee and Power*. For a non-Marxist version of this argument, see Samuel Z. Stone, *The Heritage of the Conquistadores*, and Deborah J. Yashar, *Demanding Democracy*. On the role of the middle class, see Dietrich Rueschemeyer, Evelyne Huber Stephens, and John D. Stephens, *Capitalist Development and Democracy*. On the role of the working class, see Ruth Berins Collier and David Collier, *Shaping the Political Arena*; and, more recently, Ruth Berins Collier, *Paths Toward Democracy*.

[34] Useful reviews of institutionalist research include Joe Foweraker, "Review Article: Institutional Design, Party Systems and Governability – Differentiating the Presidential Systems of Latin America," *British Journal of Political Science*, Vol. 28, No. 2 (July 1998), pp. 651–76; Jonathan Hartlyn and Arturo Valenzuela, "Democracy in Latin America since 1930," in Leslie Bethell, ed., *Latin America: Politics and Society since 1930* (New York: Cambridge University Press, 1998), pp. 3–66. Two particularly noteworthy (and recent) institutionalist discussions of Latin American politics are José Antonio Aguilar Rivera, *En pos de la quimera: reflexiones sobre el experimento constitutional atlántico* (Mexico City: Fondo de Cultura Económica, 2000), and Barry Ames, *The Deadlock of Democracy in Brazil* (Ann Arbor, MI: University of Michigan Press, 2000).

to spending taxes in advantageous ways and to placing followers in bureaucratic positions.[35] Especially in an underdeveloped economy where opportunities for accumulating wealth are limited, state resources allowed politicians to organize parties and to attract the support of locally based patronage networks. The benefits that public authority confers therefore acted as the glue sealing alliances between local patronage networks and national-level parties. The struggle to control the state therefore generated the conflicts that separated governmental "ins" from "outs," that undermined political stability, and that thwarted democratic reform.

We hope that *Stuffing the Ballot Box* holds up ways of integrating the sociological concerns of conventional accounts with the choice-theoretic reasoning of institutionalist research. Far from simply spinning a traditionalist yarn about "high" politics, we analyzed how parties – in the center and periphery, in urban as well as rural areas – organized themselves to fabricate votes. We also showed that the struggles among national-level politicians to define the institutions of their polity were more than simply parlor debates to entertain urban gentlemen. Even in a predominately rural society, institutional arrangements powerfully shaped the behavior of parties and voters. Indeed, the struggles over who could vote and how they cast their ballots helped to empower public opinion, improve political accountability, and therefore gradually build a social welfare state unique in the world for its commitment to human and social development.[36]

Promoting the Study of Electoral Fraud: Beyond Costa Rica

Social scientists have been aware of the existence of newspaper or archival materials on electoral fraud. Yet nearly all have shied away from using this information to make sense of politicians, parties, and their strategies. Indeed, some claim that electoral fraud cannot be studied because, as an illegal activity, its footprints are too faint or jumbled to decipher. Yet, as

---

[35] This was a point probably first made by Dana Gardner Munro, *The Five Republics of Central America* (New York: Russell, 1918), pp. 185–203. To judge from bibliographies, it is a pity that so few studies of twentieth-century Central American politics have relied upon this classic. It remains a foundation of ideas, observations, and hypotheses about the political trajectories of Central America countries.

[36] Iván Molina, "Ciclo electoral y políticas públicas en Costa Rica (1890–1948)," *Revista Mexicana de Sociología*, Vol. 63, No. 3 (July–September 2001), pp. 67–98, documents how electoral competition encouraged state officials to spend money on health care, education, and other social programs.

we show, it is possible to extract several quantitative indices from the petitions to get a sense of who was accused of violating electoral laws, how they did so, where they were doing this, and whether they met with any success. Accomplishing these objectives has been one of this book's central objectives.

Far from being a randomly occurring event, electoral fraud follows a certain logic – one that was sociologically and institutionally based.[37] Levels of fraud were higher where electorates were poorer, less literate, and more ethnically heterogenous. Parties also committed greater numbers and more severe types of infractions of electoral laws where institutions created more competitive political environments. Indeed, once we control for the size of the electorate, parties competed for fewer voters where their chances of being elected to Congress were greater. Not surprisingly, levels of fraud varied with the number of eligible voters per political party, the proportional number of local parties, and the intensity of political competition.

At the most general level, this finding suggests that the lack of competition may discourage parties from denouncing and committing acts of fraud. In situations where institutions restrict entry into the electoral arena, dominant parties may have no incentive to violate electoral laws. Especially in one-party systems, politicians can afford to run "fair" elections because they are assured of victory. And in settings where several parties exist, their leaders may collude to divvy up public offices without relying upon the use of fraud. In such uncompetitive systems, acts of fraud may nevertheless go unreported because there are no avenues for denouncing them. Alternatively, parties may believe that the possibility of legal redress is so remote that it is pointless to spend the time to document activities which, by definition, are illicit.

An implication of this line of reasoning is that the collapse of oligopolistic arrangements may fuel complaints about electoral fraud. If reports of ballot-rigging depend on overall levels of political competition, then the number of complaints should skyrocket with democratization. Studies of Mexico reveal that infractions of electoral law picked up in the 1980s and 1990s, precisely when the Institutional Revolutionary Party's (PRI) decades' long domination of politics began to crumble. Indeed, an analysis of more than three thousand municipal elections between 1989 and

---

[37] For an overview of electoral fraud, see Fabrice Lehoucq, "Electoral Fraud: Causes, Types and Consequences," *Annual Review of Political Science*, Vol. 6 (2003), forthcoming.

1998 in Mexico reveals that postelection conflicts increased where political competition was more intense and where citizens engaged in collective action.[38]

Another implication of this general finding is that electoral politics, even in so-called oligarchic regimes, has been a lot more competitive than previously imagined. In his magisterial study of nineteenth-century Brazil, Robert Graham analyzes a political system where parties missed no opportunity to impugn the behavior of their rivals and to use violence to win municipal, state, and central state elections.[39] And in her study of the Second Reich in Germany, Margaret Lavinia Anderson shows that, after the 1867 declaration of universal manhood suffrage, electoral politics was competitive and involved parties arguing about procedure, outcomes, and rules.[40] In a series of fascinating studies, Argentine historians reveal that elections since the mid-nineteenth century were highly competitive and filled with denunciations of fraud.[41] Similarly, scholars of U.S. politics show that allegations of fraud in local, state, and federal systems were highest where elections were the most contested.[42]

If regime change fuels electoral fraud, then it should not be surprising that electoral formulae and other properties of electoral systems also shape the nature, distribution, and magnitude of ballot-rigging. One way to shed

---

[38] Todd A. Eisensadt, "Weak Electoral Institutions or Legacies of Social Conflict? Modelling Causes of Mexico's Local Post-Electoral Mobilizations, 1989–1998," paper presented at the 1999 Annual Meetings of the American Political Science Association, Atlanta (2–5 September). Also, see his "Observancia de las normas legales por los partidos de oposición y autonomía de los tribunales electorales en la transición democrática de México," *Foro Internacional*, Vol. 38, Nos. 2–3 (April–September 1998), pp. 340–91, his "Instituciones judiciales en un régimen en vías de democratización: solución legal frente a solución extralegal de los conflictos poselectorales en México," Ibid, Vol. 39, Nos. 2–3 (April–September 1999), pp. 295–326, and his "Measuring Electoral Court Failure in Democratizing Mexico," *International Political Science Review*, Vol. 23, No. 1 (January 2002), forthcoming. Also, see his "Courting Democracy in Mexico: Party Strategies, Electoral Institution-Building, and Political Opening," unpub. Ph.D. diss. University of California, San Diego, 1998.

[39] Richard Graham, *Patronage and Politics in Nineteenth-Century Brazil.*

[40] Margaret Lavinia Anderson, *Practicing Democracy: Elections and Political Culture in Imperial Germany* (Princeton, NJ: Princeton University Press, 2000).

[41] See Natalio R. Botana, *El orden conservador: la política argentina entre 1880–1916* (Buenos Aires: Editorial Sudamericana, 1979), as well as Hilda Sabato, *La Política en las calles: entre el voto y la movilización, Buenos Aires, 1862–1880* (Buenos Aires: Editorial Sudamericana, 1998).

[42] See Peter H. Argersinger, "New Perspectives on Election Fraud in the Gilded Age," in his *Structure, Process and Party: Essays in American Political History* (New York: M. E. Sharpe, 1992), pp. 107–8, for an overview of these issues.

light on the validity of this proposition is to study electoral fraud in places that permit varying both institutional and social structural arrangements. We should try to see if a key finding of this study – that accusations of fraud occur more frequently in majoritarian than in multimember districts using proportional representation – holds true in other places and times. It would be useful to discover whether this relationship is part of a more general pattern, one that holds that the denunciation of fraud varies positively with the competitiveness of electoral laws (and where competitiveness is defined as the average margin separating winners from losers), even when controlling for sociological conditions. If true, this finding will go a long way to indicating exactly how institutions shape partisan behavior.

These (and other) studies therefore suggest the need to jettison the assumption that dominant classes necessarily control political outcomes. Instead, we need to think carefully about how institutional arrangements and social structure shape the nature of political competition in systems that are experimenting with republican forms of government. If the nature and rhythm of fraud vary in response to institutional change, then analysts need to analyze the electoral politics of the Americas, Asia, Europe, and Africa by using a common set of methods to evaluate similar hypotheses about the impact of institutional change on political behavior. Electoral fraud, after all, does not obey spatial and temporal boundaries; where laws are lax and democratic institutions are new, parties will exploit legal opportunities to fabricate votes in their quest for the state.

Reformulating Existing Accounts of Institutional Reform

How to convince enough of the political class to loosen its grip on the state is the problem that reformers face. The difficulty of accomplishing this objective explains why office-seeking approaches are a very useful way to make sense of when politicians do and, most importantly, do not promulgate far-reaching institutional reforms. The validity of reelection-minded theories is upheld by the fact that, over a fifty-year period in Costa Rica, almost three-quarters of all presidential administrations and their legislative counterparts never proposed electoral reform. Furthermore, only a handful of presidents supported reform. Even fewer succeeded in assembling legislative coalitions to approve their bills.

Multiparty coalitions easily enacted reforms only when they expected their consequences to benefit each party equally. For example, two-thirds of all deputies amended the constitution to create direct elections for all public offices in 1913 because this prototypical efficient reform ended the principal-agent problem parties had with indirect elections. Because voters cast ballots for second-stage electors at four-year intervals, parties had a difficult time retaining the loyalty of electors in midterm and even in general elections. By abolishing the intermediaries between voters and their representatives, this constitutional amendment also advanced the interest that all parties held in preventing the president from jailing several hundred electors to impose his successor on the presidency.

A handful of presidents, nevertheless, did manage to break out of the equilibrium of regularly scheduled but fraud-ridden elections. As sociological approaches suggest, such individuals tended to be political outsiders, even if they did not represent the emergence of new generations or class actors. Both Jiménez (1910–4, 1924–8, and 1932–6) and Picado (1944–8), the two presidents who did most for the cause of electoral reform, were not party hacks. They were national-level figures who used their reputations to appeal to larger sectors of an electorate growing in size and in importance.

Yet, it would be a leap into voluntaristic faith to claim that uniquely gifted politicians are capable of single-handedly transforming institutional arrangements. First, parties reformed institutions in a world where existing rules acted as constraints – that is, placed restrictions on what politicians could and could not do. Rules about amending the constitution (approval by absolute majorities of all deputies in two different Congressional sessions) and the passage of laws (approval by a majority of deputies present during three separate readings of the bill) required reformers to build stable and broad-based coalitions to overturn the status quo. Unlike enacting constitutional reforms, creating or modifying laws also required the approval of the president as well as of Congress.

Second, institutional arrangements must exist that generate incentives for political entrepreneurs to build coalitions in favor of change. As in most presidential systems, the constitution barred chief executives in Costa Rica from holding office for consecutive terms, even though they could launch bids after spending a term away from high office.[43] If they could free themselves from party pressures, the ban on consecutive reelection – but the

---

[43] In 1969, legislators reformed the constitution to prevent the nonconsecutive reelection of presidents. At the beginning of the twenty-first century, politicians are beginning to reconsider this decision. See Fabrice Lehoucq, *Lucha electoral y sistema político en Costa Rica, 1948–1998* (San José: Editorial Porvenir, 1997), pp. 23–4.

possibility of returning to the presidency – allowed them to pursue policies not possessing short-term political benefits. Indeed, the ability to run again for high office created an opportunity for them to appeal to the common interests of the entire electorate. Indeed, reformers, especially successful ones, had a ready-made set of issues to overcome the tensions between self-interest and national interests; they could credibly claim that they were concerned with common interests, an incredibly useful weapon to vanquish rivals on the road to the presidency. Unlike locally minded legislators, chief executives did possess an interest in spearheading the democratization of the polity.

In control of the presidency, reformers could also exploit another institutionally generated opportunity to advance their agendas. If elections produce a legislature where no party holds a majority of seats, presidents can use the threat of their veto to play government and opposition against each other. By catering to the opposition's interest in gaining control of the state, chief executives can use their role as pivots to assemble coalitions of antigovernment and independent deputies to promote reforms more extensive than any legislative faction endorses. Through deft use of their veto powers, they can torpedo opposition projects unless their adversaries back meaningful electoral reforms. As along as their proposals do not encourage antireform deputies to form a two-thirds coalition to override an executive veto, reformist presidents can obtain a lot more from a Congress where, curiously enough, their party does not hold a majority.

Third, our research suggests that a constituency of reform must exist to implement far-reaching institutional reforms.[44] Without public demand for institutional change, no politician would promote policies most of the political class opposes. Embracing controversial causes is worthwhile only if their long-term electoral rewards are greater than the cost of alienating legislators and party officials uninterested in increasing the uncertainty of political competition. Indeed, the payoff for making elections fairer becomes larger with the expansion of the electorate and the consolidation of democratic politics because the size and importance of the constituency

---

[44] This argument is consistent with the finding that governments with new or, we would suggest, invented electoral mandates can propel major institutional reforms. See John T. S. Keeler, "Opening the Window for Reform: Mandates, Crises, and Extraordinary Policy-Making," *Comparative Political Studies*, Vol. 25, No. 1 (January 1993), pp. 433–86.

for reform increases. The success, in fact, of a reformist project hinges upon matching public demand for political change with institutions that encourage politicians to supply reformist projects.

Our analysis of electoral reform should therefore not be read as an endorsement of the use of executive power to solve intractable economic, political, and social problems.[45] What our analysis really demonstrates is that it is the complex interplay of institutionally based incentives, electoral constituencies, and strategic conditions that determines the success of far-reaching reforms. Strong presidential institutions alone are not of much use to advance institutional change. Indeed, Costa Rican presidents more frequently abused the powers of their office when they were at their strongest. And, as we have pointed out on several occasions, most Costa Rican presidents did nothing to promote electoral reform. The prohibition on consecutive reelection and the requirement of winning majority support created opportunities that were simply too dim for most executives to perceive. Though far-reaching reforms require politicians to be ambitious, only institutions and the "right" circumstances can encourage them to commit their time and energies to pursue policies whose benefits they will reap in the future.

Appropriate conditions, we find, consist of political crises that serve to embolden presidents and legislators to complete the reformist project. By threatening the rapid and perhaps irreversible change in the balance of power among political forces, crises can harden resolve in the face of

---

[45] Curiously, the ability to appeal to national interests is what many contemporary critics decry in presidential forms of government. See Juan Linz, "Presidential or Parliamentary Democracy: Does It Make a Difference?," in Juan J. Linz and Arturo Valenzuela, eds., *The Failure of Presidential Democracy* (Baltimore, MD: Johns Hopkins University Press, 1994), especially pp. 6–8. But, the capacity to employ such a device is what students of U.S. presidentialism suggest is responsible for major periods of innovation like the New Deal. For an argument similar to the one advanced here about how legislatures can retard needed reforms, see Ronald P. Archer and Matthew Soberg Shugart, "The Unrealized Potential of Presidential Dominance in Colombia," in Mainwaring and Shugart, eds., *Presidentialism and Democracy in Latin America*, pp. 110–59. For arguments that call for the creation of strong presidential systems to solve difficult economic and social problems, see the essays by Kurt von Mettenheim and Valerie Bunce in von Mettenheim, ed., *Presidential Institutions and Democratic Politics: Comparing Regional and National Contexts* (Baltimore: Johns Hopkins University Press, 1997). For efforts by new institutionalists to come to grips with this aspect of the presidency, see Gary J. Miller, "Formal Theory and the Presidency," and Terry M. Moe, "Presidents, Institutions and Theory," in George C. Edwards, III, John H. Kessel, and Bert A. Rockman, eds., *Researching the Presidency: Vital Questions, New Approaches* (Pittsburgh, PA: University of Pittsburgh Press, 1993), pp. 289–336, 337–86.

uncertainty about the effects of far-reaching reforms that unsettle so many politicians. The existence of a regime crisis is, in fact, why parties did not complete the overhaul of electoral laws until the mid-1920s. Despite the opposition of his party's dominant faction, Picado was able to gain the support of PRN independents by playing upon their preference for stability, even at the risk of loosening the PRN's grip on state power. When combined with the support of opposition deputies, who were concerned with facilitating their party's access to elected office, his presidential administration was able to muster a bare majority to approve the Electoral Code that remains the cornerstone of existing electoral legislation of one of the world's most stable democracies.

Index

Index

district administrators (*jefes políticos*),
45; popular election of, 63, 65,
67–70, 76–7
divided vs. unified government, 40,
244
Dobles, Luis, 216
dominant class, 63–4, 232, 263
Downs, Anthony, 7, 245
Durán, Carlos, 82

Echandi, Alberto, 109–10, 112–3, 138,
240
economically active population, 38,
42–3
El Republicano, 76
elections, direct, 68, 70, 77, 84, 86–8,
92–4, 116, 240, 246, 264; see also:
elections, indirect; elections,
second-stage; electors
elections, general, 39, 43, 59, 44, 86,
88, 90, 92–3, 105, 160–2, 171, 174;
of 1913, 2, 72, 83, 80, 88, 114; of
1919, 90, 92–3; of 1923, 30, 88, 92,
106, 108–9, 117, 240, 243; of 1928,
93, 145, 150, 158, 248; of 1932,
160–1, 177; of 1936, 165, 167; of
1940, 182; 195, 220; of 1944, 157,
169, 182, 190; of 1948, 160, 196,
205, 209, 212, 214, 221–2, 228;
popular, 35, 91, 116; of 1901, 91,
52, 228; of 1905, 53, 239–40, 243;
of 1909, 6, 39, 53, 63, 65, 67, 71;
midterm, 44, 59, 88–9, 92–3, 105,
114, 116, 160–2, 171, 174–5; of
1915, 89, 93, 95–6, 108; of 1921,
18, 92–3, 106, 110; of 1925, 128,
144–5, 150, 253; of 1930, 19, 146,
175; of 1934, 173; of 1938, 171,
175–6; of 1942, 180, 190; of 1946,
182, 185, 201, 207, 211–3
elections indirect, 59–60, 63, 69–71,
73, 84, 90, 93, 114, 240, 246, 253,
264; see also: elections second-stage,
electors
elections, majoritarian or plurality, 63,
80–1, 83, 125, 229–30, 261;

nonconsecutive, 64, 68; run-off,
120, 125, 139, 141
elections, second-stage, 35, 50–1,
86–7, 116; midterm of 1904, 51, 54;
of 1908, 65; presidential of 1902,
51; see also: elections, indirect;
electors
Electoral Code of 1946, 2, 7, 12, 32,
197–9, 206–9, 211–2, 215, 219, 225,
231, 248, 253, 255, 267
electoral constituencies, 231, 256,
265–6
electoral cycle, 72
electoral formula, 229
electoral fraud, 12, 17–9, 31, 204,
228–32, 238–9, 241, 255, 260,
262–3; accusations against indirect
elections, 45–53; accusations against
popular elections, 49–50, 54,
charges against polling stations,
49–50, 96–102, 165–72, 185–8;
charges, most serious, 50, 61–2, 87,
96, 99, 102, 105, 114–5, 157, 163,
165, 169, 171, 182–9, 191–3;
charges of procedural sort, 2, 17,
49, 61–2, 87, 99, 102, 115, 163, 165,
171, 185, 191, 239, 242;
institutional controls, 54–5, 106–8,
175–8, 188–91; intensity and
magnitude, 52–3, 62, 104–6, 116,
157, 171–5, 239; levels or rates, 48,
157, 165, 184–5, 192, 229, 233, 235;
nature and spatial basis, 45, 47–52,
94–104, 163–71; polling stations
disqualified, 52–3, 105–6, 173–4,
190–1, 193; social structural vs.
institutional arguments, 48, 61, 94,
96, 115, 157, 162, 185, 232–8;
theory and methodology, 12–24, 35,
229–41, 255–63; underreporting,
52, 239; vote deflation, 104, 106,
116, 171; vote inflation, 104, 106,
116, 165, 171, 188
electoral governance classical
approach, 5, 30, 33, 39–40, 62, 80,
106, 178, 225, 230, 238, 241–2

271

Index

Index

LaVergne, TN USA
10 November 2010
204264LV00004B/76/A